Ascetic Figures before and in Early Buddhism

# Religion and Reason 30

*Method and Theory*
*in the Study and Interpretation of Religion*



Mouton de Gruyter
Berlin · New York

# Ascetic Figures before and in Early Buddhism

## The Emergence of Gautama as the Buddha



Martin G. Wiltshire



Mouton de Gruyter
Berlin · New York 1990

Mouton de Gruyter (formerly Mouton, The Hague)
is a Division of Walter de Gruyter & Co., Berlin.

⊗ Printed on acid-free paper which falls
within the guidelines of the ANSI to ensure
permanence and durability.

*Library of Congress Cataloging in Publication Data*

Wiltshire, Martin Gerald.
Ascetic figures before and in early Buddhism ; the emergence of Gautama as the Buddha / Martin G. Wiltshire.
p. cm. — (Religion and reason ; 30)
Based on the author's thesis (Ph. D.) — University of Lancaster.
Includes bibliographical references (p. ) and index.
ISBN 0-89925-467-5 (alk. paper)
1. Gautama Buddha. 2. Asceticism—India. 3. Asceticism—Buddhism. 4. Buddha (The concept) I. Title. II. Series.
BQ894.W55 1990
294.3′63—dc20 90-13283
CIP

*Deutsche Bibliothek Cataloging in Publication Data*

**Wiltshire, Martin G.:**
Ascetic figures before and in early Buddhism : the emergence of Gautama as the Buddha / Martin G. Wiltshire. — Berlin ; New York : Mouton de Gruyter, 1990
(Religion and reason ; 30)
ISBN 3-11-009896-2
NE: GT


Printing: Ratzlow-Druck, Berlin. —
Binding: Lüderitz & Bauer, Berlin. Printed in Germany.

*To Harry Scragg*
*in memoriam*

## Preface

This book has grown out of my doctoral thesis, entitled 'The Origins of the Paccekabuddha Concept', submitted to the University of Lancaster. It puts forward a theory that attempts to identify with more exactitude than hitherto achieved the ascetic milieu to which the Buddha belonged , and to locate the Buddha firmly within this milieu. It also sets out to demonstrate that the 'followers of the Buddha', the 'sangha', were aware of the Buddha's identity as part of this milieu and accordingly constructed the doctrine of the Buddha's uniqueness as a response to this awareness and as a way of establishing and consolidating their own identity. This work, therefore, represents both a piece of historical inquiry and the application of a sociological approach. In this latter respect it seeks to use the sociological concept of the 'new religious movement' and its typical behavioural traits as a way of explaining and shedding light on developments that marked the beginnings of the Buddhist tradition.

How far it succeeds in this it will be for the reader to judge, but I hasten to add that the book is conceived as a preliminary exploration and the author will be more than satisfied if it spurs others into responding to and following up some of the issues raised here.

The chief resource for research has been the Pali Text Society edition of the Nikāyas. Translations from the Pali cited here have been taken from the PTS editions unless otherwise stated. In terms of coverage of the wider ascetic background of the early Indian religious tradition I have drawn upon a number of key Jain and Brahmanical texts in the original and in translation.

Many of the terms occurring in this work exist in both Pali and Sanskrit (sometimes in Prakrit also) e.g. P.**paccekabuddha**, **isi**, **samaṇa**; Skt. **pratyekabuddha**, **ṛṣi**, **śramaṇa**' Pkt. **patteyabuddha**. If a term with more than one rendering is mentioned in connection with a specific textual source then the rendering preferred is the same as occurs in the source; otherwise in general discussion the Pali rendering is preferred. One exception to this principle is the adoption of the locution 'Śramaṇa Tradition' or 'Śramaṇa Movement' when the subject is discussed at the broadest historical level.

I would very much like to thank Professors Ninian Smart and Trevor Ling for encouraging me to go to print. Needless to say they are not answerable for the ideas and argument contained in this book. Thanks are also due to Professor Jacques Waardenburg in accepting the work into the series 'Religion and Reason', and for his manifest patience and understanding with regard to any delays there may have been in forwarding the manuscript. I am indebted to Jackie Brienne and Enid Adam for help with proof-reading and to the Western Australian College of Advanced Education for assistance with production of a camera-ready copy. A special thanks to Eunice Fitzhenry who retrieved the manuscript from a potentially disasterous situation in the city of Liverpool. And to my wife, Jean, who throughout has acted as 'a remover of obstacles' enabling me to apply time and energy for the completion of the book.

Martin G Wiltshire
Perth W.A.
March 1990

**Table of Contents**

# Introduction

Among the wide variety of ascetics, philosophers and teachers forming the backcloth to the life and legend of the Buddha there is mention in Buddhist sources of mysterious ascetic figures called **paccekabuddhas** (Skt. **pratyekabuddha**). Although surrounded by obscurity, their peculiar distinctiveness lies in the fact that they are regarded as 'enlightened'. They alone among all the groups of ascetics share with the Buddha the honour of this distinction. Our curiosity as to their real identity is further increased when it is realised that they are a category of ascetic recorded in Jain as well as Buddhist sources.

Although the subject of **paccekabuddhas** has been variously studied by European, Singhalese and Japanese scholars no one to date has provided a theory of the historical identity of these figures and succeeded in situating them with some degree of precision in the religious and social context of their time.[1] Perhaps the closest anyone has come to providing a successful explanation of their identity is Richard Gombrich. In a review (OLZ, 74, 1979) of Kloppenborg's 'The Paccekabuddha, A Buddhist Ascetic' he has suggested that they have no basis in historical fact but are merely a classificatory abstraction devised by Buddhist doctrine. Although Gombrich's 'fiction' theory possesses the merit of coherency we subscribe to the view that there actually existed an identifiable ascetic phenomenon corresponding to the figure of the **paccekabuddha**. It is the principal intention of this book to argue this case and to show how important to our understanding of Early Buddhism is the question of the identity of these ascetics.

What Buddhism essentially teaches about **paccekabuddhas** is they achieve the summum bonum of Buddhist experience, enlightenment (**bodhi**), without contact with the Buddha or his teaching. They are not like the traditional followers of the Buddha, the monks and laity, who acquire their identity as a result of hearing and responding to the Buddha's word (**buddha-vacana**). **Paccekabuddhas** realize enlightenment by their own efforts, having never heard or come to rely upon the Buddha's teaching. Not only does this fact set them apart from the mainstream of tradition, it raises important issues in respect of the import and status of that tradition. In the first place it raises questions with regard to the alleged uniqueness of the Buddha himself if he is not the only being imputed to have achieved enlightenment entirely by his own efforts. Secondly, how ought we to understand the role and function of his teaching and his significance as a mediator if, in principle, beings can achieve the same end by their own efforts? These queries, it must be appreciated, do not take the form of criticisms launched from without the Buddhist tradition. They arise from within, since references to **paccekabuddhas** and the assertion that they are 'enlightened' ascetics are to be found within the Buddhist scriptures themselves. How can these scriptures affirm the sui generis nature of the Buddha and, at the same time, admit the existence of **paccekabuddhas**? It is hoped that this study will make a significant contribution to the resolution of this fundamental paradox.

The first step we have taken in the direction of resolving this paradox is to ascertain the accepted and standard meaning of the term **paccekabuddha** in Early Buddhism. With this in mind we have divided the Pali sources into three groups corresponding respectively to earlier-Nikāya, middle-Nikāya, and later and post-Nikāya periods of composition. To the first group may be assigned the earliest strata of material within the Nikāyas, exemplified by such texts as the Sutta-nipāta and by verse sections occurring elsewhere in the Nikāyas. The main body of the Nikāyas belongs to the 'middle' period, and most of the fifth Nikāya belongs to the 'later' period together with, of course, the post-Nikāya commentarial literature.

Throughout these sources there are just two sorts of **buddha** mentioned: the **sammāsambuddha** and the **paccekabuddha**. Sākyamuni, the historical founder of Buddhism, is a **buddha** of the former kind by virtue of being that category of person who, in a given dispensation (**sāsana**), brings into existence a body of teaching (**dhamma**) or a path (**magga**) by which, **nibbāna** can be realized, and who also creates a community (**saṅgha**) of followers. The status of the **paccekabuddha** within Early Buddhism can best be summarised in the form of three distinct but interconnected propositions:

(i) The **paccekabuddha** is the same as the **sammāsambuddha** in that he achieves enlightenment (**bodhi**) without assistance from a teacher (**satthar**).[2]

(ii) In contrast to the **sammāsambuddha**, the **paccekabuddha** does not, after his enlightenment, become a teacher (**satthar**) in the sense that he does not promulgate a **dhamma** and found a **saṅgha** or **sāvaka** (disciple) tradition.[3]

(iii) The **paccekabuddha** cannot co-exist with a **sammāsambuddha** and therefore belongs to a different era.[4]

It remains unclear whether any or all of the doctrines expressed by these propositions pertains to **paccekabuddhas** in the earliest historical stages of Buddhism. The question of the relative status of the two sorts of **buddha**, for example, is not addressed until the period of the composition of the later and post-Nikāya texts. The term **paccekabuddha** does not appear at all in the earliest strata of the Nikāyas and when it does first appear, in the middle period, there is no reference to these or similar doctrines. The obscurity surrounding its first usage leaves open the possibility that the concept of a **paccekabuddha** underwent some alteration of meaning in the various phases of the composition of the sources.

Some explanation is therefore required as to why **paccekabuddhas** are not specifically mentioned in the oldest strata and why, when they are referred to in the middle period, there is no attempt at doctrinal interpretation. In view of these obscurities we have searched the earlier and middle strata of sources for any evidence of a distinction of kinds of **buddha** such as that exemplified by the categories **sammāsambuddha** and **paccekabuddha**.

This investigation resulted in us spotlighting the ascetic figure referred to as the **muni**. The usage of the term **muni** in canonical sources is accompanied by considerable obscurity but one noticeable feature is its association with the Buddha and with the **paccekabuddhas** rather than with disciples of the Buddha or non-Buddhist ascetics. The term **muni** it would seem represents a blanket concept for an 'enlightened' being, together with an implication that the notion of **buddha** might at one time have been an entirely singular concept. We have therefore formulated the hypothesis that the **muni** represents a proto-Buddha figure who antedated the distinction between **sammāsambuddha** and **paccekabuddha**. We therefore seek to demonstrate that what was at first one type of 'saint' in due course became bifurcated into the categories of **paccekabuddha** and **sammāsambuddha**. Over a longer period Buddhism filled in the outlines of the distinction by providing full doctrinal justification for the two categories of **buddha**.

In those passages where **paccekabuddhas** are first mentioned these figures are not only linked with the **muni** but with the ascetic categories of 'seer' (P.**isi**; Skt.**ṛṣi**) and 'renouncer' (P.**samaṇa**; Skt.**śramaṇa**). The discovery of these additional associations has further helped our quest after the historical identity of the **paccekabuddha**. Since **isi**, **samaṇa** and **muni** are not only Buddhistic terms but trans-sectarian then an investigation is warranted into their significance in relation to the wider context of the Jain and Brahmanic traditions. We therefore have resolved to explore each of these categories within both Buddhism and the wider ascetic milieu of the period.

In Buddhist sources, terms such as **isi**, **muni**, **samaṇa** and a further counterpart, **brāhmaṇa**, are used attributively (describing the ascetic ideal) as well as indicatively (denoting a social identity). In Pali canonical texts, for instance, the application of the term **isi** to an ascetic signifies his possession of 'religious potency' and is used of both Brahmanic and non-Brahmanic ascetics. **Samaṇa** signifies a 'renouncer', one who has abandoned household existence in order to become a religious mendicant; he is categorically not a Brahmanic ascetic. Besides denoting one who has reached the height of spiritual perfection, **muni** is always understood as the Buddhistic counterpart of the Brahmanic priest. Both the Buddha's and the **pacceka-buddhas'** own particular distinctiveness lie in the fact that they are characterised by all three of these nomenclatures. All sorts of ascetics are characterised as **isi** or **samaṇa** but significantly the term **muni** is reserved for the Buddha and the **pacceka-buddha**.

The qualities by which an ascetic deserves the title **isi** are quite varied: Whereas the 'religious potency' of the Brahmanic **isi** consists in his ownership of ascetic power (**tapas**), sacred formulae (**manta**) and his right and ability to perform **śrauta** rites, the use of the term **isi** to describe the **paccekabuddha** denotes his possession of 'magic power' (**iddhānubhāva**). One of the dominant themes in the representation of the **paccekabuddha** within earlier and later Buddhist literature, (and one scholars have tended to overlook), is his close association with displays of 'magic' (P.**iddhi**; Skt.**ṛddhi**), notably his practice of 'flight' or 'levitation'. These references to his 'magic powers' occur almost entirely within Buddhist narrative literature. Traditionally in Buddhism, such displays were for the purpose of proselytising; nevertheless they were regarded as a poor alternative to proselytising by the method of 'verbal' instruction (**anusāsana**). Canonical Buddhism teaches that a person can only become a **sāvaka** (disciple) by receiving 'verbal' instruction. Exhibitions of 'magic' can do no more than impress the onlooker, whereas 'verbal' instruction communicates itself directly to a person's understanding.[5] The **paccekabuddha** is an ascetic who employs 'magic' more often than 'verbal' instruction, and he is never seen to make persons into **sāvakas**. **Paccekabuddhas** display their magic in order to win the allegiance or vindicate the devotion shown to them by the layperson.

The **paccekabuddha**'s identity as a 'renouncer' (**samaṇa**) in canonical sources serves as an important clue in deciphering his historical identity. In this connection there survives a legend in Buddhist and Jain literature which tells how four proto-**śramaṇa** kings (**kṣatriyas**) become **paccekabuddhas**. Close scrutiny of extant recensions of the legend reveals that it is very old, probably antedating the formation of these two distinct traditions, and represents an archetypal account of the origins of the non-Brahmanic custom of 'renunciation', namely, the beginnings of the Śramaṇa Movement. The legend, therefore, seems to link **paccekabuddhas** with an archaic ascetic tradition. This interpretation receives corroborative evidence in the Isigili Sutta, the earliest Buddhist canonical reference to the **paccekabuddha**. The following questions therefore present themselves: Could the **paccekabuddha** have been the source of the ascetic phenomenon of 'renunciation' in India? Could he have represented the common ascetico-religious background tradition which manifested itself ultimately in the sectarian forms of Buddhism and Jainism? Certainly the theory would account for the presence of this mysterious figure in both Buddhism and Jainism, and also would help shed light on the historical origins of these traditions and their similarities in doctrine, ethics and mythology.

Further confirmation of the theory that **paccekabuddhas** were proto-**śramaṇas**, arises out of the way in which Buddhist sources describe the experience of **paccekabodhi** (the form of enlightenment which gives rise to the concept **paccekabuddha**). This experience is represented as happening only to householders and occurs simultaneously with the decision to become a 'renouncer'. In short, there seems to exist a definitive connection between the attainment of **paccekabodhi** and the act of 'renouncing' household life. The theory which interprets the **paccekabuddha** as an ascetic figure antedating the rise of Buddhism and Jainism also helps to explain his equation with the **muni**. For the figure of the **muni** is mentioned as far back as the later portions of the Ṛg Veda, such as in the Keśin Hymn, where he is depicted as a mysterious ascetic with extraordinary powers.

Searching for the historical identity of the **paccekabuddhas** by investigating their connection with the ascetic categories of **isi**, **samaṇa** and **muni**, has provided us with sufficient evidence to produce a cogent and coherent explanation of the **paccekabuddha** concept. This explanation can be summarized as follows: The Buddhist and Jain traditions had their origin in the Śramaṇa Movement which began as a protest by **kṣatriyas** against the Brahmanic stranglehold on religion and society. This protest expressed itself in the adoption of an ethic of world-renunciation. The movement redefined and gave its own significance to many traditional Brahmanic concepts as it grew in momentum and challenged the hegemony of the Brahmanic tradition. After some time the cultural phenomenon of 'renunciation' developed sectarian differences within its own tradition. The period from the beginnings of 'renunciation', whilst the movement was still principally a maverick phenomenon, until the period prior to sectarian divisions can be said to mark the epoch of the original **muni**, the proto-**śramaṇa** or proto-**buddha** figure. The concept of the **paccekabuddha** in the post-Buddhist and post-Jain period is an anachronism for this figure. Here lies the original significance of that concept.

This theory provides a comprehensive explanation of the doctrine of the **paccekabuddha** in Canonical Buddhism as expressed in the three propositions (supra) defining their status and their relationship to the figure of the Buddha. The first proposition, that no form of **buddha** has a teacher, can be read as evidence that the Buddhistic tradition had its roots in the heuristic principle of discovering truth through one's own experience rather than by accepting the teaching and authority of another. With regard to the second proposition, it is to be noticed that notions of a **dhamma**, **saṅgha** and **sāvaka** (disciple) together with the notion of a 'founder', are all corollaries of a sectarian based organisation. The doctrinal affirmation that **paccekabuddhas** are not themselves 'founders' of a **dhamma** or a **saṅgha**, is consistent with them belonging to the pre-sectarian stage of the tradition. The idea that the **paccekabuddha** is incapable of teaching **dhamma** can itself be understood as a dogmatic overlay of interpretation on a de facto state of affairs - the **paccekabuddha** existed prior to the emphasis on distinct teachers with their own doctrine and principles of practice. So we see the rise of historical Buddhism as corresponding to the growth of a **sāvaka** tradition, where initiation involves the principle of following the teaching of one man. Once this principle becomes enshrined, the idea of realising a spiritual goal without the assistance of another begins to decline.

The third proposition, that **paccekabuddhas** cannot exist at the same time as a **sammāsambuddha**, marks the full adoption and investiture of the principle that a teacher is a sine qua non for salvation. If **paccekabuddhas** were admitted to exist it would undermine the rationale of a **sāvaka**-based organization. In canonical theory there survives two forms of **buddha**, but in practice there is only one: he who justifies the existence of the **sāvaka** tradition - Sākyamuni Buddha. It is to be observed that such a proposition occurs only in the later and post-Nikāya period, at a time when the Buddhist tradition had acquired an established organizational structure. Prior to that time there is evidence to suggest that the attitude toward the attainment of enlightenment was a good deal more fluid.

The interpretative framework which we have found best assists the clarification of these historical and doctrinal developments is a sociological one. The sorts of events that characterize the emergence and rise of Buddhism as a major religion are seen to be those which follow a similar pattern sociologically to that of many new religious movements. In particular, to see the Buddha as a successful charismatic leader and to see the demise of the notion of 'freely-realizable' enlightenment as part of the process whereby the movement successfully achieves 'routinization' of that charisma, helps to make sense of the sorts of doctrinal developments that have been outlined above. We have, therefore, decided to utilise the term 'cultus' (worship) to represent the behaviour of the Buddhist tradition in its origins and inception. This term has been chosen advisedly for two reasons: firstly, because of its associations with the word 'cult'. We have deliberately not used the word 'cult', for obvious reasons, but we are aware that the study of so-called 'cults' has and can prove instructive for the understanding of more enduring religious movements. We would like this association borne in mind throughout this study. Secondly, the word 'cultus' perhaps represents for us an interpretative key for analysing traits and trends of behaviour exhibited by Early Buddhism. In particular it is a term which adequately conveys the dynamic driving principle underlying the growth of Buddhism, the principle of the uniqueness of Sākyamuni and his teaching. In this respect, Buddhism was operating no differently than its sectarian rivals. Brahmanism, for instance, assimilated salvation to the notion of dutiful performance of 'sacrificial rites' and represented the **brāhmaṇa** as the sole mediator. Buddhism displays a similar structure: the figure of Sākyamuni becomes the sole mediator and his teaching (**dhamma**) the means of salvation. We have, therefore, considered it appropriate to refer to Buddhism in its beginnings as "the Sākyamuni 'cultus'". In short, the rise of historical Buddhism was inspired by the belief in the *sui generis* character of the Buddha and his teaching.

In giving accentuation to the importance of these particular features in the origins of Buddhism we may lay ourselves open to the accusation that we have altogether ignored the paramount role of the 'moral' and 'reformative' factors in the emergence of Buddhism, its critique of caste and of animal sacrifice, or have undervalued the originality of the Buddha and his teaching. It is not our intention to denigrate these factors or underestimate the ethical dimension of Buddhism, and we do not see our thesis as detracting from them. Indeed, it will be seen that a main pillar of this thesis is the argument that the primary impetus behind the disaffection with Brahmanic religion and the mores of existing culture was the affirmation of the religious and moral postulate of **ahiṁsā** (non-injury). That at some point in society's emergent moral sensibilities and ascetico-religious techniques a figure such as that of the Buddha should have encapsulated and given new direction and initiative to those developments is no surprising observation in respect of comparisons with the sociological beginnings of other faiths with historical founders. To see the Buddha as part of a wider currency of values operating at the time and to see him as a focus of special 'worship' is not to cast aspersions on his originality or the moral force of his message. Our foremost object has been to understand the way in which he was apprehended by his followers. Here the very existence of the category of ascetic known as **paccekabuddha** as well as the construction placed upon that category by his followers is highly pertinent to the issue of that apprehension.

## Primary Sources

As far as we are aware the **paccekabuddha** is not mentioned in other than Buddhist and Jain literature. This is only to be expected, since the term has doctrinal significances specially associated with these representative traditions of the Śramaṇa Movement. In Buddhist literature our analysis of the subject of the **paccekabuddha** concentrates mainly on the Pali corpus of texts and Buddhist Sanskrit sources. Within these sources material on the **paccekabuddha** (Skt.**pratyekabuddha**) can be classified on a two-fold basis, according to 'genre' and 'topics'. There are two kinds of genre: narratives (stories and legends) and expositions of doctrine. It is often the case that doctrinal expositions are integrated into the narrative. Doctrine may be expounded at various points during a narrative; alternatively, the narrative itself may be taken to illustrate doctrinal truths.

All material on the **paccekabuddha** can be subsumed under the following six topics:

1. Scenes of 'devotional acts' towards a **sammāsambuddha** - these result in the attainment of **paccekabodhi** in some future rebirth.

2. Scenes showing 'devotional acts' or acts of'abusive behaviour'towards **paccekabuddhas**, where reference is made to resultant 'merit' (P.**puñña**; Skt.**puṇya**) or 'demerit' (P.**apuñña**; Skt.**apuṇya**).

3. Scenes that depict persons becoming **paccekabuddhas** (attaining **paccekabodhi**)

4. Alleged sayings of **paccekabuddhas** (e.g., the stanzas of the Khaggavisāṇa Sutta of the Sutta-nipāta).

5. Enumeration of (a) those attributes of the **paccekabuddha** which make them an exemplar of spiritual attainment. (b) the path of the **paccekabodhisatta** (i.e.,**paccekabuddha-to-be**) over numerous existences during which the requisite attributes are brought to fruition.

6. Concise statements of dogma or doctrinal formulae relating to **paccekabuddhas**.

## Alleged Sayings of Paccekabuddhas

In the Buddhist and Jain traditions there are a small number of groups of 'sayings' ascribed to **paccekabuddhas**. These 'sayings' are representative of a long-standing tradition of gnomic and didactic literature in India. In the Pali tradition, the 'sayings' are preserved in 'metrical form' (i.e., **gāthā**) and are of two kinds: **udāna** (moral utterances) and **subhāsita** ('well-spoken' words). According to Buddhist Commentarial tradition, the **udāna** states succinctly the prime cause of the **paccekabuddha**'s enlightenment, and is spoken upon the occasion of his enlightenment or immediately before his death (i.e., **parinibbāna**); it is further remarked that the **paccekabuddha** makes his **udāna** either in response to a question (**puṭṭha**) or according to his own measure of understanding if there is no question.[6] These utterances are sometimes also referred to as **vyākaraṇa** (explanations).[7] It is possible that they were given as mantras to meditate upon.[8] A **subhāsita** consists, on the other hand, of a form of 'admonition' or 'general moral advice' (**ovāda**) intended to save people from the four hells (**apāya**).[9] Quite clearly, the distinction between the **udāna** and the **subhāsita** shows that some 'sayings' were spoken to the ears of lay people who were regarded as potential initiates into the life of a **bhikkhu** and some to those who were not regarded so. In short, there seems to have existed an esoteric-exoteric distinction.

According to the later Nikāya and Pali commentarial tradition the stanzas of the Khaggavisāṇa Sutta (Sutta-nipāta vv.35-75) are **udānas** of **paccekabuddhas**.[10] They are composed in **triṣṭubh** metre which marks them as belonging to the oldest stratum of Pali verse. These same stanzas have also become incorporated within the Paccekabuddhāpadāna section of the Apadāna (pp.7-14). In addition there is a somewhat truncated and repetitious Buddhist Sanskrit version to be found in the Mahāvastu (I.357) which likewise identifies the stanzas as **udānas** of **pratyekabuddhas**. The Mahāvastu identifies the authors as belonging to a tradition of 'five hundred' **pratyekabuddhas** who resided at Vārānaṣī and passed away into **parinirvāṇa** on learning of the imminent birth of the **bodhisattva**. In the Pali tradition, the commentaries to the Sutta-nipāta and the Apadāna, called the Paramatthajotikā and the Visuddhajanavilāsini respectively, describe how these stanzas came to enter the Buddhist tradition.[11] Both commentaries agree that the stanzas were first transmitted by the Buddha in response to an inquiry from his disciple Ānanda about the meaning of **paccekabuddha** and **pacceka-bodhi**. The Paccekabuddhāpadāna version reads:

> 'When the Tathāgata was dwelling in Jetavana The Vedeha **muni** (i.e. Ānanda), first paying homage, asked: "Wise one, there are said to be **paccekabuddhas**, how do they come to be?" '

The commentarial version reads:

> 'Whilst he was dwelling in solitariness and seclusion, the following thought occurred to Ananda: "The aspirations (**paṭṭhāna**) and resolves (**abhinīhāra**) of Buddhas is known, likewise of **sāvakas**, but that of **pacceka-buddhas** is not known. Let me question the Lord on this." Rising from his solitariness, he approached the Lord and asked him about this matter. Thereupon, the Lord taught the saying on 'strivings in former existences' (**pubbayogāvacare**): "There are five results of 'strivings in former existences':-
>
> One achieves knowledge (**aññā** i.e.,**bodhi**)
> (1) before death
> if not then (2) at death
> if not then (3) as a god (**deva-putta**)

if not then (4) through 'sudden intuition' (**khippābhiñña**) in the presence of **buddha**.
if not then finally, (5) as a **paccekabuddha**.

In the course of his description and definition of **paccekabuddha** the Buddha transmits to Ānanda the stanzas which came to comprise the Khaggavisāṇa Sutta. These stanzas are understood to represent the definitive collection of **paccekabuddha** 'sayings' from the point of view of the Buddhist tradition.

However there are a number of miscellaneous stanzas occurring in the Jātakas also imputed to be sayings of the **paccekabuddha**. The most important of these are the so-called eight **samanabhadra gāthā** (stanzas about the blessings of being a 'renouncer') stating why life as a **samana** is preferable to life as a **gahaṭṭha** (householder). They are part of the moral instruction (**ovāda**) that a **paccekabuddha** called Sonaka imparts to a king.[12] Once again an equivalent version is found in the Mahāvastu.[13]

## Pali Literature

Most of the Pali literature on the subject of the **paccekabuddha** belongs to the fifth Nikaya and the Commentaries, for the reasons we have stated earlier in the introduction. The sections of the Paramatthajotikā and Visuddhajanavilāsini that comment upon the Khaggavisāṇa stanzas are almost identical.[14] They follow the traditional commentarial method: a gloss on the terms in the original together with an illustrative tale; in this case the tale depicts the circumstances in which an individual stanza or group of stanzas came to be uttered. Altogether there are forty tales, each relating how a particular King of Bārāṇasī renounced his throne and attained **paccekabodhi**. These tales represent the fourth kind of topic, scenes in which persons become **paccekabuddhas**. The non-narrative portions of these two Commentaries provide us with material relating to topics five and six. There are also tales featured within the Commentaries which describe acts of 'service' or 'abuse' to **paccekabuddhas** (topic two). Of especial note among the commentarial tales, however, is the one depicting the birth and enlightenment of the legendary 'five hundred' **paccekabuddhas** referred to in the Isigili Sutta.[15]

In Pali sources the most important corpus of 'narratives' about **paccekabuddhas** occurs in the Jātakas. These ascetics are mentioned in more than thirty Jātaka stories and figure prominently in at least ten of these. The Kumbhakāra (J.III.377ff.) and the Pānīya Jātakas (J.IV.114ff.) together furnish nine individual examples of persons becoming **paccekabuddhas**. Jātaka material is also significant in two other respects: Firstly, some of the imagery is the same or similar to that occurring in the Khaggavisāṇa stanzas; secondly, the stories figure within the framework of 'dynasty' myths. In this kind of myth the allegedly significant religious history (the former existences of the **bodhisatta**) of pre-Sākyamuni times is charted according to 'dynasties'. Each story begins with a reference to the name of the dynasty and the particular ruler at the time the events described took place. There is no systematic or chronological scheme (except for the final Jātaka which depicts the last human existence of the **bodhisatta** prior to his entry to the

Tusita heaven). However, Buddhist chronologies of pre-Sākyamuni dynasties are found in the Mahāvaṁsa and the Dīpavaṁsa Chronicles and with the aid of these we can acquire a general picture of 'historical' or 'mythical' succession. We have therefore been able to show which stories purportedly belong to which era, and on this basis make inferences about how the Buddhists viewed the times prior to the advent of Gotama Buddha.

## Buddhist Sanskrit Literature

Buddhist Sanskrit literature falls broadly into two categories: Mahāyāna and non-Mahāyāna. In the Mahāyāna, the **pratyekabuddha** has no longer a quasi-historical or mythical dimension but operates entirely at a doctrinal level to signify the idea of one who is selfish and spiritually shortsighted for not acting in the best salvific interest of others. Mahāyāna texts, therefore, have no direct relevance to the subject of this book and, with one exception, are disregarded. This exception is a short Mahāyāna text devoted entirely to the subject of the **pratyekabuddha**, and known as the Pratyekabuddhabhūmi. When some of the pronouncements on the **pratyekabuddha** in the Sanskrit Avadāna sources are paralleled in the Pratyekabuddhabhūmi, we have seen fit to draw attention to this. There may also be individual terms and concepts we come across in the course of our discussion which receive fuller expression in the Mahāyāna; in such circumstances the Mahāyāna conception will be found useful in clarifying or amplifying the meaning.

Amongst non-Mahāyāna sources we have drawn heavily upon the Sanskrit Avadāna literature, notably, the Mahāvastu, Divyāvadāna and Avadāna Śataka. The Avadāna texts are a literary genre designed to bolster the Buddhist doctrine of **karma** by using 'narratives' to show how present and prospective mundane and supramundane accomplishments are the result of (past) deeds; hence the name **avadāna** (heroic deed or act). These texts have proved important to our study because they provide a non-Theravada window on the subject of the **pratyekabuddha**: the Avadāna Śataka and Divyāvadāna are presumed mainly Sarvāstivādin works and the Mahāvastu is a product of the Lokottaravādin branch of the Mahāsamghikas. Doctrinally this gamut of literature, in contrast to the Pali, represents a shade of opinion within the **bhikkhu-saṅgha** more tolerant of the exhibition of 'magic powers' by Buddhist ascetics. So, for instance, displays of 'magic power' are often used by **pratyekabuddhas** to rouse devotional responses, as well as themselves being a form of response by **pratyekabuddhas** to devotional acts of service from the layperson. The difference is important because in one case it is the **buddha** and in the other the devotee who instigates the 'religious' or 'revelatory' experience; a difference functionally corresponding to the distinction between prevenient and cooperating grace in Christian theology.

The Avadāna Śataka is a work that warrants especial mention. The third decade of the one hundred tales (Nos.21-30) of which this work is composed are devoted entirely to the theme of **pratyekabodhi**. Two of these tales (Nos. 21 and 24) describe how in previous eras certain persons become **pratyekabuddhas** as the karmic consequence of performing 'devotional acts' towards the Buddhas Kaśyapa and Vipaśyī. Both these stories give an account of the sorts of circumstances and experiences that result in **pratyekabodhi**. Candana

(No. 21), for instance, attains his **pratyekabodhi** as a result of contemplating a withering flower which in Buddhist literature is the most regularly depicted manner of realising that goal. The eight remaining stories describe how the performance of 'devotional acts' towards the Buddha Sākyamuni will lead the individual to have auspicious future rebirths and eventually to the realisation of **pratyekabodhi** itself. These stories all share the same basic format:

1. The devotee usually belongs to a lower social status.
2. He/she espies the Buddha.
3. He/she offers a gift or performs some cultic act of devotion to the Buddha.
4. The Buddha performs a feat of magic (**ṛddhi**) that brings a faith (**prasāda**) response.
5. (Sometimes) the devotee declares aloud his particular wish or aspiration (**praṇidhāna**).
6. The Buddha smiles and utters a 'prediction' (**vyākaraṇa**) - a verbal guarantee - that **pratyekabodhi** will take place for that person in some future rebirth.
7. The 'mundane' consequences of the devotee's act of merit are outlined.
8. It is stated what will be the devotee's name as a **pratyekabuddha**. The name is always derived from association with the type of cultic act which secured the assurance of **pratyekabodhi**.

The striking doctrinal feature of these stories about **pratyekabodhi** is that this attainment is only made possible by the mediation of the Buddha or Buddhas. All those who achieve **pratyekabodhi** at some point during their sequence of rebirths perform an act of devotion to a **samyaksaṁbuddha** (**sammāsambuddha**), and this act is represented as the necessary and sufficient condition of that achievement. In other words, the authors of the Avadāna Śataka have assimilated the notion of the **pratyekabuddha** within a **samyaksaṁbuddha** qua Sākyamuni 'cultus' framework. In addition to this decade of stories,the **pratyekabuddha** features in eleven other stories from the Avadāna Śataka (Nos.17,41,44,80, 87-90,94,98,99) as an object of alms-giving or maltreatment. Finally we have included as Appendix II a table showing recurrent formulae (topic six) used of **pratyekabuddhas** in the Avadāna Śataka and the Divyāvadāna.

## Jain Literature

Jainism has a doctrinal equivalent to the notion of the **paccekabuddha** in its own religious tradition, the figure of the (Pkt.) **patteyabuddha**.[16] The distinction between the **paccekabuddha** and **sammāsambuddha** which exists in Buddhism has its counterpart in the Jain doctrine of the **patteyabuddha** and **svayambuddha**. Evidence suggests, as in respect of Buddhism, that the actual term **patteyabuddha** was not known to the authors of the oldest sections of their canon. According to Schubring, the term first occurs in the Viyahapannatti, one of the eleven **angas**, where it is mentioned without any form of definition. **Patteyabuddha** first appear in narratives in the Āvaśyaka Mūla-sūtra. However, the most important Jain texts on the subject are the Uttarādhyayana Sūtra and the Isibhāsiyāiṁ.

Charpentier describes the Uttarādhyayana as a work "in its original contents more like the old Buddhist works, the Dhammapada and the Sutta-nipāta".[17] Although dating Jain canonical texts is notoriously difficult and hazardous Charpentier assigns the composition of the essential text to a period (circa 300 BCE) similar to that when the Sutta-nipāta is believed to have been composed.[18]

The Uttarādhyayana contains a collective reference to four kings who are later identified by the Commentaries as **patteyabuddhas**. These same four kings also appear in early Buddhist legend and are identified as **paccekabuddhas** by Buddhist Commentaries too. We analyse the substance of this legend in chapter three and show how it sheds light on the **paccekabuddhas** early śramaṇic identity.

The Isibhāsiyāiṁ (sayings of the Ṛṣis) is a text whose diction and vocabulary suggest contemporaneity with the first two and probably oldest of the extant Jain **aṅga**, the Ācārāṅga Sūtra and Sūtrakṛtāṅga, as well as with the Mūla Sūtras, Uttarādhyayana Sūtra and Daśavaikālika. Schubring considers the Isibhāsiyāim to be among the most ancient of Jain texts with origins circa 300 BCE.[19] Interestingly, however, it is not included within the Jain canonical corpus and may therefore be said to hold an apocryphal status. The text first became known to Western scholars in a printed edition, Indaur 1927, entitled 'Śrīmadbhiḥ pratyekabuddhair bhāṣitāni Ṛṣibhāṣitasūtrāni' which also included an appendix with compendiums (**samgahaṇī**) of the **ṛṣi**'s names and their associated maxims. The work has since been re-edited by Schubring (Isibhāsiyāiṁ. Ein Jaina Text der Fruhzeit, NAGW, 1942,- pp.489-576; 1952, pp.21-52) but has not yet been translated into a European tongue. The text is composed of 45 sections (**ajjhayaṇa**), each section comprising the sayings of an individual **ṛṣi**. As the title of the Indaur edition and an inscription on the manuscript (op. cit., p.490) indicate, these **ṛṣis** are to be equated with **patteyabuddhas**. This might explain the apocryphal as opposed to the canonical status of the work. Each section has the same fourfold structure: the maxim of the **rsi**; name of the **rsi**; an account of his accomplishment; and a conclusion. A single formula is used to introduce the said name and author of the maxim e.g., **'Vajjiyaputteṇa arahatā isiṇā buitaṁ'** (said by Vajjiyaputta the **arahata**, the **isi**), likewise, a common formula is used for the conclusion: **'evam se buddhe virate vipāve dante daviealam tāī no punaṛ-avi icc-atthaṁ havvam āgacchati tti bemi'**. We have not examined this text in great detail since a translation and thorough analysis of it would constitute a major feat of scholarship and linguistic enterprise in its own right.[20] Instead we briefly draw attention to certain features relevant to the main thrust of our enquiry:

a. The text is an indication that **pacceka-buddhas** held a similar status in Jainism to that in Buddhism; for their 'sayings' were considered to be of sufficient value to be retained and cherished within both traditions.
b. The Isibhāsiyāiṁ and the Khaggavisāṇa Sutta are early texts within their respective traditions. This supports our theory that the **paccekabuddha** has a significance which pertains to the early stages of these traditions.
c. Schubring points out that the concepts of the Isibhāsiyāiṁ are neither highly technical nor doctrinally sophisticated. This observation is important to our theory of the **paccekabuddha's** pre-sectarian identity.
d. Within it are repeated many of the concepts which we discuss in connection with the figure of the **paccekabuddha** in the Buddhist sources e.g. **muni**, **vimutti**, **paccayya**, **bhaya**, **bandhana**, **savvadukkham**, etc.
e. There is no mention of the term **patteya-**

**buddha** in the sections, but the **isis** are nevertheless categorized as **buddha**. In other words this text corroborates the argument that the concept of the **paccekabuddha** is later than the ascetic figure whom it was used to denote.

This study has been arranged into four chapters. The first chapter serves very much as the pyramidical base. Here we examine and seek to clarify the meanings attached to the figures and notion of **paccekabuddhas** in the earliest references to them in the Buddhist sources. It is from this examination that we discover the idea of their archaic identity and their link with the concepts of **isi**, **samaṇa** and **muni**. We go on to amplify the significance of their association with these categories by seeking to establish the full connotation of these terms. Each of the three remaining chapters take respectively as their theme, **isi**, **samaṇa** and **muni**, and explore the implications of their association with the **paccekabuddha** in a wider trans-sectarian context and in respect to their projected archaic identity. Each category therefore serves as a discrete but complementary avenue of investigation, and when taken together provide a comprehensive testimony to the thesis that the word **paccekabuddha** denoted the historical forerunners of Buddhism. In the final part of the fourth chapter we evaluate the import and significance of this evidence for scholarly understanding of the origins of Buddhism.

**Notes**

1. The main works on the subject of **paccekabuddhas** to date are Pavolini,

(1899) Sulla Leggenda dei Quattro Pratyekabuddha, Actes du XII Congres d'Oriental, I. pp.129ff; J. Charpentier, (1908) Paccekabuddhageschichten, Uppsala; L. de la Vallee Poussin, (1918) 'Pratyekabuddha', ERE. Vol.10. pp.152-4; H. Sakurabe, (1956) 'On Pratyekabuddhas' (Engaku ko), Otani Gahuho, XXXVI, 3, pp.40-51; Cooray, (1957) 'Paccekabuddha', pp.57-63 (an unpublished Article submitted to EB); K. Fujita, 'One vehicle or Three', J.I.P. Vol.3. Nos 1/2, March/April 1975 (published in Japanese, 1969); R.Kloppenborg, (1974), 'The Paccekabuddha - A Buddhist Ascetic. A study of the concept of the paccekabuddha in Pali canonical and commentarial literature', E.J.Brill. An amended and slightly attenuated version has since been published by the Buddhist Publication Society in Kandy (1983). Malalasekera's article (s.v., 'paccekabuddha') in DPPN is also a significant contribution to the subject; K.R.Norman, (1983), 'The Pratyekabuddha in Buddhism and Jainism' in Buddhist Studies Ancient and Modern, Ed. P.Denwood and A.Piatigorsky, Curzon Press Ltd., London.

2. Pb.Ap.3:'they attain **paccekabodhi** without (the instruction of) **buddhas**' (**vināpi buddhehi...paccekabodhiṁ anupāpuṇanti**).
   At Pug.14/70/73 both the **paccekabuddha** and the **sammāsambuddha** are defined as a person who 'comes to the knowledge of the **dhamma** on his own, without having heard the truths before' (**pubbe ananussutesu dhammesu sāmaṁ saccāni abhisambujjhati**). This formula appears as early as the Majjhima Nikāya (II.21) but is there used only of the Buddha.

3. 'their consideration for the world is not the transcendental (**lokuttara**) but the

mundane (**lokiya**) welfare of persons' (Mahāvaṁsa-ṭīkā - cite Cooray p.59). '**buddhas** bring themselves and others to enlightenment; **paccekabuddhas** bring themselves to enlightenment but not others' (Sn.A.51). Unlike the **sammāsambuddha**, the **paccekabuddha** attains neither 'omniscience' (**sabbāññu**) nor 'mastery of the fruits' (**phalesu vāsibhavam** - Pug.73). Hence he lacks the faculties considered necessary for the creation of **sāvakas**.

4. cf., for example, Pb.Ap.2: 'Ye **sabbabuddhesu katādhikārā aladdhamokkhā Jinasāsanesu**' (Those who honoured all **buddhas** without attaining liberation during the dispensation of a Jina); Sn.A.51: '**paccekabuddhā buddhe appatvā buddhānaṁ uppajjanakāle yeva uppajanti**' (**paccekabuddhas** are those who do not become **buddhas** in the time of the appearance of **buddhas** [i.e., **sammāsambuddha**]). See also S.A.III.189,208; A.A.I.194; II. 192; Sn.A.128-9.
5. infra pp.49-51
6. Sn.A.46. See, also, the Kumbhakāra and Pāṇīya Jātakas where the **bodhisatta** asks each of the novitiate **paccekabuddhas** what 'theme' (ārammaṇa) had decided them to become **bhikkhus**. In response each **paccekabuddha** divulges his own 'theme' in the form of 'a single stanza' (**ekekaṁ gāthaṁ**).
7. According to Pb.Ap.6 and Ap.A.151/Sn.A.63 the **gāthās** of the Khaggavisāṇa Sutta constitute **vyākaraṇas** and **udānas**. When a **paccekabuddha** provides another with a **vyākaraṇa**, he in fact informs that person of the 'subject of reflection' (**ārammaṇa**) which resulted in his **pabbajjā/paccekabodhi**. See J.IV.116-117; Sn.A.95.

8. See, for example, J.III.472-3; the Nikayas acknowledge that in pre-Sakyamuni times **mantas** were used to evoke some forms of awakening: mantāya **bodhabbaṁ** (awaken through **mantras**) - A.IV.136-7/ D.II.246.
9. Ap.A.205. Subhāsita (Skt.**subhāṣita**) is a recognised genre of Indian literature and is to be found in most Sanskrit works (Sternbach IBG Vol.I.p.2). There is a **sutta** in the Sutta-nipāta (pp.78-9) on the subject of **subhāsitas**. Examples of the **subhāsitas** of **paccekabuddhas** may be found at Pb.Ap.55,56; J.III.241-245.
10. Sn.A.46/Ap.A.138-9; Nd.II318ff.; Ap. p.8.
11. Sn.A.147; Ap.A.139.
12. J.V.252-3.
13. Mvu.III.452-3.
14.

| **Ap.A** | | **Sn.A.** |
|---|---|---|
| pp.128-138 | | - |
| 138-142 | = | 46-51 |
| 142 (slight variation) | | 51 |
| 142-145 | = | 51-54 |
| 145 (l. 10-24) | | - |
| - | | 54(l.20)-55(l.29) |
| 145ff. | = | 55ff. |
| - | | 130-131 |
| 202-206 | | - |

15. There are two versions of this tale: A.A. I.345-56; Thig.A.182-190.
16. The concept of the **patteyabuddha** in Jainism has the same significance doctrinally as in Buddhism. The principles of the three propositions which we have used in the introduction to summarise Buddhist doctrine on the **paccekabuddha** may also, therefore, apply to the Jain doctrine. For example, proposition.(1) "Not having heard" means like the **pratyekabuddha**: '**asoccā yathā pratyekabuddh'adih**', quoted by J. Deleu, Vihāyapannatti, Brugge, 1970, p.160. cf.

also A.M. Ghatage, 'Kahanaya-tigam: A Prakrit Reader', Kolhapur 1950, p.49: Jacobi SBE. XLV.Pt.II. p.35 n.2; Schubring p.23; Stevenson p.171.
Prop.(ii): Isibhāsiyāiṁ p.490-491.
Prop.(iii):Isibhāsiyāiṁ p.492.

17. Charpentier (1) p.40.
18. ibid., p.48.
19. Schubring p.81.
20. The text has been studied by Dr.H.Nakamura in two articles entitled, 'The Buddhism of the earliest period, as typified by Sāriputta' (Sāriputta ni daihyo-sareta sai shoki no Bukkyo), Indogakaku Bukkyokagu Kenkyu 14.2.1966, pp.1ff.; 'The Sage Yājñavalkya in the Jain Tradition' (Tetsujin Yajinyavarukya - Jaina-kyo no shoden) op. cit. 15.1.1966, pp.29ff.

Chapter One
# The Paccekabuddha in Early Pali Sources

In this opening chapter we examine the conception of the **paccekabuddha** according to the early and middle period of the composition of the Pali Nikāyas. Our intention is to survey the earliest available textual evidence on the subject for the purposes of constructing a picture that can be compared with the established conception of the **paccekabuddha** in later Buddhist dogma. In this oldest material, three types of passage are found to be relevant to our inquiry: a) those in which the term **paccekabuddha** occurs, b) those in which there is no explicit mention of **paccekabuddhas** but some evidence to suggest they are being referred to; c) the stanzas of the Khaggavisāṇa Sutta of the Sutta-nipāta which later tradition ascribes to be 'sayings' of **paccekabuddhas**. Through a careful analysis of these types of passage we shall show how **isi**, **muni** and **samaṇa** emerge as the key terms for deciphering the identity of the **paccekabuddha**. Accordingly we shall then proceed to analyse their wider usage in the Nikāyas with a view to clarifying the precise significance of their application to the figure of the **paccekabuddha**.

## Explicit References to the Paccekabuddha

Explicit references to the figure of the **paccekabuddha** are relatively sparse in early

Pali sources. In fact, there are only eight passages in the first Four Nikāyas in which the term **paccekabuddha** is found to occur. The fact that it is not found in the Sutta-nipāta, for instance, but in the later portions of the four Nikāyas shows that the actual term itself was either not familiar or not important to the authors of some of the oldest strata of the Buddhist scriptures. This would indicate that the term **paccekabuddha** itself was coined sometime when the Nikāyas were in the process of composition or that it was assimilated from without during that same period.

Six out of the term's eight occurrences figure in the context of classificatory lists: three occasions in connection with the subject of the merit acquired through almsgiving; twice in connection with the subject of '**ṭhūpa**-worship'; and once with regard to the categorisation of types of **buddha**. The remaining two occurrences are in passages which are more extensive. One comprises a brief narrative about a **paccekabuddha** called Tagarasikkhī; the other represents the most prolonged and crucial mention within the early sources, where an entire Sutta, the Isigili, is devoted to the subject of **paccekabuddhas**. We shall supply a brief description of each of these passages but concentrate in especial detail on the Isigili Sutta.

## Dakkhiṇeyya

**Paccekabuddhas** happen to be included among those categories of being who according to Buddhist teaching are worthy of a gift (**dakkhiṇeyya**) of alms. As such they are here shown to depend upon the laity for their livelihood.

In the Dakkhiṇavibhaṅga Sutta of the Majjhima Nikāya (III.254) the **paccekabuddha** is placed second only to the **sammāsambuddha** within a hierarchy of fourteen kinds of individuals worthy to receive offerings. In this list he is given precedence over the **arahant** (a disciple that has realized **nibbāna**) and over those who are on the path to becoming an **arahant**.

In the Book of Tens from the Aṅguttara Nikāya (V.23) the **paccekabuddha** is again placed second to the **sammāsambuddha** within a hierarchy of ten persons said to be 'worthy of worship (**ahuneyya**), reverence (**pahuneyya**), offerings (**dakkhiṇeyya**), salutations with clasped hands (**añjalikaranīya**), a field of merit unsurpassed for the world' (**anuttaraṁ puññakkhettaṁ** lokassa). The eight remaining kinds of persons are the various types of **sāvaka** listed in the Canon: one released both ways (**ubhato-bhāga-vimutta**) one released by insight (**paññā-vimutta**), the body-witness (**kāya-sakkhī**), the (right) view-attainer (diṭṭhippatta), one released by faith (**saddhāvimutta**), one devoted to the doctrine (dhammānusāri), one devoted through faith (**saddhānusāri**), one who has entered the family [of sons of Buddha] (**gottabhū**).[1]

In the Book of Nines (A.IV.394-5) the **paccekabuddha** is again placed higher than the **arahant**: the fruit (**phala**) of a donation (**dānam**) of food to one **sammāsambuddha** is greater than donations to one hundred **paccekabuddhas** and the fruit of a donation to one **paccekabuddha** is greater than donations to one hundred **arahants**. In the Mahaparinibbana Sutta of the Dīgha Nikāya(II.142-3) and the Book of Fours from the Aṅguttara Nikāya (II. 245) the **sammāsambuddha**, **paccekabuddha**, tathāgatasāvaka (disciple of the Buddha) and **cakkavatti** (universal monarch) are the four beings alone considered 'worthy of a ṭhūpa' The Mahāparinibbāna Sutta explains the religious and doctrinal significance of the **ṭhūpa**: a **ṭhūpa** has the effect upon the people (**bahujana**) who adorn it with garlands, perfumes, and paint, that is, who 'honour' (**abhivaddeti**) and perform devotional acts (**pūja**) of 'arousing faith in their heart' (**cittaṁ pasādeti**) and consequently they will be reborn in a heaven (**sagga-loka**).[2]

**Buddha**

In the Book of Twos from the Aṅguttara Nikāya (I.77) the **sammāsambuddha** and the **paccekabuddha** are listed as the two persons (**puggala**) who are **buddha**. This constitutes an important basic reference, for it shows, firstly, that the Nikāyas acknowledge two types of **buddha** proper, and, secondly, that the **paccekabuddha** was not considered a category of disciple (**sāvaka**).

**Tagarasikkhī**

In the Dutiya-Vagga of the Saṁyutta Nikāya (I. .92) King Pasenadi questions the Buddha on the subject of the 'miser' (**asappurisa**: 'a person that does not share'). The king cites an example of a notorious miser who had recently died and asks how he came to be both wealthy and miserly in the same lifetime. The Buddha replies by saying that in a former life the miser had once given a **paccekabuddha** called Tagarasikkhī some alms but then afterwards regretted it. The Buddha explains to the king that the miser acquired his 'wealth' by virtue of the gift but inherited an incapacity to enjoy that wealth because he subsequently regretted making the gift.

There are three significant items of information regarding **paccekabuddhas** which can be gleaned from this narrative. In the first place, the **paccekabuddha** Tagarasikkhī is referred to as a **samaṇa**. Secondly, significant 'merit' (**puñña**) or 'demerit' (**a-puñña**) is seen to result from service or disservice to a **paccekabuddha**. Thirdly, we are informed that a time-span of seven existences in the **sagga-loka** elapsed between the incident with the **paccekabuddha** and the man's rebirth as a miser. Therefore we are led to understand that the **paccekabuddha** Tagarasikkhi lived in the distant past.

All but one of the aforementioned references to the **paccekabuddha** occur within the context of 'lay' Buddhist practice - **dana** and **pūja**. Before we proceed further on this point it is important that we define what we understand by 'lay' and 'monachist' practices and values in the context of our discussion. By 'lay' practices we refer to the householder's (**gahaṭṭha**) performance of concrete acts of service and devotion to those who have renounced the household life. By 'lay' values we mean the householder's concern with the fruits or consequences of those acts, notably his belief that they conduce to a better rebirth. His religious practice is aimed at improving his circumstances within the conditions of **saṁsāra**. These values are indicated by the term **lokiya** (this-wordly) in Canonical Buddhism, to distinguish them from those values which have a transcendental frame of reference. By 'monachist' practices we understand the **bhikkhu**'s mode of livelihood as a '**pabbajita**', 'one who has gone forth' from home to the homeless life and its associated forms of conduct. The **bhikkhu**'s values are centred upon the spiritual attainments made possible by the act of going forth (**pabbajjā**) from household life - **pabbajjā** confers upon him a unique social identity and assists his religious objective of detachment and an end to rebirth. These values are described as **lokuttara** (world-transcending).[3]

## Isigili Sutta

The Isigili Sutta (M.III.68-71) is the only discourse of the Buddha concerned exclusively with the subject of the **paccekabuddha.**[4] Albeit the Sutta is comparatively short. It has both metrical and prose sections which Barua takes to be evidence of the Sutta being a later work within the Nikāyas. It shares the same pattern as recognised later works like the Dīgha Nikāya and Buddhist Sanskrit texts.[5] In the most general terms the Sutta features an aetiological myth which is intended to explain the origins of the name Mount Isigili, one of the five hills that surround the town of Rājagaha, the capital of Māgadha. From a consideration of references to the mountain of Isigili in other parts of the Nikāyas it seems it was a place strongly associated with non-Brahmanical ascetics. In the Majjhima Nikāya it is named as a place where **nigaṇṭhas** (Jain monks) performed their austerities.[6] In the Saṁyutta Nikāya it features as a site where ascetics performed ritual suicide.[7] Elsewhere it is said to be the favourite residence of the Buddha's chief disciple, Mahā-Mogallāna, who is distinctive for his possession of powers of magic (**iddhi**).[8]

The theme of the Isigili Sutta is as follows: the Buddha tells a group of **bhikkhus** that Isigili acquired its name from an association with **paccekabuddhas** who existed 'in a former time' (**bhūtapubbam**). He explains that five hundred **paccekabuddhas** had once resided on the mountain. People (**manussa**) who witness them enter (**pavisanta**) the mountain and disappear (**na dissanti**), would exclaim: 'This mountain swallows these seers' (**ayaṁ pabbato ime isī gilatīti**). This is how the mountain came to acquire the name 'Isigili'; the people, envisaged the **pacceka-buddha** as a **seer** (P.**isi**; Skt.**ṛṣi**). The Sutta mentions the names of ninety-one of the five hundred **paccekabuddhas** said to inhabit the mountain, listing them and their respective virtues in the form of a hagiology. The Buddha concludes his discourse with a doxological refrain which comprises one of the earliest doctrinal pronouncements on **pacceka-buddhas**: 'These and other **paccekabuddhas** are of great power (**mahānubhāva**); they have stopped the flow of phenomenal existence (**bhāvanetti-khīṇā**). Praise (**vandatha**) all these immeasurable (**appameye**), great seers (**mahesī**) who are freed from all fetters (**saṅgā**), completely cooled (**parinib-buta**).'[9]

Listing the names of ascetics in the Sutta would seem to imply that **paccekabuddhas** held or were intended to hold some special significance for those to whom the Buddha's discourse was addressed. It therefore indicates that some form of 'cultus' must have existed in respect of them. Cooray, who has made a comparative analysis of names of **pacceka-buddhas** listed in the Isigili Sutta and its Commentary as well as in the Apadāna Commentary to the Khaggavisāṇa stanzas, remarks 'It is likely.that the original purpose of the list was to include the names of pre-Buddhist sages whom the people held in high esteem, especially in the localities where the cult of **paccekabuddhas** had its origins.'[10] Two facets of information gathered from our reading of later sources supports the notion of a 'cultus'. Firstly, a **paccekabuddha** is generally assigned a name whose significance relates to the specific nature of his spiritual attainment. In the introduction we noted that in the Avadāna Śataka **paccekabuddhas** come to acquire their names in this way. Every name therefore enshrines within itself a spiritual quality or property and can be used as a focus of inspiration and meditation. Secondly, the Isigili Sutta itself has been adopted by Singhalese tradition as a text for recital in Pirit ceremonies.[11] This goes to show that the **paccekabuddha** was seen as a special source of 'protective' power.

What are we to understand by the motif in which the **paccekabuddhas** mysteriously vanish into the mountain? It might simply be a dramatized account of ascetics entering the recesses of mountain caves which were their natural place of residence or retreat. Alternatively, it could be an allusion to ascetics exercising their 'magic power' (**iddhānubhāva**). It could refer to any one of a number of 'forms of magic' (**iddhividhā**) recognised in the Pali Canon. For instance, there is the power of making oneself invisible, or going, 'feeling no obstruction, to the farther side of a wall or rampart or hill (**pabbata**),as if through air'.[12] This utilization of magic appears the most plausible of the two explanations since the disappearance becomes a puzzle to the onlookers: the mountain 'swallows','devours' the **paccekabuddhas** and they mysteriously vanish. A naturalistic explanation is hardly sufficient to account for the dramatic tone of the incident. If, in fact, this is the correct construction to place upon the passage, then we already have in the earliest specific mention of **paccekabuddhas** their representation as ascetics who exercise 'magic' (**iddhi**). This interpretation is further confirmed by the **paccekabuddha**'s description as **mahānubhāva** (of great power) in the doxology section of the same Sutta.

It is not without significance that those people (**manussa**) who observe the ascetics disappear recognise them as **isis**. **Manussa** is here preferred to **jana** (viz.**mahājana**, **bahujana**), the latter being the more common Pali expression for a gathering of persons. **Manussa** is the standard Pali term for 'humankind' and is most often used in juxtaposition to other classes (**jāti**) of being (**satta**), such as the **devas** and the **petas**. Therefore the alignment here of **manussa** and **isi** possibly has the implication that the **paccekabuddhas qua isi** are a different (higher) category of being. Their sudden and inexplicable disappearance is evidence enough to the ordinary lay person that they are in possession of 'supra-normal' powers and therefore a fortiori are more than human (**uttari-manussa**).[13]

Other salient factors which emerge from an analysis of this Sutta are these: In the first place, three of the named **paccekabuddhas** are given the epithet **muni**. Secondly, the Sutta provides us with a definition of the word **paccekabuddha**: 'ye...**paccekam ev'ajjhagamuṁ subodhiṁ** (those who individually have come to right enlightenment).[14] This inclusion of a semantic definition of the word **paccekabuddha** would seem to suggest the term and its significance required explanation and clarification for those to whom this discourse of the Buddha was addressed. In short, it would suggest the relative unfamiliarity of the term. To this we would add that the general impression arising from the Sutta is of the comparative obscurity of these ascetics. We may note too that **paccekabuddhas** are depicted in the 'plural', that is, as a group or class of holy-men or ascetics. This is not the sort of evidence to support Gombrich's theory that the **paccekabuddha** is purely an hypothetical concept. On the contrary, there is every reason to suppose that the Sutta has come into existence on the basis of the conviction that there existed a class of ascetics for which **paccekabuddha** came to be the appropriate term. One of the points the Buddha communicates in his discourse is that **paccekabuddhas** are a very long-standing, time-honoured tradition. To this end he chooses the device of linking them with the name of a mountain that stems back to antiquity. The discourse makes it quite clear that they are, to quote the well known phrase, 'as old as the hills'. It therefore seems that its main purpose is to furnish the Buddhist tradition with some chronological or historical roots of its own. Making known (hence the significance of assigning names) the existence of antecedents or predecessors would provide the Buddha's own tradition of lay-followers and monks with a sense of historical continuity by showing them they have their very own tradition of forebears.

The three main points which emerge from our examination of the eight references to the **paccekabuddha** in the four Nikāyas are: firstly, he represents a long-standing tradition; secondly, he is regarded as a bona fide **buddha** or enlightened person and, thirdly,he is of considerable interest to Buddhist lay practice. We shall briefly comment on these points in turn. The reference to him as 'worthy of praise' **(vandatha)** in the Isigili doxology and as worthy of offerings **(dakkhiṇeyya)** and other aspects of homage might be taken to imply that he was a phenomenon which existed at the time of the Buddha. However, there is no corroborative evidence elsewhere supporting the theory that **paccekabuddhas** were contemporaries of the Buddha. In fact, the Isigili Sutta leads us to the conclusion that if Isigili mountain was at one time the residence of **paccekabuddhas** it quite evidently is not any more!

Nikāya doctrine makes it quite clear that there is only one buddhological counterpart to the **sammāsambuddha** and that is the **paccekabuddha**. However, it should be noted that whereas the term **paccekabuddha** occurs in this stratum of material we are considering, the word **paccekabodhi** does not. The word which the Isigili Sutta uses to designate the enlightenment of **paccekabuddha** is instead **subodhim**, a term occurring nowhere else in the four Nikāyas.[15] If the term **paccekabuddha** is comparatively late in terms of the composition of the four Nikāyas, then the term **paccekabodhi** evidently is even later still. **Paccekabodhi** becomes the stock term for the **paccekabuddha**'s enlightenment in the later canonical and post-canonical sources; that it is not used here presumably indicates that it was not yet in currency. This is an important observation, since it would appear to demonstrate that whilst there were two kinds of **buddha** there was only one form of **bodhi** (enlightenment). This would mean that the distinction which came to apply between a **sammāsambuddha** and a **paccekabuddha** was intended to be understood as soteriological not buddhological; that is to say, it had to do with their function in relation to others rather than with any intrinsic difference in their goals of attainment. The fact, however, that this holy-man was esteemed as a **buddha**, shows nevertheless that the Buddhists thought of him as organically related to their own tradition. And it should be stressed too that we have found no evidence to suggest that the **paccekabuddha** is denigrated in any way as, for example, in later sources with regard to his failure to teach; on the contrary, he is always referred to honorifically.[16]

We have seen that in the greater number of

the passages under discussion the **pacceka-buddha** is mentioned in the context of merit earning, clearly evincing his strong significance for 'lay' practice. This emphasis on merit-earning suggests the existence of a devotional 'cultus' among the laity. The fact of such a 'cultus' has been corroborated by the discovery of **paccekabuddha** images, by references to them in rock inscriptions, and by reports in Buddhist literature of stupas erected to **paccekabuddhas** in accordance with canonical injuctions.[17]

Finally, we have noticed that the **pacceka-buddha** is associated with just three categories of ascetic which feature in the ancient Indian religious tradition: isi (Skt.**ṛsi**), **muni** and **samaṇa** (Skt.**śramaṇa**). We shall consider the significance of this association after we have first discussed other passages in the early canonical sources that possibly relate to this ascetic figure.

## Passages which might refer to the Pacceka-buddha

There are some passages occurring in the four Nikāyas and elsewhere which do not explicitly mention **paccekabuddhas** but which nevertheless provide fairly strong grounds for supposing that they are being referred to. We shall cite a passage or passages taken from three different contexts and forward reasons why it is arguable they allude to these specific ascetics. We hope to show that the descriptions in these passages bear some relation either to some specific attribute or to the general picture of the **paccekabuddha** presented elsewhere in Buddhist literature. The first group of passages occur in the context of the story of Gautama Buddha's hesitation to teach. There are two passages, one taken from the Catūṣpariśatsūtra, which forms part of the Vināya of the Sarvāstivādins, and one from the Mahāvastu. The Pali equivalent is of no immediate interest here. However, the Pali tradition does have a comparable allusion but this occurs in the Mahāpadana Sutta, where it is Vipassī Buddha's enlightment not Gotama's that is being related. We see fit to cite this also. The Catūṣpariśatsūtra reads: 'The **dhamma** obtained by me is profound, of deep splendour, difficult to see, difficult to understand, incomprehensible, having the incomprehensible as its scope, fine, subtle, the sense of which can only be understood by the wise. If I were to explain this to other people, and if other people were not to understand it, that would mean weariness and distress to me and also depression of mind. Shall I retire, alone, to a forest hill-side, practising the discipline of those who abide in happiness?'[18] We may ourselves ask whether the Buddha's question at the end is a purely rhetorical one or whether it refers to an actually existing phenomenon of, solitary, forest-dwelling ascetics. The Mahāvastu version is the same as this, except for the final sentence which reads: 'Let me then abide in silence all alone in a tract of wilderness.'[19]

In the story of Vipassī's enlightenment as told in the Mahāpadana Sutta, it is said that after renouncing household existence, Vipassī is followed by a vast throng of eighty four thousand people. This circumstance he perceives to be intolerable if he is to make any definite spiritual progress. He therefore determines to: 'dwell alone, apart from the group (**eko gaṇasma**)...the eighty-four thousand **pabbajitas** went one way and Vipassī the **bodhisatta** went another way.'[20]. Having obtained his seclusion Vipassī goes on to develop the insight that results in his enlightenment.

The one common factor in all of these passages is the idea that the experience of **bodhi** belongs within the context of physical isolation from others. For our own purposes the Sarvāstivādin passage is the most indicative, for it implies an already existing tradition or custom of solitary ascetism - 'practising the discipline of those who abide in happiness'. As we have indicated this allusion may be nothing more than the use of literary licence in order to impart greater dramatic effect to the event of the Buddha's hesitation. Nevertheless, one of the distinctive features of the **paccekabuddha** is his solitary individualism as we shall shortly see from an analysis of the Khaggavisāṇa Sutta. In which case the words here ascribed to the Buddha may represent an oblique allusion to this particular ascetic phenomenon.

The second passage for discussion is found in the Saṅgārava Sutta of the Majjhima Nikāya.[21] Here the Buddha distinguishes from among **samaṇas** and **brāhmaṇas** three sorts of persons who have 'attained in this life super-knowledge which is perfect and transcendent', (**diṭṭha dhammābhiññā vosāna pāramippattā**). The first two sorts of persons are the three-veda (**tevijjā**) **brāhmaṇas** who rely upon tradition, and the reasoners and investigators (**takkī-vimaṁsī**). The third category of persons are those 'who come to the knowledge of the **dhamma** on their own, not having heard the truths before' (**pubbe ananussutesu dhammesu sāmaṁ yeva dhammam abhiññāya**). It is to this last category that the Buddha attaches himself. By so doing he implies that, as far as method and attainment goes, he himself is not entirely unique. This third category could of course be referring exclusively to

**sammāsambuddhas**, but there is nothing in the text itself to give substance to this interpretation. In fact there is no evidence of any sort of distinction between kinds of **buddhas** in this passage. The same formula occurs again in later Pali tradition and is there interpreted to mean both **sammāsambuddhas** and **paccekabuddhas**. That there is no mention of these two classes of **buddhas** in the earliest occurrence of the formula suggests the 'two-fold' distinction had not yet come into existence.

The third passage under consideration features a dialogue between the Buddha and a **brāhmaṇa** named Saṅgārava who is adviser to the king. The subject under discussion is **iddhipāṭihāriya** (the extraordinary phenomenon of magic). When the Buddha politely asks Saṅgārava what had been the topic of conversation between the king and his courtiers for that day, Saṅgārava replies that it was about the idea that fewer monks (**bhikkhu**) existed in the olden days: a greater proportion of them possessed supra-normal powers (**uttarimanussadhammā**) and, therefore, 'the extraordinary phenomenon of magic' was witnessed more often in those times. On hearing this the Buddha points out to Saṅgārava that 'magic (**iddhi**) is not the only type of extraordinary phenomenon (**pāṭihāriya**) that exists; there is also mind-reading (**ādesanā**) and verbal instruction (**anusāsanī**), and among these three the last is superior. One reason for us suggesting that those here referred to as monks of former times might be **paccekabuddhas** is that **paccekabuddhas** too are strongly associated with magic power in the mind of the laity. Whether or not this similarity presents itself as sufficiently convincing, it remains of considerable interest and worthy of note that this passage points to the existence of an increasing trend in the direction of monachism but, at the same time, a corresponding decline in yogic powers. We shall have occasion to remark further on this point in chapter four.

## The Sutta-nipāta

Before considering the Khaggavisāṇa Sutta it is necessary to make comment upon the work in which it occurs, the Sutta-nipāta. The term **paccekabuddha** is not found anywhere in the Sutta-nipāta, and the counterpart term, **sammāsambuddha**, occurs there only rarely. Terms such as **buddha** (v.545,571) **sambuddha** (v.178,180,1031), **buddhaseṭṭha** (v.1126), **tathāgata** (v.251,1031), **cakkhuma** (v.1132), **mahesi** (vv.176-7,356,481,915,1060,1082) **muni** (v.164,550,700 et seq), **satthar** (v. 545), **ādiccabandhu** (v.540) are those more commonly used to denote the person of Gotama Buddha. When **sammāsambuddha** is found to occur (p.106 and v.565), it is in the soteriological context of teaching the **dhamma**. The absence of the word **paccekabuddha** and the corresponding infrequence of **sammāsambuddha** in the Sutta-nipāta, together with their later juxtaposition together in the Book of Twos, suggests to us that the two terms functioned doctrinally in contradistinction to one another and were therefore meant to be understood as counterparts: the one denoting a soteriological, the other a non-soteriological **buddha**. If we are correct in postulating their doctrinal interdependence, then the absence of the one and relative scarcity of the other would seem to indicate that the greater part of the Sutta-nipāta was composed either prior to or in ignorance of this particular distinction.

The Sutta-nipāta is acknowledged by linguists as having some of the oldest examples of Pali verse.[22] Fausböll, who completed the first English translation of the work, says in his introduction that 'in the contents of the Sutta-nipāta we have ... an important contribution to the right understanding of Primitive Buddhism, for we see here a picture not of life in monasteries, but of the life of hermits in its first stage'.[23] The theory that the idea of two kinds of **buddha** was not at first part of Buddhism serves to explain why an early text like that of the Sutta Nipāta does not provide us with the information that the Khaggavisāṇa **gāthās** are specifically words of **paccekabuddhas**. With regard to the dating of these **gāthās**, both Cooray and Norman have pointed out that they must be comparatively early in composition, in view of the fact that a Commentary to them already occurs in the Pali Niddesa.[24]

We propose to argue, on the basis of material principally located in the Sutta Nipāta, that **muni** represented the original term for one who is considered 'enlightened' (**buddha**, **sambuddha**), and that the qualities or properties of the **muni** are synonymous with those characteristics of the holy-man who came to be designated **paccekabuddha** in the middle period of Nikāya composition. We shall further argue that the terms **sammāsambuddha** and **paccekabuddha** were introduced in order to supersede the singular **muni** conception and formed part of a project to establish a Sākyamuni 'cultus' in which boundary lines marking him off from other supposedly enlightened persons were introduced.

As the early schools of Buddhism share the view that the verses of the Khaggavisāṇa Sutta are 'utterances' of **paccekabuddha**, we shall regard the verses themselves as shedding light conceptually on these ascetics. We shall also regard certain other sections of the Sutta Nipāta as having a special relevance, for instance the Muni Sutta (vv.207-21), the Sundarikabhāradvāja Sutta (vv.462-84), the second section of the Nālaka Sutta (vv.699-723), the Māgandiya Sutta (vv.835-47) and Attadaṇḍa Sutta (vv.935-54). In commentarial tradition these Suttas are referred to collectively as the **moneyya suttas**. As the title **moneyya** (state of **muni**) denotes, these sections of the Sutta-nipāta have as their principal theme the subject of the **muni**. It is the similarity between the conception of the **muni** here and themes within the Khaggavisāṇa Sutta which has led commentarial tradition itself to remark that the **moneyya suttas** may as well appply to **paccekabuddhas**.[25] We shall therefore regard all these **gāthās** as a unified corpus of material.

Given this working hypothesis the first major observation to me made is that this material provides a monachist vista or perspective upon the ascetic, referring to the qualities which relate to the life of a renouncer (**pabbajita**) or monk (**bhikkhu**) and to its projected goals. By contrast, we have seen that most of the references to the '**paccekabuddha**' in the four Nikāyas refer to him in the context of 'lay' practice - giving (**dāna**) and devotional acts (**pūja**).

## The Khaggavisāṇa Sutta

In Pali there are two versions of the Khaggavisāṇa Sutta. One belongs to the Sutta-nipāta and the other is found in a section of the Apadāna known as the Paccekabuddhāpadāna. The Paccekabuddhāpadāna version has one more stanza than the Sutta-nipāta version, but in all other respects is identical. Accordingly, for the sake of simplicity, we shall confine all further discussion to the Sutta-nipāta version only. Each stanza (with the exception of Sn.45 which forms a duad with the succeeding stanza) concludes with the injunction 'one should wander alone like a rhinoceros' (**eko care khaggavisāṇakappo**). The entire collection is therefore known as The Rhinoceros Discourse, and the **paccekabuddha** has come to be metaphorically alluded to throughout Buddhist tradition as the single-horned rhinoceros who fares alone. The injunction to emulate the rhinoceros and fare alone is a figurative way of urging a person to become a **pabbajita**, defined in the Pali Canon as 'one who goes forth from a household to a homeless life' (**agārasmā anagāriyaṁ pabbajita**).[27] We shall henceforth use the term **pabbajjā** (Skt.**pravrajyā**) to mean the initial decision and act of leaving the household life, and the term **pabbajita** (Skt.pravrajita) to denote one who has made that decision and act.

The refrain '**eko care khaggavisāṇa-kappo**' quite evidently constitutes an exhortation to abandon life as a householder. The underlying theme of the stanzas is the contrast between the constraints upon the life of a householder and the freedom which characterises the homeless life. One is enjoined not only to physically separate oneself from family and social ties (vv.2,44,60,64-5) but to separate oneself in spirit from all types of dependence (v.43, 74). Happiness (**sokhya** - v.61) cannot be achieved within traditional society because social relationships involve physical (v.35) and emotional (vv.36-8) constraints. Affection (**sneha** - v.36; **pema** - v.41), resentment (v.49) and sensuality (**kāmaguṇa** - vv. 50-1) come from social interaction (**saṁsagga**-v.36) and result ultimately in states of fear (**bhaya** - v.37,49,51) and situations of peril (**ādīnava** - v.36,69). Concepts and metaphors of attachment abound within these stanzas: bonds (**bandhana** - v.44), bondage (**paṭibaddha** - v.37,65), fetters (**saṁyojana** - v.62,64; **saṅga** v.43,61); net (**jala** v.62, 71) and fish-hook (**gaḷa** - v.61). On the other hand, the **pabbajita**'s sense of freedom is conveyed by comparisons with wild-life: the rhinoceros, the deer (v.39), the elephant (v.53), the lion (vv.71-2).[28] The choice of 'wild animal' analogies is indicative not only of the kind of environment inhabited by the ascetic but represents a rudimentary or non-doctrinal mode of classification. There is one exception to the stress upon individualism in the Khaggavisāṇa Sutta and that consists of the verses (vv.45-7,58) which refer to the idea of the teacher and example: friendship with such a person is to be encouraged. As for the rest of mankind there are hazards in close ties with them. The suggestion that spiritual preceptors are hard to find almost implies that the stanzas were composed outside the context of the Sākyamuni 'cultus'.

Although these stanzas are traditionally associated with the **paccekabuddha** they, do not include the term **paccekabuddha**. The term which is used to personify the spiritual and ascetical ideals here expressed is **ekacarin**. Insofar as the stanzas of the Khaggavisāṇa Sutta represent the teaching of **paccekabuddhas** the notion of the **ekacarin** may be taken to represent the embodiment of the **paccekabuddha** ideal.

### The Moneyya Sutta

The concept of the **muni** requires some detailed analysis as it forms a vital piece of weaponry in our argument that the **muni** corresponds to a proto-**buddha** figure. Certain striking similarities between the **muni** and the **ekacarin** will hopefully become apparent in the course of this analysis.

According to the **moneyya suttas** the **muni** is one who has abandoned household life (vv. 220-1) because he has discerned (**dassati**) the futility of living as a householder. He has therefore conformed with the injunction of the Khaggavisāṇa Sutta to become a **pabbajita**, a solitary wanderer (**ekaṁ carantaṁ** v.208,213,218,718f; also vv.844-5,1078), dwelling on the outskirts of the forest (**vananta** - v.709; see also v.221,708) near to human habitation (vv.710-11). He subsists on the food given him by local villagers (v.217, 221, 708-13); he is therefore a mendicant (**bhikkhu** - v.221). He meditates (**jhāyati**) in the forest (v.709,719,221; cf. also v.165). He is distinctive for his behaviour qua mendicant: whatever befalls him he accepts with complete equanimity (**samāna-bhāva** - v.702; **sabbadhī samo**: 'remaining the same in all circumstances' - v.952; see also vv.226-17). Avoiding extremes (v.839,851, vv.854-5,858), he responds with neither pleasure nor displeasure (v.811; cf. also v.954), with neither desire nor grief (v.948) and reacts to neither praise nor calumny (v.217,702); consequently he is a model of restraint (**yatatta** - v.220, 723) and decorum (vv.852-3). He is specifically distinctive for his control of speech (v. 217,850) and he conducts his alms-round in silence (vv.711-13). He is described as dumb without being dumb (v.713), silent like the vast ocean (v.720), and calm (**santam**) like a deep pool (v.721). On the subject of 'speech' the figure of the **muni** is contrasted with the **samaṇa**: the latter 'while knowing, teaches **dhamma** and speaks much' (v.722); the former, 'while knowing, is restrained and speaks not much' (v.723). The **muni** is described as 'freed like the moon from Rāhu's grasp' (**cando va Rāhu-gahaṇā pamuttā** - v.465).

Above all, the **muni** is known as he who discerns (**dassati**):'he who discerns the end of rebirth' (**jātikhayantadassī** - v.209); 'through understanding the world, he who discerns the supreme' (**aññāya lokaṁ paramattha-dassiṁ** - v.219); 'he has discerned the state of tranquillity'(**addakkhi so santipadaṁ** - v.208). The muni's transcendence is otherwise represented as the attainment of 'tranquillity' (**santam** v.208,721,848,857,861) and as the ending of rebirth (v.209), that is, as the crossing over (v.857) of becoming (**bhāva**). His means to that transcendence is 'discernment' (**dassana**). Because he is free from **bhava** he no longer belongs within time (**kappa** v.860,911, 914) or to any category (**sankha** v.209) of being (**gati**; cf. also vv.1074-6). Thus the **muni** has entirely transcended the realm of this world (**loka-dhātu**). His detachment is frequently conveyed by reference to the metaphor of the lotus (**paduma**) rising above the murky water (v.779,812,845,913).

## The Terms Muni, Isi and Samaṇa in the Early Pali Sources

We have shown that the **paccekabuddha** is referred to as a **muni**, isi and **samaṇa**. It is now our purpose to examine the meaning and usage of these three ascetic nomenclatures throughout the early sources.

### Muni

In both the four Nikāyas and the Sutta-nipāta the term muni is used in two principal ways:

(i) To denote a person who possesses certain paradigm qualities and accomplishments by virtue of which he qualifies to be **mona** or **moneyya**:

| | |
|---|---|
| Sn 723 | **sa munī monam arahati, sa munī monam ajjhagā** (the **muni** is worthy of **monam**, the **muni** has attained **monam**). |
| Sn 698 | **moneyyaseṭṭhaṁ munipavaraṁ apucchi** (he questioned the eminent **muni** (i.e., Gotama) about the best **moneyya**). |
| Sn 484 | **muniṁ moneyyasampannaṁ** (the muni is endowed with **moneyya**). |

Here two abstract nouns **mona** and **moneyya** are used to elucidate the meaning of the concrete noun, **muni**. We have preferred to leave them untranslated since in early Pali sources they occur solely in conjunction with the concept **muni** and their meaning is entirely bound up with that concept. Interestingly, the term mona is found in the Sutta-nipāta, but not in the four Nikāyas. It would therefore be presumptuous of us to translate it by 'wisdom', as the later Niddesa defines it, or by 'silence', the later meaning of its Sanskritic equivalent. What is apparent from the two terms' usage in Pali is that they function as superlatives.

(ii) As a title of distinction and as a form of address: Sn 1075 '**tam me munī sādhu viyākarohi tathā hi te vidito esa dhammo**'. (Explain this thoroughly to me, O Muni, for this **dhamma** is well known to you'). In the early sources the use of **muni** as a title is reserved for the Buddha, for **paccekabuddhas** and, in a single isolated case, for an **arahant** named Brahmadeva. All of these are persons who have attained **nibbāna** (that is, who have become **arahants**) and, with the exception of Brahmadeva are **buddhas** in the technical sense of the word. Brahmadeva serves as the exception which proves the rule, for we shall shortly see that his predicates are exactly those which are elsewhere listed as **muni** attributes.

## The Buddha as Muni

The Buddha possesses the title Sākya-**muni** and is referred to throughout the Nikāyas as **muni** and **mahā-muni**.[29] One particularly significant use of the term in connection with the Buddha occurs in the episode in which he predicts his own death.[30] When Ānanda fails to request the Buddha to remain alive for an entire aeon (**kappa**), and Māra fails to persuade the Buddha to succumb to immediate death, the Buddha announces that his own **parinibbāna** will take place in three months time. This announcement is accompanied by an earthquake and storm. In the wake of this portent, the Buddha pronounces that he is a **muni** who has transcended (**avassajati**) becoming (**bhāva**). Here the concept of the **muni** is once more associated with the formative idea of transcending death and rebirth. Māra, of course, is the personification of **bhāva**. It is therefore fitting that immediately subsequent to Māra's worsting on this occasion, the Buddha should refer to himself as a **muni**; for he is elsewhere acclaimed as 'the **muni** that conquers Mara' (**Mārabhibhū muni**).[31]

## Paccekabuddhas as Muni

We have already noted, firstly, that some of the **paccekabuddhas** in the Isigili Sutta list are referred to as **muni** and, secondly, that there are strong parallels in the Sutta-nipāta between the conception of the **ekacarin** and the figure of the **muni**. In later Pali literature **paccekabuddhas** are also classed as '**mahāmuni**'[32], giving a clear indication of their elevated buddhological status.

## The Arahant Brahmadeva

The story of Brahmadeva is to be found in the Pathama-vagga of the Saṁyutta Nikāya.[33] Brahmadeva is the son of a Brāhmaṇiyā (female Brahmin) who is initiated into **pabbajjā** by the Buddha and becomes an **arahant**. On one occasion whilst on his alms-round he approached the house of his own mother who, at the time, was preparing an offering (**āhuti**) to the god Brahmā. Conceding that Brahmadeva was a more worthy recipient of the offering than himself, Brahmā decided to intervene. He instructed the woman to give the offering to Brahmadeva on the grounds that he is 'one who is no longer subject to rebirth' (**nirupadhika**), one who has 'attained beyond the **devas**' (atidevapatta), who is 'worthy of an offering (**dakkhiṇaṁ dakkhiṇeyya**) and offerings' (**āhuneyya**), who has 'laid down the **danda** against the weak and the strong' (**nikkhittadaṇḍa** tasathāvaresu), who is a **muni**.[34] The epithets here applied to Brahmadeva are recognisable as predicates frequently occurring within the **moneyya suttas**. For example, the equation of the concept of the **muni** with one who has laid aside the **daṇḍa** (that is, laid aside 'harming') is the central theme of the Attadaṇḍa

Sutta.[35] Most strikingly, however, Brahmadeva's story provides a particular illustration of the way in which the concept of the **muni** is viewed as a direct alternative to beliefs and practices of Brahmanic religion: the message of this discourse is that the offerings intended for the deity Brahma should be given instead to this worthy ascetic.

## The Muni and the Brāhmaṇa Contrasted

**Muni** happens to be the title which the **brāhmaṇas**' prefer to use for the Buddha.[36] On those occasions that the Buddha teaches **dhamma** to **brāhmaṇas** he is imputed to be 'the **muni**' who teaches them about **moneyya** or **muni** qualities.[37] And these same **brāhmaṇas** question the Buddha about the meaning and significance of the appellation **muni**.[38] And not only Brahmadeva but the **muni** generally is regarded as a more worthy recipient of offerings (**dakkhiṇā**) than are the **brāhmaṇas**.[39]

Of particular significance is the occurrence of a certain stock formula within the Nikāyas in which the muni is identified with **tevijjā** (i.e. the three highest 'special-knowledges' - **abhiññā**).[40] **Tevijjā** is the dogmatic counterpart within Buddhism of the three Veda - that which is reckoned as **śrūti** and the sole and sufficient receptacle of truth according to Brahmanism. The formula reads

> 'He who has knowledge of former lives,
> Who sees heaven and hell
> And has attained the end of rebirth
> The one who has obtained the special
> knowledges is a **muni**.'[41]

The first three lines of the above stanza list respectively the three special knowledges (**abhiññā**). These are the three highest of the standard list of six 'special knowledges' categorized in Buddhist doctrine: remembrance of former existences (**pubbe-nivāsānassati**), divine eye (**dibba-cakkhu**) and extinction of the cankers (**āsavakkhaya**) which terminates rebirth.[42] The formula therefore demonstrates that the concept of the **muni** is formatively linked with the acquisition of the three highest **abhiññās** which elsewhere in Buddhism play a significant part in the doctrine of the Buddha. For example, the Buddha's own experience of enlightenment is represented in terms of his realisation of these **abhiññās**.[43] And soon after his enlightenment the Buddha uses the **abhiññā** of the 'divine eye' (**dibba-cakkhu**) to assist his salvific enterprise. Thereafter the special powers of the **dibba-cakkhu** and **pubbe-nivāsānusati** continue to play a key role in his teaching.[44] The doctrine of the Buddha's 'omniscience' (**sabbaññū**) in the later Pali texts means that he possesses the 'knowledge of former lives' and the 'knowledge of people's **kamma**' to a greater degree than anyone else.[45] A word must be said about the imagery in the above stanza. Essentially, the world is transcended by the power of 'cognition': the faculty of seeing/knowing (**dassana**). We have already pointed out the frequent use in the **moneyya suttas** of the verb **dassati** (to discern) in connection with the **muni**. In the light of this observation each line of the stanza may be summarised as follows:

a. The temporal dimension of the cosmos is transcended (by knowledge).
b. The spatial/hierarchical dimension is transcended (by seeing).
c. Rebirth is ended.
d. The one who has achieved all this is a **muni**.

In providing an interpretation of this stanza, one perceives a logical connection between attainments (a) and (b) and the realization of (c): In (a) the **muni** masters 'time' and in (b) 'space'; and these together entail the termination of the relentless cycle of birth and death. It may be recalled how a recurrent theme in the **moneyya suttas** is the one of the **muni** no longer belonging within time **(kappa)** or to any category **(sankha)** of being. Since 'space and time' and 'the cycle of birth and death' are really the same thing - **saṁsāra** - it must follow that rebirth is stopped when 'space' and 'time' are transcended in this way. Conceptually, therefore, the supreme religious attainment is represented as the traversing of space and time.

## The Non-Affiliated Aspect of the Muni

The figure of the **muni** depicted in the Nikayas is not one who belongs to a specific religious or ascetic group, nor is he identified with any particular historical or mythical epoch. Instead he is equated solely with the concept of a **buddha** or one who has ended rebirth. Since he is qualitatively unique he exists outside the conception of a sectarian tradition. To illustrate this we cite a passage from the Nandamāṇavapucchā Sutta of the Sutta-nipāta:

> "They say there are **munis** in the world", said the Venerable Nanda. "What does this mean? Do they describe him as a **muni** because of his knowledge or because of the way in which he lives?"
> "The good say, Nanda, that a **muni** is not one who has a view **(diṭṭhi)**, a tradition **(suti)** or knowledge **(ñāṇa)**.

> I say that **munis** are those who having disarmed (themselves of a view, a tradition etc.) wander calm and content."'[46]

Here, Nanda's question about munis resembles Ananda's fundamental question about **pacceka-buddhas** that we referred to in the introduction.[47] Both questions are prefaced by references to their alleged existence, or existence by hearsay **(janā vadanti/kīra nāma honti)**, and both constitute forms of enquiry about the real identity of these figures. Here the **muni**'s identity is evidently something of a mystery just like the **pacceka-buddha**'s in the Isigili Sutta. The explanation why the **muni** defies categorisation in terms of conventional standpoints and affiliations is that his own position cannot be reduced to either a 'metaphysical view' **(diṭ-ṭhi)**, a 'body of revelation' **(suti)** or a 'form of gnosis' **(ñāṇa)**. It is only to be defined in terms of freedom from dogmatic stances or viewpoints.[48] In relation to the philosophical and religious disputations that characterised other types of ascetic, the **muni** is here described as a non-combatant or nonparticipant: **visenikatvā** (lit. making armyless). This term has a number of significant connotations: 'army' **(sena)** implies warfare, conquest, killing. **Visenikatvā** can therefore be read as a synonym for **avihiṁsā** (non-injury). The **muni** is principally distinguished as an exponent of **avihiṁsā**. In practical terms he has 'disarmed' the passions: he is without **igha** (der.√**ṛgh**: to tremble, rage) and **āsā** (longing, discontent). In body and mind he is at peace. And he has disarmed himself of dogma. Although not explicitly stated, the **muni** exemplifies the principle of the middle way.

## Textual Usage of Muni

With one apparent exception, the term **muni** is found only in the metrical sections of the Sutta-nipāta and the four Nikāyas.[49] This indicates that the word belongs to some of the oldest material contained within the Sutta Pitaka. We are, however, led to ask why its usage is restricted to the metrical sections and does not figure more prominently later in the prose works. In response to this question we may suppose that either the word has a special significance which confines it to metrical usage, or that it fell into comparative disuse in the early stages of Buddhism's development.

## Conclusion on the Term Muni and its Significance

The outstanding features of the use of the term **muni** in the early Pali sources can be summarised in the form of three distinct points. In the first place the prevailing significance of the word **muni** is buddhological: The images of stark contrast with Brahmanism; the prominence of the themes of conquering Māra, acquiring the **abhiññās** and ending rebirth; the observation that the **muni** does not derive from a recognised tradition; the use of the term on all but one occasion as an epithet of **buddhas**. All these features reinforce this interpretation. Secondly, themes which elsewhere are distinctive of the **ekacarin** and the Buddha coalesce in the image of the **muni**. Thirdly, there must be some explanation why its usage is confined to the metrical sections of these sources. Any attempt at an explanation must be consistent with the first two points. Given these factors we propose the following interpretation: The usage of the term **muni** in the early sources antedates the contradistinction between the **paccekabuddha** and the **sammāsambuddha** and hence the usage of these two terms. Owing to the emergence of certain 'cultic' and 'dogmatic' factors, a distinction of two types of **buddha** - the **paccekabuddha** and the sammāsambuddha - arose and, consequently, the term **muni** suffered an early redundancy gradually becoming an anachronism. We can in fact, detect some small intrusion of cultic and dogmatic elements into its interpretation whilst the term is still in currency. So, for example, the Buddha is not a **muni** per se, but a 'distinctive' or 'great **muni**' (mahāmuni), an 'eminent **muni**' (**muni pavaram**) and a teaching **muni**;[50] this latter aspect contrasts with the general tenor of the muni as non-disposed to speaking. We here glimpse attempts by the followers of the Buddha to modify the term's apparently non-sectarian significance in the transition from the pre- to the post-Sākyamuni era. Both the **sammāsambuddha** and the **paccekabuddha** are encompassed within the notion of the **muni**. Their formulation as categories and their introduction into Buddhist doctrine,however, signified the replacement of a single conception of a **buddha** by a dual one. Subsequently, the **paccekabuddha** qua **ekacarin** serves as a paradigm for the Buddhist monk to emulate on the grounds of his **muni** status. With respect to the figure of Sakyamuni, however, **muni** characteristics form only one element of his conception. He is something more: a **muni-pavaram** and a **sammā-sambuddha**.

## Isi

In the early Pali sources the term **isi**

(**seer**) is applied to a wide variety of ascetics: non-Buddhist as well as Buddhist ascetics, ascetics of former times as well as contemporary ascetics.

## Seers of Former Times (Pubbakā Isayo)

The ten authors of the Vedas are called 'former **brāhmaṇa isi**'(**brāhmaṇaṁ pubbakā-isayo**).Buddhists denied that these 'seers' saw or knew Brahma, claimed infallibility or possessed the **abhiññās**.[51] In this respect they may be contrasted with the figure of the Buddha, who is **brahmabhūta** (become-**brahma**),whose word is authoritative (**suta**) and truth (**sacca**) and who has himself acquired the **abhiññās**. According to the Brahmanadhammika Sutta, **brāhmaṇa** ascetics in olden times were more moral than their contemporaries because they did not perform animal sacrifices, rather they exemplified virtue and upheld **dhamma**.[52] These **brāhmaṇas** are referred to as **pubbakā isayo** too. One who refrains from animal sacrifice is therefore praised as a **mahesi**.[53] The Buddha alludes to Kanha, a former ascetic adept in **brahmamanta**, as a 'mighty seer' (**uḷāra isi**).[54] The six **titthakaras** who taught the **brahma-vihāra** meditations in an era preceding that of Sakyamuni, and who as a consequence attained rebirth in the world of Brahma (**brahma-loka**),are described as 'seers who are outside' (**isi-bāhirakā**) the Buddhist order.[55]

## Contemporary Seers

Those **brāhmaṇas** who practise divination - the discernment of auspicious signs (**P.lakkhaṇa**; Skt.**lakṣaṇa**) and identify the Buddha's status as a 'great man' (P.**mahāpurisa**; Skt.**mahāpuruṣa**) shortly after his birth - are called **bahirakā isayo**, the same as the six **titthakaras**.[56] Asita (the so-called Buddhist Simeon) and Pingiya, both **brāhmaṇa jatilas** (ascetics with matted hair), are referred to respectively as **isi** and **mahā-isi**.[57]

## Royal Seers (Rājīsi)

**Isi** also occurs in the compound **rājīsi** (royal seer) where it is given two distinct senses; this distinction is vital to our argument later. Firstly, isi can denote a universal sovereign (P.**cakkavatti**; Skt.**cakravartin**) who performs extensive animal sacrifices.[58] Secondly, it can denote a universal sovereign who decides to become a renouncer (**pabbajita**).[59] It is evident that when the Buddhists use it in the first sense they are adopting the Brahmanic conception, for in the Brahmanic tradition a **rājīsi** (Skt.**rāja-ṛṣi**) is one who reaches heaven or the desired religious goal through the performance of prescribed rituals.[60] When they use it in the latter sense it is a modified, Śramaṇic adaptation. In Buddhist sources the first is used in a disapprobatory, the second in an approbatory sense.

## Buddhist Isis: Paccekabuddhas

We have seen in the Isigili Sutta that the **paccekabuddha** is referred to as both **isi** and mahesi). Later narrative literature contrasts the figure of the **paccekabuddha** with the Brahmanic isi. So, for example, a **paccekabuddha** is sharply differentiated from the **tāpasa** (brahmanic ascetic) in the story of the Bhikkhā-parampara Jātaka.[61] The purpose of the **jataka** is to show that among all social and religious dignitaries the Buddhist **bhikkhu** (exemplified here by the figure of the **paccekabuddha**) is the most worthy (**dakkhiṇeyya**) to receive alms. That the **paccekabuddha** should have been selected to illustrate this principle is further endorsement of the auspiciousness he is renowned for in the four Nikāyas. Those whom the **jātaka** lists as persons to whom it is appropriate to make a gift are, in order of increasing priority, **rājā** (king), **purohita-brāhmaṇa** (king's counsellor and priest), **tapasa** (brahmanical ascetic), and **pacceka-buddha**. The story goes that a landowner gives some food to a king who regards it as more meritorious to pass it on to his **purohita** than to eat it himself; for the same reason the **purohita** passes the food on to a **tāpasa** who, in turn, gives it to a **paccekabuddha**. The **paccekabuddha** eats it, since there exists no one more worthy to receive it than himself.

## Buddhist Isis: the Muni

In a stanza of the Muni Sutta the **muni** is referred to as the great **isi** (**mahesi**) who has discerned the state of tranquillity (**santim**).[62] This usage illustrates our earlier point that whilst the **muni** can be an **isi**, the **isi** cannot be a **muni** unless he is also **buddha**.

## Buddhist Isis: the Buddha

Sākyamuni is accorded the superlative title of **issisattama**. **Sattama** can be translated either as the 'best' or, following the commentaries, the 'seventh'(in the sequence of teaching Buddhas enumerated in the mythology of the four Nikāyas).[63] In order to create suitable prestige for their own tradition the Buddhists have here appropriated the sense in which it applied to the Brahmanic ṛṣis that composed the Vedas. The Buddha, in fact, is rarely referred to simply as an **isi**, nearly always superlatively as a great seer (**mahesi**),[64] bull among seers,[65] (**isini-sabha**) and divine seer (**devīsi**),[66] a way of setting him apart from other ascetics, especially non-Buddhist ones. Whereas the term **isi** can denote more-or-less any ascetic phenomenon or tradition, **mahesi** is reserved for those who merit the special approval of Buddhists.

## Buddhist Isis: the Saṅgha

**Bhikkhus** who dwell with the Buddha at Jeta-vana are referred to by onlookers as seers of the Buddhist Order (**isisaṅgha**)[67] and, elsewhere, the Buddha's chief disciple Sāriputta is called an **isi**.[68] It may be noticed how **isi** seems to be the accepted appellation of the common populace for both **paccekabuddha**, as witnessed in the Isigili Sutta, as well as for the **saṅgha**.

## Isi Characteristics

The theme most commonly associated with the occurrence of the word **isi** is the one of power over the phenomenal world. There is, for instance, an **isi** called Rohitassa who possesses the power of flight, who can tra-verse the distance from the eastern to the western ocean in a single step but cannot tra-verse the entire world.[69] Asita possesses a similar power that enables him to perceive (**dassati**) and visit the world of the thirty three gods (**tāvatiṁsadevaloka**), in order to hear of the impending birth of the **bodhisatta**.[70]

There are some **isayo** whose magic power expresses itself in the form of 'cursing' (**abhisapeti**). In the Assalāyana Sutta, for example, a group of brahmanic **isayo** with pernicious views (**pāpakaṁ diṭṭhigataṁ**) try to impose a curse on the aforesaid Asita.[71] By the power of their austerity (**tapas**) they attempt to burn him to a cinder.[72] But Asita's own **tapas** is greater than his opponents and he thwarts their attempt. This story shows that the Buddhists did not see all **isis** as virtuous. In another story some seers living on the sea-shore find themselves in danger (**bhaya**) from the perennial skirmishes between the **devas** and the **asuras** (demons). They therefore seek a 'safety-pledge' (**abhayadakkhiṇa**) from Sambara, the leader of the **asuras**. Accusing them of being supporters of Sakka, Sambara refuses their request and threatens them with **bhaya**. By invoking a form of curse themselves, the **isi** turn Sambara's threat upon himself so that he becomes subject to never-ending fear (**akkhayaṁ hoti te bhayaṁ**).[73]

## Comparison of the Terms Muni and Isi

The meaning and usage of the terms **isi** and **muni** may be directly compared and contrasted on a number of fronts. The term **muni** is applied solely to **arahants**, whereas **isi** can describe non-Buddhist as well as Buddhist ascetics. It is quite evident that the texts use **isi** in its derived Brahmanic sense, by referring, firstly, to the authors of the Veda as **isi** and, secondly, to kings who observe elaborate sacrificial rituals as **rājīsi**). When **isi** is used of Buddhist ascetics then it becomes apparent that either. the Buddhists adopted it from its Brahmanic usage for their own purpose, as seems to be the case in its later application to their own tradition of seven **sammāsambuddhas**, or that it happened to be predicated of Buddhist ascetics (**paccekabuddhas** and the **saṅgha**) by the common people, a designation the Buddhists were content to accept. By contrast, the figure of the **muni** is presented as one who is in every respect superior to, and to be differentiated from all non-Buddhist ascetics, Brahmanic and non-Brahmanic.

Another important observation is that the term **isi** nearly always conveys asceticism as a 'corporate' notion e.g. the ten authors of the Veda, the six **titthakaras**, the seven **sammāsambuddhas**, the five hundred **paccebuddhas**, the Buddhist **saṅgha**. The **isi** is invariably depicted as representative of some group, sect or tradition. On the other hand, the **muni** is disinguished as a singular individual, a spiritual exemplar who exists outside the context of a collectivity or tradition. Whereas **isi** conveys the sense of a religious tradition, **muni** simply conveys the idea of absolute transcendence and thereby conceptually excludes all relative or functional values. In short, **muni** is a thoroughly 'buddhological' concept. By contrast, in its application to Buddhist personnel, isi is a 'mediating' or 'soteriological' concept, for it has connotations relating to the Brahmanic tradition.

**Muni** and **isi** are both concepts denoting 'religious power'. Their respective powers may be defined in relation to the world system (**lokadhātu**). The **isi** possesses powers (e.g., magic: **iddhi**; asceticism: **tapas**) which operate in terms of the structure or governing principles of the **lokadhātu**; he has the power to alter forms (**nama-rupa**) only. The **muni's** power, by contrast, consists not in any capacity to change forms or appearances but to go beyond the **lokadhātu**, to transcend its basic conditions of birth and death. The function of the two terms **isi** and **muni** may be seen, therefore, to correspond to the recognition that there is a religious distinction between power to 'transform' forms and power to 'transcend' forms. Furthermore, the application of both terms to **buddha** signifies that they possess both kinds of power. Nevertheless the balance between the **muni** and **isi** dimension of religious experience constituted a very delicate problem for Buddhism. This becomes all too apparent from considering the question of how far the use of magic (**iddhi**), that mode of asceticism most characteristic of the **isi** concept, was an acceptable part of spiritual practice in Early Buddhism.

## Iddhi

**Iddhi** presented a problem to Early Buddhism in so far as it could be used by its own adepts as a means of winning adherents; in short, it was sometimes adopted as a 'non-verbal' method of transmission, a proselytising device. It is necessary to stress that the use to which **iddhi** is put would not have presented itself as a problem at all had the phenomenon not been regarded by Buddhists as forming a legitimate expression of their own ascetical experience. An entirely negative dogmatic standpoint could not be adopted in view of the recognition that 'magic power' (**iddhānubhāva**) supervened upon the attainment of the fourth **jhāna**, and indicated that the adept was making progress in his steps toward the ultimate conquest of becoming (**bhāva**). In spiritual terms it represented, according to the Sāmañña-phala Sutta, attainment of the first **abhiññā**.[74] There is evidence to suggest that a relapse in a person's spiritual state led to a decline in his **iddhānubhāva**; the figures Devadatta, the Buddha's cousin, and Pāṭikaputta the naked ascetic are a case in point.[75]. The metaphysics underlying the conception of **iddhānubhāva** in the Nikāyas consists of an alchemical conception of matter.[76] All matter is composed of a limited number of basic elements (**bhūta/dhātu**) e.g. air, water, earth, fire etc. A physical object can take on a different appearance or form when one of these elements is increased, and, correspondingly, others decreased. So, for example, through the meditational technique of **tejo-dhātu-samādhi** a person takes on the form of fire.[77] 'Transformation' is not accomplished by physical or chemical experiment, however, but by the 'power of mind' (**cetovāsippatta**).[78] The 'various forms of magic' (**aneka vihitam iddhividhaṁ**) acknowledged to exist by Canonical Buddhism are said to result from 'applying and bending-down the mind', having prior to this achieved knowledge and insight (**ñāṇadassana**) concerning the impermanence of the (physical) body, and the mind-made body (**manomaya kāya**).[79]

## Buddhist Criticism of Iddhi

There are a number of respects in which **iddhi** becomes the subject of qualified criticism in early Pali texts. In the first place, it does not produce 'transcendence' of the phenomenal world. Transformations within the world are effected by it but not translations beyond it. We have instanced the case of the **isi**, Rohitissa, who found that he could not reach the end of the phenomenal world although he could cover vast distances by the power of 'flight'. A similar example is to be found in the Kevaddha Sutta: A certain member of the **bhikkhu-saṅgha** ascends by means of **samādhi** technique to the worlds of Brahmā, hoping at some juncture of his ascension to discover from one of the deities where the four great elements (**mahā-bhūta**) come to an end. But no one knows the answer, not even the god Brahmā himself. The **bhikkhu** then realises that this technique is not the solution to his problem.[80]

In the second place, the early Pali texts evince a critical attitude to those who 'display the phenomenon of magic' (**iddhi pāṭihāriyam dasseti**) to impress others. On many occasions the Buddha exhibits magic power for others to see but he always combines the display with verbal instruction. According to Vināya tradition, the Buddha used his magic to assist him in winning some of his first converts.[81] The Buddha in fact established a wide reputation for his **mahānubhāva** (great power) and **mahīddhi** (great magic).[82] It was this very reputation which caused one **bhikkhu**, Sunakkhatta, to become a dissatisfied member of the **saṅgha**. He was disappointed that the Buddha had shown him no magic and failed to live up to his reputation. When the Buddha at last decides to demonstrate his magic to him, Sunakkhatta fails to recognise its significance, thereby proving that magic does not evoke faith (**pasāda**) but can only enhance faith that is already present.[83]

Probably the clearest formulation of the criticism of the use of **iddhi-pāṭihāriya** occurs in the Book of Threes.[84] Here, **iddhipāṭihāriya** together with **ādesanā-**

**pāṭihāriya** (the phenomenon of mind-reading) are placed a poor second to **anusāsana-pāṭihāriya** (the phenomenon of teaching or instruction) as devices for converting people. We are told that **iddhi-pāṭihāriya** and **ādesanā-pāṭihāriya** seem like an illusion. This should not be taken as entirely dismissive but more as an indication of how **iddhi-pāṭihāriya** and **ādesanā-pāṭihāriya** actually work, that is, on the level of forms and appearances. They belong to the phenomenal world which is characterised by change and impermanence. By contrast, **anusāsana-pāṭihāriya** provides others with the possibility to achieve a state of permanence outside the phenomenal world. The account of **iddhi-pāṭihāriya** and **ādesanāpāṭihāriya** is accompanied by the statement 'the one who does it experiences (**paṭisaṁvedeti**) it, it is exclusive to him'.[85] This is a pointed criticism. The adept does not communicate to the audience anything which they can experience (**paṭisaṁvedeti**) and realise themselves. They are in the position purely of spectators who have to rely upon the testimony of their eyes (senses) because the powers are, by definition, superhuman (**uttara-manussa**). By contrast, that which the verbal instruction communicates can be realised and tested (**vitakka**) by the listener himself, because it is directed at his understanding, at his own level (**vihāra**) of spirituality. Nevertheless, the three types of **pāṭihāriya** are seen to some extent as integrated; none of them are prohibited from forming part of the basic materials (**sappāṭihīrakataṁ**) of the **bhikkhusaṅgha**. The Sutta under discussion here is the one which states that there were fewer **bhikkhus** in former times but a preponderance of these exhibited **iddhi-pāṭihāriya**. It, therefore, seems as if the Buddha was trying to give some sort of directive away from what at one time had been a growing trend in displaying magical powers.

The Kevaddha Sutta shows the Buddha to have firm views on the question of the abuse of magical power.[86] He confesses to being troubled (aṭṭiyati) and vexed (**harāyati**) in regard to **iddhi-pāṭihāriya**, and avoids it because he sees 'peril' (**ādīnava**) in it. The Buddha saw it as a potentially dangerous phenomenon because the capacity to produce feats of magic was not exclusive to the Buddhist tradition. The attainment of **iddhānubhāva** was not only available to other traditions through the **jhānic** method but similar powers it seems could be reproduced by the use of 'spells' or 'charms' (**vijjā**).[87] Consequently, the use of just **iddhi** to persuade people to become Buddhist was seen as disingenuous, owing to the fact that non-Buddhist adepts could replicate the same powers. In order to surmount this problem, the Buddha, firstly, forbids the **bhikkhu-saṅgha** from using it solely for the purpose of impressing lay-followers and, secondly, determines to give a new directive to the concept of **iddhi** itself: traditional forms of **iddhi** are designated as **no-ariya** (that is, as not integral to the Buddhist path); then he defines **iddhi** in its **ariya** form as consisting simply of the practice of equanimity (**upekhaka**) and mindfulness (**sati**).

**Summary**

As an aspect of the practice of 'concentration' (**samādhi**), the various sorts of magic (**anekavihitaṁ iddhividdhaṁ**) were a recognised part of Buddhism's own religious heritage. Buddhism did not, however, regard magic power (**iddhānubhāva**) as a salvific means to transcending the world and ending re-birth.

But it was a power which nevertheless testified to the existence of a world of phenomena (inhabited by **deva** who by nature possessed that power) that lay between the mundane world and transcendence.

The Buddha himself is represented as using **iddhi-pāṭihāriya** didactically only. He always augmented it with verbal teaching. But there was invariably the danger that members of the **saṅgha** might use it just to 'show off' in front of the laity. The fact that the Canon provides evidence of attempts to 'emasculate' or 'bowdlerize' it by substituting for it the doctrine of **upekhaka** and **sati** is sufficient to show that a trend away from emphasis on the acquisition of magic power accompanied the growth of the **sāvaka** tradition. Since the **paccekabuddha** has strong associations with the acquisition and use of 'magic' and would appear to represent a tradition much older than the teaching of Sākyamuni then we can regard the above observations as providing prima facie evidence in support of the theory that the relationship between the **paccekabuddha** and **sāvaka** tradition was one of historical continuity and transition.

## Conclusion on Muni and Isi

Our discussion of the doctrinal status of **iddhi** in Early Buddhism has shown that the **isi** dimension to the Buddhistic 'holy-man, his identification with **iddhānubhāva**, is viewed with reservation, if not criticism, both as a form of religious potency and as a converting device. This means that with respect to the two recognised dimensions to Buddhist spirituality - **muni** and **isi** - the one is more highly valued than the other. The significance of the terms, therefore, lies as much in their antithesis as their complementarity, indicating essentially the presence of two different strains within early Buddhism - this worldly and other wordly - broadly corresponding to the respective aspirations of the Buddhist 'monk' and Buddhist 'layperson' outlined earlier. In chapter two we shall show that the **muni** and **isi** dichotomy was the inevitable outcome of a tradition's evolution from a non-sectarian to a sectarian basis. Qualities which were nondifferentiated or conciliative in the figure of the **paccekabuddha** begin to acquire a separate significance when the tradition started to think of itself as a potential proselytising force. At this point in time the image which it projected to others became a primary consideration in determining the movement's general ethos.

## Samaṇa

We shall now consider the meaning and usage of the term '**samaṇa**' in the early Pali sources. Samaṇa is the third and last ascetic category with which the figure of the **paccekabuddha** is identified. The key to what the Buddhists understand concerning the origins of the Śramaṇa Movement is to be found in the Agañña Sutta.[88] It here states that the **samaṇa-maṇḍala** (**samaṇa** group) originated when individuals from the four established **maṇdalas** within society (i.e. **khattiya, brāhmaṇa, vessa, sudda**) found fault (**garahati**) with their own respective social station (i.e. **dhamma**) and therefore decided to renounce their previous social identity and lead the life of homeless ascetics. Thus **samaṇas** are **pabbajitas** drawn from all four classes of

Indian society. As a result they in turn come to comprise a fifth socially identifiable group (**maṇḍala**). To confirm this it is added the **samaṇa** is recognised by his 'shaven-head' (**muṇḍaka**).[89]

The **samaṇa** movement therefore originated as a form of disaffection with the existing status quo. The same Sutta explains the origin of the **brāhmaṇa-maṇḍala** likewise in terms of both disillusionment with society and renunciation, but at an earlier stage in society's evolution. It is said that, long ago, those who rejected (**bahenti**) the growing immorality of society and went to live apart in the forest came to be designated **brāhmaṇas**. It stresses, however, that the great majority of **brāhmaṇas** have since abandoned the practice, and therefore the notion of **brāhmaṇa** no longer has that significance.[90] The propitious origins of the **brāhmaṇa** class would help to explain why the term **brāhmaṇa** can have a normative as well as a descriptive significance in Buddhist sources.

Since the person who becomes a **samaṇa** does so by rejecting his traditional role within the socio-economic framework, he no longer has a **dhamma**. Over a period of time, however, the strength and autonomy of the Śramaṇa Movement became such that **samaṇas** acquired a separate distinctive **dhamma** of their own. In other words, the traditional fabric of society officially recognised the **samaṇas** by acknowledging that they too performed a positive 'social' function. The social function or dhamma ascribed to them was that of 'teacher' or 'moral instructor'. The **samaṇa** is society's conscience and the conscience of the king. The **samaṇa**'s own, individual, **dhamma** consists in instructing the rest of society on matters relating to its own **dhamma** (duty). In exchange for this service, society, especially the king, furnishes him with alms. Therefore the term **samaṇa** is seen to connote three things: A movement of 'renunciation' having specific historical origins; one who renounces the world and lives on alms; and one who on the grounds of his renunciation is especially qualified to teach others. In view of the **paccekabuddha**'s alleged archaic identity we shall show in chapter three how the primary significance behind his description as a **samaṇa** lies in the fact of his identification with the proto-**samaṇas**, those who initiated the renunciation movement.

## Conclusion

From an analysis principally of the early and main Nikāya sources we have shown the **paccekabuddha** was understood to represent a tradition ante-dating Sākyamuni but, nevertheless, was recognised by Sākyamuni and his followers as authentically 'buddhological'. The air of obscurity which surrounds the figure of the **paccekabuddha** may be accounted for, firstly, on the basis of his relatively archaic identity and, secondly, on the grounds that the notion of enlightenment outside of the context of the teaching transmitted by Sākyamuni could present a possible threat to a movement whose main thrust centred upon the uniqueness of one single figure. We have also been required to explain why the term **paccekabuddha** does not occur in the oldest sections of the Canon. The real key to providing an explanation lies, we have argued, in the figure and concept of the **muni**, who is prominent in the oldest sections and seems to represent the conception of a **buddha** ante-dating the specific **sammāsambuddha-pacceka-**

**buddha** distinction of classical Buddhist doctrine. In brief, there is evidence in the early sources to indicate that originally there was a single buddhology.

The few details of the **paccekabuddha's** ascetism which do emerge indicate two distinct conceptions 'lay' and 'monachist'. The former sees him as one endowed with strange, magical powers; the latter as a solitary wanderer **(ekacarin)** who embodies and illustrates the spiritual heights attainable by self-mastery. In a more general way the **paccekabuddha** is identified with three specific ascetic categories: **muni**, **isi** and **samaṇa**. We have tried to amplify the significance of this identification by examining the meaning and use of each of these categories in the early sources. These findings may briefly be summarised as follows: **Isi** is the exoteric term for anyone who possesses religious potency **(mahānubhāva)** irrespective of their tradition. **Samaṇa** denotes a non-**brāhmaṇa**, one who belongs to the tradition of 'renunciation'. **Muni** is one who has achieved 'absolute detachment' or 'transcendence'. This last term is used to denote one who exists outside a 'sectarian' context, and who stands in antithesis to members of the Brahmanic 'cultus'. None of these terms are found to be mutually exclusive; that is to say, they can all be used of the same figure. Hence they can be understood as providing different perspectives or vistas on a given ascetic phenomenon. Taking account of these significances, we shall devote the remainder of this study to deciphering the meaning of their application to the figure of the **paccekabuddha** in terms of shedding light on the question of his historical identity.

Since we have shown there is no evidence in the earliest sources of the forms of denigration characterising viewpoints of the **pac-**

**cekabuddha** in later tradition, then we are left with the problem of explaining how and why this denigration came about. Having argued that the oldest form of 'buddhology' did not differentiate **buddhas** into separate categories, then it must be the case that the downgrading of the **paccekabuddha** corresponds to the upgrading of Sākyamuni. In other words, the explanation which presents itself is that a special 'cultus' formed itself around the figure of Gotama the Buddha. In the ensuing chapters we shall adduce evidence in support of this hypothesis.

**Notes:**

1. Nyanatiloka, Buddhist Dictionary, 3rd Ed. Frewin Colombo, 1972, sv '**ariya-puggala**'.
2. D.II.142. On the ritual of 'stupa-worship' see S.Dutt, Buddhist Monks and Monasteries of India, Allen and Unwin, 1962.pp.185-186.
3. On an early definition of **lokiya** and **lokuttara**, see M.III.72. Note that both **lokiya** and **lokuttara** come under the denomination of'right view' (**sammā-diṭṭhi**). It is important to understand that a person chooses the life of a '**bhikkhu**' that he may transcend all opposites, that means **puñña** as well as **pāpa** (wrong-doing). See Sn.547,636, 790; Dh.39,267, 412. For a comprehensive analysis of Pali and Mahāyāna teaching on the advantages of becoming a **bhik-khu**, see Vimalakīrti, p.75 fn.71.
4. On the difference between the Chinese and the Pali version of the Isigili Sutta, see Fujita, JIP.p.129,fn.97ai.

5. Barua pp.529-30
6. M.I.92.
7. S.I.120f. III.121f.
8. S.I.194.
9. The significance of the term '**vandatha**' (praise!) can be deduced from the use of the same verb at Sn.573: '**bhikkhavo tisatā ime tiṭṭhanti pañjalīkatā; pāde vīra pasārehi, nāgā vandantu satthuno 'ti**' (These three hundred monks wait with clasped hands stretch forth your feet, O hero, let the Nāgas pay homage to the master.) The **paccekabuddha** is referred to many times as **mahesi**: Pb.Ap.5; Ap.248(No.301); J.VI. I.46 g.143; Mc.42-3.
10. Cooray pp.61-2.
11. See Dial. Pt.III.p.185; Kloppenborg (1) p.49.
12. Dial. Pt.I pp.88-9.
13. On the meaning and connotations of **manussa** and **uttari-manussa**, see each term respectively in PED. At Sn.1043-1045, **issayo** are differentiated from **manujā** (= **manussā** Nd.2. 96).
14. Horner's translation, M.L.S. Vol.III. p.185 Compare (1) Kloppenborg's translation(p.97) of **pāṭiyekkam** at Sn.A.92. The sentence can also be translated 'those who have come to right enlightenment separately (from one another)'.
15. Norman has pointed out to me that **ajjhagamuṁ subodhiṁ** may be a transcriptional error for **ajjhangiṁsu bodhiṁ** but that - on the other hand - the term **subuddha** does occur at Thag.212 (for stylistic reasons). He translates this sentence of the Isigili Sutta as 'individually they arrived at a good enlightenment'; Fujita (op. cit. p.126 fn.81) translates it as 'they have by themselves attained to subtle, enlightened

intuition'.

16. Fujita (op. cit. p.99) tells us that there is one passage in the Chinese **agama** (T2.676c) which attests to the **paccekabuddha**'s failure to teach **dharma**:'The **pratyeka** has no **dharma** such as these: He has no **varsa**, no disciples. He goes alone, without companions, and preaches no Dharma for others.' In his view, however, the passage is the only case of the kind in the entire Āgama/Nikāya complex, and must therefore be considered a later interpolation. By way of contrast, he cites a passage from the Mahāparinirvāṇa Sutta (T1.200a) which implies that the **pratyekabuddha** fulfilled a positive soteriological role: 'The **pratyekabuddha**, by contemplating the **dharma**, independently intuits the way, and is also able to bring happiness and advantage to the people of all the world.'

17. An Epigraphical Summary, CJS., 1930, p.101 reports the existence of an inscription dated 1st century AD on a rock in the Kurunagala District of Sri Lanka, reading 'Dasavana Paceka Budaha tube' (The stūpa of the tenth **paccekabuddha**) Unfortunately no vestiges of a stupa are to be found in the vicinity of the rock. The expression 'tenth' **paccekabuddha** shows that there was, at the time, a list of **paccekabuddhas** who were worshipped in Ceylon. The scene of the final demise of **paccekabuddha** prior to the advent of Gotama is depicted much later on a bas-relief at Borobudur, Java. An inscription in Gāndhārī Pkt on a silver scroll found by John Marshall at Taxila and dated 136 AD makes reference to the triple categories of Buddhas, **paccekabuddha** and **arahant**

as worthy of reverence (**pūyae**). See Kloppenborg (1), p.10. In the later sources the erection of **ṭhūpas** to **paccekabuddhas** is mentioned at Ap.498; J.III.434,440; Av.Śat. Nos.21-24, 88-90. See also Buddhist Records of the Western World trans. by S.Beal, Trübner 1884, (Oriental Reprint 1969) p.XXVI,209.

18. CPS ch.8.v.3.
19. Jones Vol.3.p.303.
20. D.II.30.
21. M.II.211.
22. See Winternitz pp.92-8; Geiger p.14; Pande pp.51-65.
23. SBE Vol.X. p.xii.
24. Cooray p.61; Norman p.102.
25. Nd.II.58.
26. For a discussion of whether **khagga-visāṇa** means 'rhinoceros' or 'rhinoceros horn', see Kloppenborg (1) p.59, fn.10; Jones p.250 fn.1; BHSD sv **khaḍg-visāṇa**. That the expression 'one should wander alone like a rhinoceros' has a wider significance than its Buddhist usage is shown by the occurrence of the same or similar expression in Jainism also. In the Kalpa Sūtra it is said that Mahāvīra 'was single and alone like the horn of a rhinoceros' (SBE.Vol.XII. Jaina Sūtras, trans. H.Jacobi, pt.1. p.261). cf also Mvu.III.144. See Pb.Ap. 52; Nd.2.217; Vism.234; Mvu.I.301. for the use of this epithet in connection with the **paccekabuddha**.
27. See Sāmañña-phala Sutta (esp. D.I.62 et seq.).
28. cp. 'The monks (of Gautama) live unfettered lives and roam about free as d-eer' (Jones Vol.3.p.421). In the Sumañgala J.(III.440), a hunter shoots a **paccekabuddha** with an arrow, mistaking him for a deer.

29. The use of **muni** as an epithet for the Buddha occurs, for example, at DII.107, 157; M.I.79; S.I.187; Sn.414,508,541 et seq. **Mahā-muni** occurs at S.I.196; Sn. 31.
30. D.II.108; S.V.263; A.IV.312.
31. Sn.545
32. Pb.Ap.44; Bv.A.43.
33. S.I.140-2.
34. ibid. I.14.
35. Sn.935-54.
36. M.II.144; S.I.168,175; A.I.165; Sn.1074, 1089.
37. Sn.251,461-2,484.
38. Sn.1077ff.
39. S.I.174-5.
40. M.II.144; A.I.165,167; cf. also Dh.423. The association of the figure of the **muni** with 'knowledge is not confined to Buddhist sources. The Bṛhad.Up.(IV. 4.22) states '**etaṁ eva viditvā muni bhavati**; knowing (the **ātman**) one indeed becomes a **muni**'. The Katha Up. (II.1.15) talks of the **muni** who has understanding. In Jainism it too says (Utt.XXV.32) '**nāṇeṇa ya muni hoi**' (one becomes a **muni** by knowledge).
41. **pubbe nivāsam yo vedi**
    **saggāpayañca passati**
    **atho jātikkhayam patto**
    **abhiññāvosito muni**
42. See BD. sv **abhiññā** for a list of all six 'special-knowledges'.
43. M.I.22-3; 248-9. See also Mvu.I.228-229; II.228-229; Lal.344-345; Lamotte pp.17-18.
44. On his use of the **dibba-cakkhu** see, for example, Pāṭika S.(D.III.1ff.); Devaduta S.(M.III.178ff.); on his use of **pubbe nivāsānussati**, see the early **jātaka** stories in the four Nikāyas. e.g., Mahā Sudassana S.(D.II.169ff.);

Mahā Govinda S.(D.II.220ff.); Makhādeva S.(M.II.74ff.).

45. See Vism.411. Of the 'ten powers' (**dasabalāni** - M.I.69-71; A.V.33-36) which distinguish a tathāgata or **sammāsambuddha**, three comprise **abhiññās** 4-6 and the remaining seven are, in fact, variations or elaborations of these same **abhiññās**. See Jayatilleke p.470, para.805.

46. **Santi loke munayo' icc-āyasmā Nando**
**janā vadanti, ta-y-idaṁ kathaṁ su:**
**ñānpapannam no muniṁ, vadanti**
**udāhu ve jīvitenūpapannaṁ,**
**na diṭṭhiyā sutiyā na ñāṇena**
**munīdha Nanda kusalā vadanti,**
**visenikatvā anighā nirāsā**
**caranti ye, te munayo ti brūmi** - Sn. 1077-8.

47. supra p.15.

48. A similar interpretation of the **muni** is given in the Māgandiya Sutta (Sn.835-47). See especially the opening line of stanza 839.

49. The reference to **muni santo** at M.III. 239 is not a true exception since it is quite evident, from the bracketing of the passage in the PTS edition and the context in which it occurs, that the reference is an interpolation.

50. See M.II.169,200.

51.

52. Sn.284ff.

53. S.I.76

54. D.I.96-7

55. A.III 373; IV.136

56. D.III.145

57. Sn.679, 1008

58. A.IV.151; It.21.

59. D.III.60.

60. See, for example, Mbh (3) Vol.VIII.p.13.

61. J.IV.369-74.

62. Sn.208.
63. Sn.356; M.I.386; S.I.192.
64. Sn.176-7,356,481,915,et seq.; M.II.100.
65. Sn.698.
66. Sn.1116
67. M.III.262; S.I.33,55.
68. S.I.61; A.II.49-50.
69. S.I.65
70. Sn.679-85.
71. M.II.154ff.
72. According to M.I.377 'reducing an opponent to cinders' is achieved through **iddhi** and 'thought power' (**ceto-vasi**).
73. S.I.227f.
74. D.I.75-9.
75. A.III.123 and D.III.12-27.
76. cf. E.J.Holmyard, 'Alchemy', Pelican 1957, pp.19-21; Johansson pp.37-39.
77. This is one form (together with **apodhātu samādhi**: water-element **samādhi**) in which the **paccekabuddha** expressed his 'magic power'. See Sn A.54. Apparently, a way of passing into **parinibbāna** without leaving any physical remains whatsoever was for an **arahant** to enter **tejodhātusamādhi** at the moment of his passing away. This would ensure the immediate destruction of his bones as well as his flesh (see Ud.92-93). In both the Mvu (I.357ff.) and the Lal. (13-14) versions of the demise of the legendary five hundred **pratyekabuddhas** this is the manner in which they passed into **parinirvāṇa**.
78. A.III.340-1.
79. D.I.77.
80. D.I.215-23.
81. Vin.I.16.
82. M.I.392.
83. D.III.3ff.; M.I.68ff.
84. A.I.172.
85. A.I.172.

86. D.I.211ff.
87. D.I.213-4.
88. D.III.95-6.
89. Dh.264. The same definition occurs in Jainism, e.g., Utt.XXV.31: '**na vi muṇḍaena samaṇo**' (one does not become a **samana** by having a shaven-head).
90. The difference between the former righteous **brāhmaṇas** (**porāṇaṁ brāhmaṇam**) and the contemporary degenerate **brāhmaṇas** forms the theme of the Brāhmaṇa-dhammika S.(Sn. pp.50ff.)

Chapter Two

# The Paccekabuddha as Isi

In the opening chapter we observed that **isi** was a general term for anyone who possesses religious potency and that in terms of the Buddhistic tradition this potency took the form of magic power **(iddhānubhāva)**. We noted, in addition, that magic power, that is to say, **iddhi-pāṭihāriyam dasseti** (exhibiting the extraordinary phenomenon of magic) could not of itself produce converts or initiates. This could only be done through 'verbal' transmission. Hence it becomes apparent that it is not the **isi** dimension of the Buddhistic holy man that produces converts and creates a **sāvaka** tradition or a **bhikkhu-saṅgha**. This being so, the **paccekabuddha**'s significance qua **isi** must therefore relate to the ordinary layperson, to the one who may or may not happen to be a devotee but who is definitely not an 'initiate' in the technical sense of belonging to a **saṅgha**. Since standard Buddhist dogma excludes the **paccekabuddha** from creating **sāvaka**s then any soteriological significance he has must be confined to the laity. This explains why it is his relationship with the laity which receives more prominent treatment in Buddhist sources than any other aspect. In consequence, the quest for the **paccekabuddha**'s significance as **isi** involves us in an investigation of his relationship to and with the laity.

Our discussion will accordingly proceed under three distinct headings:

(a) The layperson's conception of the **pac-**

**cekabuddha**.

(b) The principle of 'transmission' governing the **paccekabuddha**'s relationship with the layperson.

(c) An assessment of the **paccekabuddha**'s soteriological significance for the layperson.

Before embarking on these matters we need to identify the relevant sources as well as what we mean by 'layperson'. We now abandon the distinction between earlier and later canonical sources so relevant to our discussion in Chapter One and concentrate almost entirely upon 'narrative' literature, a more popular genre mainly intended for consumption by the laity. The narrative material we will be reviewing occurs within Pali and also within Sanskrit Avadāna literature. Since these narratives contain scenes depicting the encounters of **paccekabuddha** with the laity then they represent the prime source of information on the subject of the relationships between **paccekabuddha** and laypersons. And since too Buddhist dogma assigns **paccekabuddha** to an era outside the Buddhist **sāsana** (dispensation of the Buddha's teaching) then the narratives in which they feature are those purporting to depict such eras. It should be noted that the **paccekabuddha** is generally referred to as a **samaṇa** in the Pali narratives, whilst in the Avadāna narratives he is more often referred to as a **ṛṣi** (P.**isi**). An explanation of why they should refer to him differently in this way will be given in the course of the discussion.

In using the term 'layperson' or 'laity' we are referring to non-ascetics or householders-(P.**gahaṭṭha**; Skt.**gṛhastha**). Among these we can make out three categories:
Firstly, those who apprehend the **pacceka-**

**buddha**'s conduct and qualities as exemplary. These are so impressed by the **paccekabuddha** that they want to know how to become one themselves. Consequently he instructs them in matters relating only to the advantages of 'renouncing' the household life.[1] Heeding that instruction, the householder becomes a **pabbajita**. Secondly, there is the category of layperson who apprehends the **paccekabuddha** as something 'mysterious' and 'supranormal' (**uttari-manussa**) but auspicious. These are inspired to make offerings (**dakkhiṇā**) and are therefore referred to as '**paccekabuddha** devotees' by us. Lastly, there is the category of those who insult or in some way abuse **paccekabuddhas**. We ourselves are only concerned with the latter two categories since the first category of layperson does not proceed beyond that point of receiving teaching on **pabbajjā** from the **paccekabuddha**. This aspect of the subject is already comprehensively covered in Kloppenborg's monograph. Most of all, we are interested in the first category of layperson, since it is this one which responds positively, not antipathetically, to an encounter with the **paccekabuddha**.

## The Layperson's Conception of the Paccekabuddha

Where the **paccekabuddha** is mentioned within Pali narratives it is usually in a specific mythical setting. We shall refer to this setting as the Gandhamādana scenario. Gandhamādana is a Himalayan mountain in which is to be found a mythical cave named Nandamūla. This cave is the acknowledged retreat of all **paccekabuddhas**. As soon as someone becomes a

**paccekabuddha**, wherever he may be, he flies directly to the Nandamūla cave to join other **paccekabuddhas**. From here they periodically fly to and fro in quest of alms, sometimes individually, sometimes in groups.

A representative description of what happens to a person when he becomes a **paccekabuddha** can be found in the Kumbhakāra Jātaka[2]. As in the Isigili Sutta, the scene is represented largely from the perspective of the ordinary layperson or onlooker, who is unconversant with the spiritual and meditational powers that create such ascetic figures as **paccekabuddhas**. The Kumbhakāra Jātaka tells how a king named Karaṇḍu attains **paccekabodhi** from contemplating some trees in his mango orchard. This experience leaves the king transfixed, as if in a trance. Noticing his apparent daydreaming but unaware of the momentous spiritual event that has just happened, his own courtiers remark: "You stand too long, O great king!" The king then declares to them that he has become a **paccekabuddha** and therefore must no longer be regarded as a king. In astonishment the courtiers protest that he cannot be a **paccekabuddha** because these ascetics have hair and beards which are shaved, dress in yellow robes, are not attached to a family **(kula)** or group **(gaṇa)**, are like clouds torn by the wind or the moon's orb freed from Rāhu, and dwell in the Nandamūla cave in the Himalayas."[3] When the courtiers finish speaking, the king lifts his hand and touches his head in a ritual gesture. Instantly, his appearance changes from a 'householder' into that of a **samaṇa** with its characteristic features of robes, bowl, razor, needle, strainer and girdle. He then levitates into the air, delivers a few words of exhortation **(ovāda)** and flies away to Mount Gandhamadana.

This tale clearly illustrates how the ordinary layperson only knows and recognises the **paccekabuddha** in terms of his general appearance and behaviour.[4] The layperson is not party to the real significance of the **paccekabuddha** as an 'enlightened being'. This he cannot be, since ex hypothesi he himself is not initiated into that dimension of spiritual reality. In the same way as we enquired after the meaning of the sudden disappearance of the **paccekabuddhas** in the Isigili Sutta, we may ask the significance here of the motif of King Karaṇḍu's sudden transformation from a 'householder' into a **samaṇa**. In an era when there is no **saṅgha**, as this story represents, there can be no procedure of ordination (**upasampadā**) into monkhood. The 'sudden transformation' motif can therefore be seen as a dramatic convention employed to compensate for not being able to portray this important Buddhistic rite of transition. An additional explanation is to be found in the different perspectives which **bhikkhu** and layperson had of the **paccekabuddha**. The layperson knows only of **paccekabuddhas** as **samaṇa** and does not comprehend the idea of how one becomes a **paccekabuddha**, notably, that **paccekabuddhas** were once 'householders' themselves. By contrast those responsible for transmitting the story (members of the **bhikkhu-saṅgha**) were, for historical and dogmatic reasons, intent on showing that attainment of **paccekabodhi** happened mostly within the situation of a 'householder' as well as showing that **bodhi** and 'renunciation' were logically connected. In view of this contrast between the layperson's and monk's perceptions of the **paccekabuddha** the 'sudden transformation' theme is introduced to give proper representation to his doctrinal as well as to his popular conception. The layperson knows only the finished product; the **bhikkhu** is interested in how that product comes to be.

Once the transformation into a **samaṇa** has taken place, the **paccekabuddha** acquires the power to fly. 'Flight' is the form of magic **(iddhi)** most characteristically associated with the figure of the **paccekabuddha** in the Pali and Avadāna narratives. The 'flight' theme should be interpreted within the entire mythological perspective which situates the residence of **paccekabuddhas** on Mount Gandhamādana in the Himalayas. Owing to its physical elevation and remoteness, Mount Gandhamādana may here be taken to represent the notion of transcendence. The **paccekabuddha** commutes back and forth from this inaccessible region to collect alms. He is able to do this instantly, without obstacle or hindrance, by flying through the air **(ākāsa)**. 'Flight' therefore operates as the linking principle or force between an inaccessible or transcendent sphere and the mundane world. The **paccekabuddha**'s capacity to fly may accordingly be said to symbolise his role as a negotiator between the disparate worlds of the transcendent and the mundane. It is to be recalled that, King Karaṇḍu effects his transformation into a **samaṇa** by touching his head with his hand. This too seems to be a gesture symbolically associated with the power to fly. In the Yogatattva Upaniṣad it states that the part of the head from the middle of the eyebrows to the crown corresponds to the cosmic element of 'ether' or 'space' **(akāsa)**. Therefore the adept who performs the meditation appropriate to this region of his body acquires mastery over that cosmic region, the power to travel through the air[5]. It would seem, therefore, that the ritual movement of touching the head functions as a symbol for the **paccekabuddha**'s mastery of this particular aspect of the empirical world.

## The Principle of 'Transmission' Governing the Paccekabuddha's Relationship with the Layperson

Since the layperson's contact with the **paccekabuddha** is more or less confined to the cultic act of alms-giving, we shall specifically examine their relationship within this situation. But where other sorts of encounter between **paccekabuddhas** and layperson may be relevant to issues we are discussing we shall refer to these as well. The process itself of alms-giving can be divided into three stages:

(i) Events 'prior to' and 'leading to' the act of giving

(ii) Events 'directly following upon' the act of giving

(iii) The kammic consequence or the 'merit' (**puñña**) earned from giving to a **paccekabuddha**, which is of two kinds: short term (in the donor's same existence); long-term (in a future birth or future births).

The 'narrative' descriptions of the donor's encounter with the **paccekabuddha** show us that almsgiving is not simply a perfunctory deed of charity but a ritual act with a deep religious significance. There is a quid pro quo basis to it: the donor surrenders a physical object or material possession and in return the **paccekabuddha** imparts an element of his spirituality or interior transcendence, that is, he effects a change of consciousness in the donor. Within the procedure of alms-giving a form of 'transmission' may be said to take place between the donor and the recipient. It is vital to appreciate that this form of transmission is generally non-verbal, since the **paccekabuddha** rarely attempts to teach or instruct the donor. In some accounts of alms-giving the donor specifies aloud the precise form he wants his merit to take. Since this is a verbal request the **paccekabuddha** is required to give a verbal assent to the request. He therefore replies with these words:

"May all you've desired and wished for take effect soon:
May every aspiration be fulfilled like the moon which becomes full.
May all you've desired and wished for take effect soon;
May every aspiration be fulfilled like the luminous jewel."[6]

This particular formula is only found in the Dhammapada, Sutta-nipāta and Apadāna Commentaries; it does not occur in the Jātaka narratives. Therefore it probably represents an early Singhalese elaboration of the alms-giving procedure. Only on certain occasions does a **paccekabuddha** acknowledge the validity of a devotional act by uttering the above formula; on other occasions he may do so simply with the words 'so be it' (**evaṁ hotu**) accompanied by a brief moral discourse.[8] The expression for the verbal response of the **paccekabuddha** is **anumodana karoti** (showing approval, acceptance, appreciation). Utterance of this phrase is a recognised procedure when the Buddhist mendicant receives alms. At the end of a meal, or after receipt of gifts, the Buddha or members of the **bhikkhu-saṅgha** demonstrate their recognition of the worthiness of the act of devotion by pronouncing their thanks in the form of a discourse or admonition.[9]

Thus 'transmission' between **paccekabuddha** and donor may be said to operate predominantly at a 'visual' level. This squares with the fact that the layperson recognises only the external characteristics of the **paccekabuddha**. These external characteristics, more precisely the features which are available to 'visual recognition', are of two sorts: his physical appearance and his 'bodily' transformations [e.g. 'exhibiting the extraordinary phenomenon of magic' (**iddhipāṭihāriyam dasseti**) in the form of levitating or flying]. These two types of transmission have significant implications in Buddhist doctrine. In chapter one we noticed that the **muni**'s transcendence expressed itself in the form of tranquillity and equanimity. In other words his 'buddhological' status is to some extent transmitted by the first type of transmission, that is by his appearance and demeanour; in both Pali and Sanskrit Avadāna literature these **muni** qualities are acknowledged to be authentic modes of transmission. So when the layperson takes note of the semblance or **muni** characteristics of the **paccekabuddha** he is acquiring definite access to 'transcendent forms'. On the other hand, the **isi** characteristics of the **paccekabuddha** (his **iddhānubhāva**), those which represent the second type of transmission, do not have the same measure of authenticity as the **muni** characteristics when considered as 'sources' of transcendence, simply because they can be reproduced or simulated by non-Buddhistic ascetics. If, therefore, a potential donor becomes a devotee of the **paccekabuddha** on grounds that he uses 'magic', there is a danger that he is misconstruing the true significance of the **paccekabuddha** - that he is **buddha**. And it must be remembered that it is by virtue of his **buddha** status that he is a powerful 'field of merit' (**puññakkhettaṁ**) for the laity. Shortly we shall see that there is a noticeable difference in the doctrinal value which different **bhikkhu-saṅgha** traditions, such as those represented by the authors of the Pali and Avadāna texts, attach to the **paccekabuddha**'s displays of magic. Both subscribe to the notion of the transmission of **muni** qualities during the first stage of almsgiving. But whereas the Pali tradition is only prepared to admit the value of transmitting **isi** qualities subsequent upon the offering of the gift, the Avadāna tradition sometimes ascribes a value to the use of magic prior to the act of giving.

## Events Prior to the Act of Giving

Although the events which lead to the act of giving are usually presented in the narrative from the standpoint of the donor, sometimes the **paccekabuddha**'s standpoint is presented as well. From the donor's perspective the encounter is a chance matter. For the **paccekabuddha**, however, it is a case of deliberate design, since he instigates the encounter by choosing beforehand the appropriate person to become donor. Since this involves the exercise of a 'supra-normal' faculty on the part of the **paccekabuddha**, we have decided to incorporate it within the theme of his use of **iddhi**.

Our discussion of the first stage of the encounter between layperson and **paccekabuddha** comes in three parts. We begin by analysing the vocabulary and symbolism used to convey the visual characteristics of the **paccekabuddha**. Then we examine the kind of impression these visual characteristics make on the prospective donor. Thirdly, we compare and contrast the mechanism of visual transmission, the hallmark of the **paccekabuddha**'s impact on the laity, with 'verbal' transmission, the distinctive feature of the Buddha's approach as represented within the Nikayas.

### Visual Characteristics

We have seen that the **paccekabuddha** belongs to the tradition of the **samaṇa** (renouncer). The qualities which he evinces qua mendicant are the **muni** ones of spirituality. The mind-states which are cultivated in meditation manifest themselves in bodily dispositions and faculties: grace and gentleness of bodily movement, and a calm and radiant countenance. When the **paccekabuddha** is mentioned in the context of alms-giving invariably his imposing beauty is mentioned. A passage from the Mahavastu can be used to illustrate this:

> 'Now a certain **pratyekabuddha** entered a village to beg for alms. He was courteous of manners (**prāsādika**) both in approaching and in taking his leave, in looking forwards and backwards, in extending and withdrawing his hand, and in carrying his cloak, bowl and robe. He was like a Nāga. He had accomplished his task; his faculties were turned inwards; his mind was not turned outwards. He was unwavering as one who had achieved harmony with **dharma**. He did not look before him farther than the length of a plough.'[10]

Elsewhere in the Mahāvāstu he is said to be 'graceful' (**prāsādika**) with reference to his bodily deportment (**īryāpatha**), which may be read as the four sorts of posture (going, standing, sitting, lying-down), in respect of which he moves in such a way as to avoid harming any creature intentionally or unintentionally.[11] We may also cite an excerpt from the Khotanese Śūrangama Sūtra, a Mahāyāna text, which draws attention to the visual importance of the **pratyekabuddha**:

'for the sake of ripening the beings, I recognised myself as Pratyekabuddha. In whatever village, district, city I dwelled, there they regarded me as a Pratyekabuddha. I exhibited the external appearance of Pratyekabuddha: I exhibited the behaviour (**īryāpatha**) of Pratyekabuddha.'[12]

The essential tranquillity of the **paccekabuddha** is frequently a subject of remark: In the Kuṇāla Jātaka a woman becomes awestruck at the sight of a motionless (**niccala**) **paccekabuddha**.[13] The Apadāna Commentary states that **paccekabuddhas** are motionless (**niccala**) because they have abandoned a turbulent (**rāga**) mind, thus illustrating the connection between mind-states and bodily disposition.[14] In a variety of Buddhist sources the **paccekabuddha** is designated by the term **śānta** (calm, tranquillity), used regularly across the whole Indian religious tradition to denote the pinnacle of meditational attainment. We have already noted that according to the Moneyya Suttas the **muni** is calm (**santi**).[15] In both the Divyāvadāna and the Avadāna Śataka the **pratyekabuddha** is described as **śānti**; in the Anavataptagāthā he is a tranquil seer (**ṛṣim śāntam**);[16] in the Mahāvāstu it says they calm their own selves (**ekamātmānaṁ śamenti**) and quell evil (**śāntaṁ** pāpam);[17] and in the Vessantara Jātaka the **paccekabuddha**'s manner of movement is taken as a paradigm, for it is said that the **bodhisatta** paced up and down in the calm manner (**upasama**) of a **paccekabuddha**.[18]

## Light Symbolism

Since the form of the **paccekabuddha**'s transmission is principally 'visual', it follows that the imagery used to describe that transmission draws heavily on the concept of 'light'. So, for example, in several alms giving scenes of the Mahāvāstu the **pratyekabuddha** is described as **tūṣṇīkaśobhana** which Jones translates by the locution 'splendid in silence'.[19] This word **śobhana** comes from the root √śubh which means 'to shine' or 'to give off a lustre' and is generally used to describe the countenance of a person who is extremely beautiful or distinguished. The epithet **tūṣṇīkaśobhana** may therefore be taken to represent the overall impression that a **pratyekabuddha** makes on the alms-giver as he approaches or stands with his alms-bowl. As a way of further stressing the radiant power of **pratyekabuddha**, objects which have been in contact with them shine (**śobhati**). Cases in point are the lotus that had once been held in a **pratyekabuddha**'s hand,[21] the wreath of flowers placed on a **pratyekabuddha**'s **stūpa**,[22] and the **pratyekabuddha**'s bowl which 'emitted an aura of light' (**obhāsaṁ muñci**) after a donor had filled it with food.[23] The idea that the aura of a **pratyekabuddha** can be transmitted into objects around him is a crucial part of the process of transmission as we shall see.

There are many other occasions on which 'light' imagery is used in connection with the **paccekabuddha**. In the Kumbhakāra Jātaka it says their **pabbajjā** shines (**sobhati**), their 'faculties are very bright' (**vippasannāni kho indriyāni**) and their 'complexion is pure' (**parisuddho chavivaṇṇo**).[24] The particular usage of one or two of these terms merits further comment. For example, **vippasanna (vi + p + pasanna)** which is here predicated of the **paccekabuddha** becomes the predominant state of mind which he evokes in the donor, thus implying it is a quality that becomes transmitted from him to the donor.

**Suddha** which is here translated by 'pure' is elsewhere used to describe the radiance of the moon and to denote a certain class of **deva** known as the **suddhavāsa devas**.[25]

**Śobha** is a term which is also used to show how the operation of **karma** is to be understood. This can best be illustrated by reference to a passage from the Maitrī Upaniṣad[26] Here karma is said to be either 'good' or 'bad', and the terms used are **śubha** and **aśubha** respectively - **śubha** literally meaning 'bright' or 'luminous', **aśubha** meaning 'dull' or 'dark'. The entire **pāda** is worth quoting because the terms are also shown to be associated with **pra-sad**: 'For by the serenity of one's thought, one destroys all action, good or bad' (**cittasya hi prasādena hanti karma śubhāśubham**).Here 'serenity of thought' (**cittasya prasāda**) is viewed as a 'transcending' agent because it eliminates **karma**. Any form of **karma** is regarded negatively because it inexorably produces the fruit which perpetuates samsaric existence. This connection between karma and 'light' is to be evidenced in Buddhist sources also. In the Mahāvāstu, the act of giving to **pratyekabuddhas** is described as a 'bright deed' (**śobhanam kṛtam**)[27] and 'a shining and lovely deed' (**śobhanam...kalyāṇam karma**).[28] The first quotation comes from a story in which there is marked use of light imagery: A servant girl gives a lotus-flower to a **pratyekabuddha**; in the **pratyekabuddha**'s hand it begins to shine (**śobhati**). Observing this, the girl asks for it back; when he puts it back into her hand, then her hand begins to shine (**śobhati**) too. The deed of giving here is not only figuratively 'lustrous' but literally so, as the object conveyed carries within it the significance of the conveying act.

There are other examples of 'light' imagery occurring in connection with **paccekabuddha**:

They are described as suns (**suriyā**) because of their likeness to them;[29] or as resembling **devas** because they possess 'flamelike' forms.[30] In both the Apadana and the Mahāvāstu the **paccekabuddha** is referred to as a lamp (**dīpa**).[31] This 'light' imagery serves to explain his salvific role in respect of the donor or devotee. The source of his spirituality, his pure mind (**mano suddhaṁ**), expresses itself in a physical dimension as 'radiance' or an 'aura of light'; 'light' symbolises his purity or holiness. When a prospective almsgiver or donor espies, that is, experiences a **paccekabuddha** visually, the light or aura which the **paccekabuddha** emits is transmitted to him and produces or evokes in him a devotional response (P.**pasāda**; Skt.**prasāda**). This sense of devotion causes the layperson to present alms to the ascetic. The symbolic significance of the 'light' motif may therefore be summarised as follows: 'Light' is a form of silent or noiseless energy which illuminates. The **paccekabuddha**'s encounter with the donor is essentially non-verbal, that is, noiseless. The **paccekabuddha**, therefore, radiates or emits a form of silent, spiritual energy which 'illuminates', that is, which makes serene the mind (**citta**) of the prospective donor.

## The Paccekabuddha's Impact on the Prospective Donor

We can discern three distinct stages to the prospective donor's initial encounter with a **paccekabuddha**. First of all, he sees the **paccekabuddha** approaching for alms. 'See' is here intended in an evaluative sense: the prospective donor 'notices' or 'perceives' something special or distinctive about the figure. Next, the spectacle of the **pacceka-**

**buddha** evokes a feeling of devotion. Thirdly and lastly, the donor offers a gift to the **paccekabuddha**. We now propose to graphically illustrate the first two stages by citing a number of passages:

(a) 'Having seen (**paśyitvā**) the deportments (**īryāṁ**) of the **pratyekabuddha**, sublime devotion (**udāraṁ prasādaṁ**) arose within the overseer's daughter.[32]

(b) 'The **paccekabuddha** stood motionless (**niccalo**). When the woman saw (**disvā**) that he was motionless, taking heed of it (**oloketvā**) she felt devotion in her heart (**cittam pasādetvā**).[33]

(c) 'Seeing (**dṛṣṭvā**) the **pratyekabuddha**, devotion arose (**prasādamutpannam**) in the wife....Because of this devotion (**prasāda**) I gave him alms'.[34]

(d) 'Seeing (**dṛṣṭvā**) the wreath (**mālā**) - (placed on the **pratyekabuddha**) - outshine (**śobhanti...atiriva**) in beauty (**rūpena**) and brilliance (**tejena**) all the other wreaths, devotion arose within her heart (**cittaṁprasādamutpannam**)'.[35]

(e) 'Seeing (**dṛṣṭvā**) the **pratyekabuddha** called Bhadrika, the mind (**manas**) of the poor man (**kṣīṇakulaputrapuruṣa**) became devoted (**prasanna**). Devoted in his heart (**prasannacitta**) he took him home and provided him with food'.[36]

(f) 'Seeing (**disvā**) the **paccekabuddha**, the king became devoted in heart (**pasannacitta**)'.[37]

(g) When the King of Bārāṇasī is shown the body of a **paccekabuddha** who has just entered

**parinibbāna** he performs **pūja**).[38]

(h) Simply by glimpsing the head of a **paccekabuddha** who has just entered into **parinibbāna**, an elder (**thera**) by the name of Vangisa in a former life, had been inspired to become a **pabbajita**.[39]

(i) Seeing (**disvā**) them (i.e., four **paccekabuddhas**), the **bodhisatta** became 'contented in heart' (**tuṭṭhacitta**).'[40]

In these citations the principal term used to express the nature of the prospective donor's response to seeing **paccekabuddhas** is devotion (Skt.**prasāda**; P.**pasāda**). The clue to understanding the significance here of **prasāda** lies in the use of the complementary term **prāsādika** (serene) as a predicate of the **pratyekabuddha**. We may recall that the **pratyekabuddha** is described as 'serene' (**prāsādika**) both in approaching and taking his leave, in looking forwards and backwards, etc. and as 'serene' (**prāsādika**) in his bodily deportment.[41] Elsewhere in Avadana sources it is said he is 'serene in body and mind' (**kāyaprāsādika cittaprāsādika**)[42] and that 'men and gods have faith in these serene ones' (**prāsādikābhiprasanna devamanuśyaḥ**. See Appendix II). We have chosen advisedly to translate **prāsādika** as 'serene' in view of the light symbolism inherent in the usage and because 'serene' is associated semantically with the concept of light. The Latin word '**serenus**' (for example) is used for 'bright' sky, 'fair' weather. In Sanskrit the verbal root **pra-√sad** is often used in a similar context to the Latin '**serenus**' to represent the 'brightness' of the sky, the 'calm' and 'tranquillity' of the sea. However, **prāsādika** has two further connotations which cannot be adequately conveyed in the translation 'serene'. They are the meanings of 'auspicious' and 'grace'. For instance, in the Śvetāśvatara Upaniṣad **prasāda** is a **bhakti** concept denoting the 'grace' of God.[43] We might also have chosen to translate the prospective donor's response, **prasāda**, by 'serene' so that for example, the prospective donor may be said to acquire 'serenity of heart' or 'mind' on seeing a **pratyekabuddha**. But in this particular case we have preferred 'devotion' since it gives a stronger indication that the response is both committed and religious in character. Alternatively, we could have translated it by 'faith' or 'belief', but such credal terms more appropriately describe the response to spoken words than to an inherently visual experience.[44] The same cognate terms are therefore used to denote both the **paccekabuddha**'s spiritual emanation (**prāsādika**) and the nature of the response - **prasāda** - which that emanation elicits in the prospective donor. This suggests that some quality or qualities are transmitted from the **paccekabuddha** to the prospective donor.

## A Comparison of Visual and Verbal Transmission

**Pasanna-citta** (devoted in heart) is a concept which also is important within the context of the Buddha's teaching. The term is used to represent the positive response of the listener to that talk which the Buddha gives prior to full **dhamma** instruction. This talk is referred to as the preliminary discourse (**anupubbikathā**). It consists of instruction on alms-giving, morality, and heaven and the perils of sensuality. If the talk is received sympathetically the Buddha proceeds with 'that teaching of the **dhamma** which the awakened ones themselves have discerned' (**atha yā buddhānaṁ sāmukkaṁsikā dhammadesanā taṁ pakāsesi**) viz. the four noble truths. The '**anupubbikathā** represents general principles of conduct applicable to the Buddhist layperson and is distinct from **dhamma** proper in that it is not concerned with penetration or apprehension of any cognitive truths. Nevertheless, it is to be seen as a necessary precursor to instruction in the four noble truths. From hearing (that is, comprehending) the four noble truths, the listener acquires the **dhammacakkhu** (**dhamma**-eye) and becomes a **sāvaka** (hearer) - one who is destined to enlightenment in this life or in some future existence.[46] In gauging the reaction to his **anupubbikathā** the Buddha looks to see if the mind (**citta**) of the listener is 'responsive'. The appropriate response takes the form of a series of graduated steps culminating in **pasannacitta**:

1. Ready in heart - **kallacitta**
2. Softened in heart - **muducitta**
3. Unbiased in heart - **vinīvaraṇacitta**
4. Uplifted in heart - **udaggacitta**
5. Devoted in heart - **pasannacitta**

The parallels that can be drawn between the positive response of the prospective donor to the visual experience of the prospective donor and the positive response of the layperson to verbal instruction from the Buddha are indicated in the following Table:

| **Sammāsambuddha (sāsana)** | **Paccekabuddha (non-sāsana)** |
|---|---|
| 1. Initial condition | |
| Hearing the **anupubbikathā** | Seeing the **paccekabuddha** |
| 2. Effect | |
| Experiencing **pasannacitta** in response to the talk of the Buddha | Experiencing **pasannacitta** in response to the sight the **paccekabuddha** |
| 3. Act | |
| On the basis of the listener's **pasanna citta**, the Buddha decides to teach the four noble truths | On the basis of his **pasannacitta** the prospective donor decides to make a gift to the **paccekabuddha** |
| 4. Attainment | |
| The listener acquires the **dhamma-cakkhu (dhamma-eye)** and becomes a **sāvaka**. He is destined to attain **bodhi**. | The donor earns **puñña** (merit) |

It is instantly noticeable that stage 2 is identical in both systems: the religious character of the response, **pasannacitta**, is the same. However, during the **sāsana** period the response is mediated by the 'spoken word'; but outside the **sāsana** period by 'vision'. The Buddha, in choosing to speak, is the active party whereas the **paccekabuddha**, in saying nothing, is passive. It can, of course, be argued that the **paccekabuddha** also plays an active role by providing the prospective donor with the opportunity to see and behold him. Where the two systems decidedly differ is in the respective responses of the Buddha and **paccekabuddha** to the individual's **pasannacitta**: the former 'teaches' the four noble truths, thereby initiating the person into **sāvaka** status; the latter 'accepts' the gift, thereby assuring the person's **puñña**. Owing to the fact that he does not respond to the devotion of the layperson with spoken instruction, the **paccekabuddha** neither instigates a **dhamma** (doctrine) nor wins novitiates (**sāvaka**). In summary, the layperson's response in these different situations of verbal and visual encounter is the same - one of 'devotion'. It is the response or reaction of the Buddha and **paccekabuddha** to the **pasannacitta** which differs.

## Events That Follow the Act of Giving

The most significant and interesting aspect of what happens after the donor has made the gift relates to magic (**iddhi**) and its uses. Since a difference is to be discerned in the salvific value that Pali and Buddhist Sanskrit sources attach to 'exhibitions' of magic, we shall look at them separately in order to show the implications of this doctrinal difference. In a number of Pali narratives **paccekabuddhas** are seen to possess the power of precognition in the matter of who will make a suitable donor. In Avadāna narratives there is no mention of them having this particular faculty. In many of the Pali narratives the **paccekabuddha** is described as residing in the meditational state of pure cessation (**nirodha samāpatti**) for periods of up to seven days. When he emerges from his meditation he is understandably hungry and so 'looks down' (**oloketi**) from Mount Gandhamādana and 'discerns' (**āvajjati**) a suitable candidate for almsgiving.[47] In terms of canonical doctrine the **paccekabuddha** is here seen to be displaying the two **abhiññā** known as the 'divine eye' (**dibba cakkhu**) and 'knowledge of other minds' (**parassa ceto-pariya-ñāṇa**). As we have seen, the latter is the faculty by which the Buddha is capable of telling whether or not a person has the requisite **pasanna-citta** to be taught the four noble truths. The **paccekabuddha** similarly uses it here to find out whether a person has the capacity for devotion (**pasāda**) or faith (**saddhā**).[48] Having located the appropriate person from afar, the **paccekabuddha** then flies from the mountain into the presence of the prospective donor. It should be stressed that in no account is there mention that the prospective donor or anyone else actually sees the **paccekabuddha** flying from Gandhamādana to the site of almsgiving. Upon alighting the **paccekabuddha** approaches the prospective donor on foot in the customary manner of a **bhikkhu**. Then the act of alms-giving proceeds. This act is to be interpreted as a palpable demonstration of the layperson's own devotion (**pasāda**) or faith (**saddhā**). That is to say, the offering of a gift constitutes the focal centre of the encounter between the layperson and the **paccekabuddha** in the sense that the relationship of the layperson to the **paccekabuddha** is assimilated to a rite or 'ritualised'. In this way an act of moral import becomes an act of religious significance. After having accepted the alms the **paccekabuddha** levitates a short distance from the ground, delivers a brief word of exhortation or moral advice (**ovāda**) and flies away to Mount Gandhamādana once again. The donor and by-standers witness this display of flying - they gaze transfixed until the ascetic disappears from view.[49] On some occasions the **paccekabuddha** makes a special resolve (**adhiṭṭhāna**) that enables onlookers to see him sharing his alms with fellow **pac-**

**cekabuddhas** after returning to the mountain.[50]

In these accounts of alms-giving the **paccekabuddha** does not display his magic power gratuitously; he only exhibits it after the layperson has demonstrated his devotion (**pasada**) by making the gift. So the exhibition of 'flying' may be understood ritually as the palpable act which the **paccekabuddha** performs in rejoinder to the layperson's palpable act of giving. Since the demonstration of faith comes first, the **paccekabuddha**'s use of magic serves to vindicate that show of faith. Meanwhile, the effect upon the donor of seeing this demonstration of magic power is to increase or expand (**vattati**) that **pasannacitta** he experienced on first beholding the **paccekabuddha**, until his entire body (**sarīra**) becomes suffused with joy (**pīti**).[51] In seeking to summarise the type of doctrinal truth here being conveyed, we can say that the **muni** dimension (the 'buddhological' attributes embodied in the form of the 'serene' ascetic) serve to elicit the initial **pasannacitta**, whilst the **isi** characteristics (viz. the use of 'magic') are assigned the auxiliary role of consolidating the **pasannacitta**.

In the Buddhist Sanskrit narratives the conception of the relationship between **pratyekabuddha** and layperson is very similar in many respects to that in the Pali sources and shares, for instance, the stress given to **muni** qualities in the moment of initial impact when the layperson descries a **pratyekabuddha**. But there are also one or two aspects in which important differences can be detected. So for example, in addition to stories of gifts to **pratyekabuddhas**, there are to be found stories of gifts to **samyaksaṁbuddhas** in which attainment of **pratyekabodhi** in a future rebirth is a feature of the resultant merit (Skt. **puṇya**). Although the Pali tradition seems to have been acquainted with the doctrinal concept of laypersons attaining **paccekabodhi** in the future through such acts of merit, it features as a much later doctrine[52] and there is no corpus of tales illustrating how it happens. In the Buddhist Sanskrit stories of alms-giving to **pratyekabuddhas** and **samyaksaṁbuddhas**, these **buddhas** often intentionally use their magic power to elicit a **prasāda**-type response from the layperson. For the purpose of analysis these stories can be separated into six main types:

a. Stories of 'devotional' acts towards **pratyekabuddhas**, where magic (Skt. **ṛddhi**) does not feature at all. Just to see a **pratyekabuddha** is sufficient to evoke 'devotion'.[53]

b. Stories of 'devotional' acts towards **pratyekabuddhas** in which they respond with a display of **ṛddhi**. The event of 'seeing' the **pratyekabuddha** plays a formative part in these stories also. So, for example, a certain beggar who sees a **pratyekabuddha** experiences intense devotion (**mahāprasāda**) and thereupon gives to him his only remaining morsel of food. In return the **pratyekabuddha** performs feats of **ṛddhi**.[54]

c. The same kind of stories as category (b) but featuring the **samyaksaṁbuddha** instead of **pratyekabuddha**. For example, a certain group of travelling players encounter the Buddha as they are passing through the gates of the town of Śrāvastī. The sight of him inspires **prasannacitta** in them and they decide to sing and dance in his honour, and to throw blue lotuses at his feet. These lotuses cling to the Buddha and emit a sapphire light which illuminates the whole of Śrāvastī.[55]

d. Stories in which some person is either ill-intentioned towards a **pratyekabuddha** or fails to recognise his **muni** attributes. The **pratyekbuddha** consequently performs a feat of **ṛddhi** in order to alter the person's attitude. **Ṛddhi** is here used to evoke devotion where the predisposition to devotion is not immediately evident. A case in point is the husband who scolds his wife for feeding a **pratyekabuddha** whereupon the ascetic flies through the air for his benefit. On seeing him fly, the husband experiences **prasāda** and apologises to his wife.[56]

e. The same kind of stories as category (d) but featuring a **samyaksaṁbuddha** instead of **pratyekabuddha**. In one such story a boatman insists on payment before he will agree to ferry the Buddha across the Ganges. The Buddha responds by flying across the river. On seeing him fly, the boatman repents (**mahā-vipratisāran**), falls at the Buddha's feet and makes him an offering.[57]

f. Stories in which a person deliberately insults a **pratyekabuddha** so that as a consequence no **ṛddhi** whatsoever is forthcoming. So, for instance, a person places an offensive substance such as urine or excrement in the pratyekabuddha's alms-bowl,[58] or a person knocks the alms-bowl out of his hand.[59] In respect of this category of tale the question might be asked why the **pratyeka-buddha** should not use **ṛddhi** to convert the offensive person, as happens in type (d) stories. In explanation of this apparent anomaly, it should be pointed out, firstly, that in these cases the degree of offense is distinctly severe and, secondly, the offensiveness itself constitutes an act or form of conduct as karmically potent as its counterpart the gift of alms. It would seem that conversion is no longer considered possible once direct contact or relations has been entered into between the lay-person and **pratyekabuddha**. This contact takes on the binding character of a contract as soon as **puṇya** (merit) or **apuṇya** (demerit) come into operation.

There are examples in Pali of stories belonging to the same categories as (a-c) and (f). It is categories (d) and (e) which are not found; those in which magic is displayed either prior to any act of alms-giving or in order to convert a prospectively 'hostile' mind to a 'devoted' mind.

## Summary of the Pali and Avadāna Understanding of 'Magic'

In the Pali narratives we have seen that the **paccekabuddha** only ever exhibits **iddhi** in response to an act or gesture of devotion- (**pasāda**) or faith (**saddhā**), signified in the alms-gift. In this respect it is the lay-person's faith which may be seen to activate it. This faith arises out of the visual contemplation of the **muni** qualities of the **paccekabuddha**. The display of **iddhi** which follows the alms-giving only strengthens or deepens the initial devotion. Therefore, it does seem some sort of distinction is intended between the **muni** and **isi** facets of the **paccekabuddha**. By contrast some of the Avadāna stories concern persons who do not respond at all to the sight of the **muni** qualities of **pratyekabuddhas** or **samyaksaṁbuddhas**. These sorts of persons are not discarded or discounted, as it seems they are in the Theravāda tradition, but means are created for them to be won over to the 'cultus'. The point to note is that the **pratyekabuddha** or **samyaksaṁbuddha** take the salvific initiative by producing displays of magic to convert the otherwise intractable layperson. Consequently, it can be said in respect of the Avadāna corpus that not only **muni** but **ṛṣi** characteristics are a recognised instrument of winning devotees. In the Pali tradition 'magic' is allowed to function as a salvific instrument only within a quid pro quo situation: the donor warrants it by virtue of his gift. In the Avadāna tradition it functions much more independently of the layperson's spiritual condition and, therefore, can be used as a tactical ploy to manipulate the right response from an uncongenial person. The soteriological perspective of the Avadāna corpus is accordingly more liberal than the Pali.

## 'Merit-Earning' from Paccekabuddhas

Direct encounters between the layperson and the **paccekabuddha** have special consequences for the former. They can significantly influence a person's spiritual destiny. They are situations with 'transforming' possibilities. This state of affairs exists by virtue of the **paccekabuddha**'s identity as a 'holyman'. Since the **paccekabuddha** embodies aspects of transcendence, the layperson's behaviour when confronted by him is an indication of his attitude towards transcendence. We therefore propose to examine the sorts of consequences or transformations which accrue from direct encounters and to investigate the nature of the power which produces these transformations. Our purpose in so doing is to unravel some of the metaphysical assumptions and premises underlying the doctrine of 'merit-earning' in order to understand better the religious significance of cultic acts.

Within the context of the doctrine of 'merit earning' (**puñña-katā**) merit can be classified as 'good' (**puñña**) or 'bad' (**apuñña**), short-term (that is, coming to fruition in the same lifetime) or long-term (in a future life or over future existences), and mundane (**lokiya**) or supramundane (**lokuttara**). We have come across only two cases of short-term merit resulting from service to the **paccekabuddha**; both of these are stories from the Pali Jātakas. We shall briefly summarise these stories as they possess a number of significant features. The first story is taken from the Sankha Jātaka and tells of a rich **brahmana** who undertakes a journey across the sea to the land of Suvaṇṇa.[60] Whilst journeying to the port of sail he is seen by a **paccekabuddha** on Mount Gandhamādana. This **paccekabuddha** 'discerns' (**āvajjati**) two things: the **brāhmaṇa** is about to board a boat that is going to be shipwrecked; the **brāhmaṇa** is predisposed to making the **paccekabuddha** an alms-gift. The **paccekabuddha** descends from Mount Gandhamādana and alights in the vicinity of the brāhmaṇa. When the **brāhmaṇa** sees the ascetic approaching in the heat and without any footwear, he offers to wash his feet and to give him his own pair of sandals. The **paccekabuddha** accepts this act of service and as a result the **brāhmaṇa** survives the journey in spite of the shipwreck.

The second story occurs in the Telapatta Jātaka and features the **bodhisatta** as one of the sons of King Brahmadatta of Bārāṇasī.[61] The **bodhisatta** asks some **paccekabuddhas** to look into the future in order to find out if he will one day become king. They tell him that he will never be king in Bārāṇasī but that if he is prepared to make the journey to Takkasilā he will become king there. They warn him, however, that the journey will involve passing through a great forest inhabited by demonesses (**yakkhinī**) who will try to seduce and kill him. The **bodhisatta** thereupon asks the **paccekabuddha** for some means of protection against the **yakkhinī**. They supply him with two protective charms (**paritta**): sand (**parittavālikā**) and a thread (**parittasuttaka**). The **bodhisatta** sprinkles the sand on his head and ties the thread around his forehead; in due course he accomplishes his journey safely.[62]

It is to be noticed how these stories share in common the theme of a safe journey. The **paccekabuddha** is represented as one who supplies protection against the hazards encountered by the traveller. In both stories too the **paccekabuddha** is seen to possess the power of precognition. In one story he foresees the shipwreck and in the other, the enthronement of the **bodhisatta** at Takkasilā.

## Bad Merit

'Bad merit' (**apuñña**) is not usually short term in its fruition. However, if the form of insult or harm is particularly heinous, such as the act of murdering a **paccekabuddha**, then the offender may die immediately and go directly to hell.[63]

## Long-Term Merit

There are three outstanding features of long-term merit: In the first place a principle of 'correspondence' is discernible between the type of action the layperson performs in regard to the **paccekabuddha** and the type of transformation which results. Secondly, there are occasions when the devotee actually specifies the particular form the accruing merit should take. One can therefore talk of 'specified' and 'unspecified' merit. Thirdly, there can be supramundane (**lokuttara**) as well as mundane (**lokiya**) consequences.

The doctrine that the fruit of an action or of an instance of behaviour shows a correspondence with the nature of the action or behaviour which produced it might appear to be self-evident. Nevertheless attention needs to be drawn to this principle of correspondence since it tells us something important about the way in which 'merit' operates. It is often the case that an act of devotion toward a **paccekabuddha** leads to alleviation in future existences of precisely those conditions which beset a person in their present existence. So, for instance, one story relates how a labourer in the hire of a treasurer fills a **paccekabuddha**'s bowl with rice which he has been striving for three years to earn. From the merit of this act he eventually becomes a treasurer himself, and never again experiences poverty in any of his future existences.[64] In another such story a beggar who happens to offer a **paccekabuddha** his last morsel of food is thereafter reborn always into prosperous circumstances.[65] And there is the story of five members of a household who, in the midst of a famine, give their last ounce of rice to a **paccekabuddha**. As a result they never experience famine again, and always return to the same family in future rebirths.[66]

The type of virtue displayed in the service of a **paccekabuddha** is also shown to have a bearing upon the particular form taken by the 'transformation' characteristics. For example, a dog who befriends and accompanies a **paccekabuddha** on his alms-rounds howls with grief when the **paccekabuddha** abandons him and returns to Gandhamādana. When the dog dies, he is reborn a god and given a voice of extraordinary power as a reward for his fidelity toward the ascetic. [67]. In another story, a servant who fetches a **paccekabuddha** alms with great speed acquires , in his future existences, the facility to travel vast distances in short periods of time [68]. Similarly, a poor man's daughter who furnishes a **paccekabuddha** with some clay that he needs, acquires skin as soft as clay in her next rebirth.[69] In another narrative, a King of Bārāṇasī is granted divine clothes because on a certain occasion in the past he had given his shawl to a **paccekabuddha**.[70]

This feature of correspondence obtains in stories concerned with the acquisition of bad merit (**apuñña**) as well as good. The young girl whose skin will become soft as clay in her next life, will also become ugly because her initial reaction toward the **paccekabuddha** had been one of anger. There are many more examples of this kind of story: a woman is reborn a hump-back because she mimics a humpbacked **paccekabuddha**;[71] the spouse of a wealthy merchant is herself reborn with a deformity because she insults a deformed **paccekabuddha**;[72] a woman who sets fire to a **paccekabuddha** dies in house-fires in her future lives;[73] a king who calls a **paccekabuddha** a 'leper' is reborn as a leper;[74] and a person who cleaves the head of a **paccekabuddha** with a potsherd becomes a 'sledgehammer' **peta** in his next life.[75]

These are just a selection of many examples showing that a principle of correspondence exists between an action toward a **paccekabuddha** and the form taken by its fruition. One striking aspect of this correspondence is the dominance of the complementary motifs of 'beauty' and 'ugliness'. Since the **paccekabuddha**'s attributes are conveyed to the lay person visually, through his own external appearance and behaviour, it would seem appropriate that the karmic consequences should have a primarily 'visual'significance. Themes of 'beauty' and 'ugliness' and their polarity are, of course, a conspicuous feature of folk-tales in general. These stories of **paccekabuddhas** are no exception. In folk-tales the possession of beauty is a token of being good, and ugliness is associated with the working of evil. Therefore, beauty and ugliness on the physical and material plane are the counterparts of good and evil on the ethical plane.

We may therefore, conclude that the operation of moral and spiritual qualities and their deficiency, when functioning within the cultic framework of encounter between layperson and Buddhist holyman, become responsible for significant 'transformations' in the physical and phenomenal world. In this scenario the **paccekabuddha**'s own 'physical' transformation, that is, his display of flight, serves to remind the devotee or potential devotee of the sorts of radical 'transformation' that can arise from service to him. The layperson relates what he sees as the'transforming' powers of the **paccekabuddha** to his own situation: if he honours and serves the **paccekabuddha** then, by virtue of this act of recognition, the same powers which produce transformations in the ascetic will work for himself.

## 'Specified' Merit

In the alms-giving procedure we have remarked that donors sometimes specify what form their merit should take. This concept is found in the Pali Commentaries and the Avadāna sources but not in canonical narratives. It would seem therefore to constitute a doctrinal and cultic elaboration of the original idea that it is auspicious to provide alms for mendicants. This particular elaboration simply formalises the original deep felt yearning and hope of the alms-giver that through his act of recognition and service better things should come to be. The donor is permitted and encouraged to articulate his aspirations in the hope that they might take on more abiding significance. In this there is an implicit acknowledgement that the question of a person's future and destiny is closely bound up with his own volition.[76] The reward that comes from his alms-giving is not ex gratia; it is the integral realisation of his most earnest aspiration. And his correct response to a first-hand encounter with 'transcendence' has already demonstrated his capacity to realise it. This is the reason why the layperson's frame of mind (viz. **pasannacitta**) plays such a crucial role in the entire proceedings.

## 'Supramundane' Merit

So far we have looked at examples of the sorts of mundane or wordly (**lokiya**) consequences which result from a person's behaviour towards **paccekabuddhas**. All types of devotional acts produce some form of mundane benefit. In some stories, however, the devotee requests that the merit that he has earned should in addition take on a supramundane (**lokuttara**) character.

The term which has given the title to an entire corpus of narrative literature, **avadāna** (heroic deed), implies that certain deeds have a special potency and, over a time-span of one or many rebirths, can produce radical forms of transformation in the agent. In the Avadāna Śataka and the Divyāvadāna, for instance, this doctrine of merit-earning has been fully systematised so that **sambodhi** and **pratyekabodhi** can only be attained through a pious action toward a **samyaksaṁbuddha**, whilst **arhant** status can only be attained through a pious act toward a **pratyekabuddha** or a **srāvakabuddha** (i.e., an **arhant**). In the Mahāvastu Avadāna there is no mention of 'supramundane' consequences of merit; and in the Pali it is confined, as far as we are aware, to the Dhammapada Commentary and the Nettipakaraṇa, both late compositions. One rather interesting exception is to be found in the Kummāsapiṇḍa Jātaka, where it is said that Sākyamuni earned his 'omniscience' (**sabbaññūtañāṇa**) as a poor man in a previous existence, by providing alms for a group of four **paccekabuddhas**.[78] The significance of the doctrine of 'supramundane' attainment through acts of merit, whether they be directed towards **sammāsambuddhas**, **paccekabuddhas** or **sāvakas**,can be stated as follows: in that the attainment of 'supramundane' goals was the traditional preserve of members of the **bhikkhu-saṅgha**, then the distinction between them and the laity (**upāsaka**) was not only the practical difference between mendicant and householder but concerned different soteriological goals. The householder was expected to strive for the attainment of rebirth in heaven (**sagga**), and the **bhikkhu** for one of the four paths (**magga**) leading to **nibbāna**. However, to recognize that the householder could perform devotional acts which conduced in the long term toward transcendental consequences, was to admit that the lay-monachist distinction is not so absolutely crucial. In other words, the laity is given access in the long term to what the **bhikkhu-saṅgha** has access to in the shorter term. In the growth and expansion of Buddhism there were increasing pressures to narrow the gap between lay and monachist salvific goals.

## The Nature of the Power Behind 'Transformation'

Our examination of those scenes containing descriptions of encounters between the layperson and the **paccekabuddha** has shown us two things: First, the response of the lay person results in a radical transformation in his or her destiny, either for good or bad, sometimes even culminating in a transformation of transcendent significance (i.e. future **arahant** status). Second, the **paccekabuddha** transforms his own body (that is, through feats of magic) in various ways to provide the onlooking layperson with some idea of the radical possibilities of transformation inherent in being a devotee. We now propose to identify and describe the power or operative principle responsible for these transformations. This will involve us in a fairly elaborate discussion of the interrelationship between the concepts **avihiṁsā** (refraining from harming) and **kamma**. In order to illustrate the nature of this interrelationship we shall refer to two tales: story (a) from the Angulimāla Sutta;[79] story (b) from the Mahāmora Jātaka.[80] Only the latter story has to do with **paccekabuddhas** but both have **avihiṁsā** as their primary theme.

The Angulimāla Sutta acquires its title from the name given to a notorious brigand and murderer who was a contemporary of the Buddha. He had achieved renown for the macabre practice of amputating his victims' fingers and making them into a garland or necklace which he hung as a trophy around his own neck (hence **angulimāla**: 'garland of fingers'). The Angulimāla Sutta tells what happens when this brigand encounters the Buddha. On a certain occasion he descries the Buddha from afar and decides to make him his next victim. Although greatly renowned for his skill and expertise in seizing his victims, Angulimala pursues the Buddha only to find that he is unable to lay hold of him; for the Buddha uses magic (**iddhi**) to stay out of his reach. The brigand is perplexed as to why he cannot catch his quarry since the Buddha appears to be travelling merely at the customary pace of a monk. In his frustration Angulimāla commands the Buddha to stand still and explain what is happening. The Buddha then speaks these words: "I, Angulimāla, am standing still (**ṭhita**), having for all beings laid aside the rod (**daṇḍa**); but you are unrestrained (**asaññato**) regarding creatures; therefore, I am standing still, you are not standing still". In this reply the Buddha is seen to connect 'stillness' with 'refraining from harming' (**avihiṁsā**): 'Stillness' is the fruit and consequence of **avihiṁsā**. There is a certain irony in the fact that the 'spiritually still' person can move faster than the 'conventionally active' person. Technically, the Buddha's 'exercise of magic' (**iddhābhisankhāra**) accounts for this, but quite clearly **avihiṁsā** is the spiritual or moral power underlying it. The story illustrates how 'real movement', that is, 'transcendence' only becomes possible through observing the ethical principle of **avihiṁsā**.

In story (b) an hunter succeeds in catching a peacock in one of his forest traps. The snared peacock turns out to be the **bodhisatta** who, on being caught, instructs the hunter on the wrongfulness of hunting. As he listens attentively to the **bodhisatta**'s words the hunter instantly attains **paccekabodhi**. At this very moment the bird is automatically released from the snare. On finding himself to be a **paccekabuddha**, however, the hunter is immediately confronted with the realization that he still has other captive animals at home. He cannot return to release them because that would be - by implication - to return to the 'household life', a situation incommensurable with his new-found status as a **paccekabuddha**. On the other hand, he is responsible for these animals remaining in captivity and so continuing to be deprived of their freedom. The hunter is shown to be incapable of solving the dilemma without the assistance of the **bodhisatta** who is stated to be omniscient (**sabbaññū**) and with a 'greater knowledge of ways and means (**upāya-pariggahañāṇam**) than a **paccekabuddha**'. The **bodhisatta** tells him that the way to solve his problem is to make an 'act of truth' (**saccakiriya**) by virtue of his realization of **paccekabodhi**. The **bodhisatta** explains that such an 'act of truth' will instantly liberate not just his own captives but all captive creatures throughout the land of Jambudīpa. Heeding the **bodhisatta's** counsel, the hunter performs an 'act of truth' and the release of all captives is instantaneously accomplished.

The concept here referred to as an 'act of truth' (**saccakiriya**) is common throughout Buddhist and Hindu literature, and Western scholars have devoted considerable attention to it.[81] Burlingame, who was among the first to discuss the concept, has supplied the following definition of it: 'A formal declaration of fact accompanied by a command or resolution or prayer that the purpose of the agent shall be accomplished'.[82] The so-called 'fact' referred to by the agent is generally some moral or spiritual quality possessed by that agent. So, for example, in the above story the hunter refers to his realization of **paccekabodhi** as the fact by which his petition will become effective. The purpose to be accomplished is something beyond the normal powers of the agent - so that the 'suddenness' of its accomplishment appears miraculous or magical. In Hindu tales, the quality or attribute a person invokes is linked closely with their dharmic role. Even persons who lead ostensibly immoral lives, such as thieves and prostitutes, can still exercise an 'act of truth' by appealing to the 'fact' that they have remained loyal to their dharmic duty.[83] The notion of an 'act of truth' is a significant piece of armoury within our argument because it points to the existence in Ancient India of a belief that power can be exerted over the phenomenal world through virtue. In this respect it may be noticed that it operates on exactly the same assumptions as the doctrine of 'merit earning', except that the latter operates within a more clearly defined cultic framework in which the concept of a power effective quality is assimilated to the notion of a specific act of virtue directed at another being. But both an 'act of truth' and an 'act of merit' produce 'radical' transformations in the agent, the one (usually) without and the other with a time-lapse. Because there is no time-lapse with an 'act of truth' it appears to operate magically. We have seen too that an 'act of merit' is like an 'act of truth' in that sometimes, it is accompanied by a verbalised resolution or petition.

To return to the subject of stories (a) and (b). Both stories are intent on showing that **vihiṁsā** (harming) is not compatible with spirituality, and both contain 'transformation' motifs as a way of illustrating this point. In story (a) the Buddha transforms himself in order to escape the prodigious clutches of the renowned bandit; in (b) the hunter is suddenly transformed into a **paccekabuddha** who then succeeds in emancipating all ensnared animals through the transformative power of an 'act of truth'. Elsewhere in canonical sources **mettā** (loving-kindness) - which is a meditational extension of the ethical principle of **avihiṁsā** - functions as a similar sort of 'transforming' agent. So, for example, in the Vessantara Jātaka, by the use of **mettānubhāva** (the power of loving-kindness) the **bodhisatta** causes all the animals within a radius of three leagues to conduct themselves kindly to one another.[84] Perhaps a more familiar story is the one in which the Buddha uses '**mettā**' to quell the ferocious elephant, Nālāgiri.[85]

Our object in reviewing these stories has been to illustrate the belief that moral and spiritual accomplishment has the potential of effecting transformations within the phenomenal world. **Avihiṁsā** is here seen to be the most powerful principle of transformation.[86] We are therefore obliged to raise the question of how **avihiṁsā** in particular conduces toward transformation. The resolution of this question requires us to look into the significance of the notion of **kamma** itself. The philosophical conception of **kamma** may be said to possess three features. In the first place there is the idea of causality: Movement (ie. action) produces impact which produces further movement, so that events or happenings do not occur in isolation or at random but as part of a sequence or a chain process. Secondly, there is the idea that causality operates on an equitable basis, namely, that 'good' volitional acts conduce proportionately toward pleasant situations or happiness (**sukha**) and 'bad' volitional acts correspondingly conduce proportionately toward unpleasant situations and suffering (**dukkha**). Thirdly, there is the underlying assumption that we are ultimately responsible for our own fate: every event that happens to us is of our own making. In the Hindu tradition this view is vividly expressed in the Maitrī Upaniṣad which says 'One's thought, indeed, is **saṁsāra** ....What a man thinks, that he becomes, this is the eternal mystery'.[87] In the Buddhist tradition, it is perhaps best illustrated in the redoubtable opening line of the Dhammapada: 'mind is the forerunner of all conditions'.

Given this state of affairs there are basically two ways of mitigating the mechanistic and relentless system of **kamma**: Firstly, one can break the chain of causation altogether; secondly, one can introduce ways of modification. Since **kamma** is the principle that movement begets further movement, the logical way to counteract it is to stop the 'movement', altogether, that is, to stand still. This we saw was the Buddha's advice to Angulimāla; and 'stillness' was to be interpreted as the practice of **avihiṁsā**. In canonical teaching **avihiṁsā** involves restraint of the triple faculties of 'mind' (**mano**), 'speech' (**vācā**) and 'body' (**kāya**). This process of restraint has the effect of starving **kamma** of its source of fuel, namely, 'purposive acts' (**sankhārā**).[88] The practice of **avihiṁsā**, therefore, gradually leads towards transcendence by the annihilation of **kamma**. Since kamma is the regular law of transformation or phenomenal change, then its annihilation means that any form of transformation - in theory at least - is possible. Hence emerges the concept of radical transformations or magic (**iddhi**).

In chapter one we saw that **avihiṁsā** and control of one's faculties were a distinctive feature of the **muni**. In view of the argument that it is **avihiṁsā** which creates the notion of transformations, we submit that it is the **muni** dimension of the **paccekabuddha** as a 'holy man' which lies at the root of his magic power (**iddhānubhāva**). Therefore, when the lay-folk apprehend him as an isi is because they apprehend his transformations as merely magical and mysterious, not comprehending the notion of volitional power underlying them. Having established this point, it is necessary to make absolutely clear that the concept of the **muni** as such has nothing to do with the question of discerning the value of displays of magic - its pedagogical use. This is an altogether different matter, a soteriological issue. Accordingly, we saw in story (b) that the **paccekabuddha** has the necessary power qua **buddha** (i.e., **muni**) to effect a transformation but needed the assistance of the **bodhisatta** to provide the 'know-how'. The **bodhisatta** possessed the requisite soteriological wisdom or insight.

With respect to the second method of mitigating '**kamma**', by modifying its inexorable character, there has come into being within the Indian religious tradition the idea that certain types of special acts or states of volition can produce or yield special effects or consequences. Here the doctrine of **kamma** is seen to operate within a cultic framework where an agent's acts are not only evaluated ethically but on the basis also of cultic criteria. Each religious tradition has subjected the philosophical conception of **kamma** to its own sectarian interpretation. So, for example, in Brahmanism the most propitious **karma** arises out of the performance of sacrificial rites. In Buddhism, on the other hand, acts of giving (**dāna**) and of devotion (**pūja**) constitute 'special' acts. Through the quality (**guṇa**) evinced in his act of giving the donor draws from the spiritual-energy resource of the **paccekabuddha** who has transcended **kamma** altogether. Hence the donor too achieves transformations. The concept of a deed or act having ethical implications therefore becomes assimilated to the concept of correct behaviour toward an object of religious veneration, in this case the **paccekabuddha** as holy-man. In the notion of a 'rite' or 'special act' the ordinary, perfunctory working of **kamma** can be short-circuited. In the Buddhist religious system, for instance, it is achieved in two ways: The gap or time-lag between the execution of a deed and its retribution or fruition can be closed-down altogether or almost altogether so there is immediate fruition. An example of this kind may be found in the Dhammaddhaja Jātaka where abuse of a **paccekabuddha** results in instant death and immediate rebirth in hell.[89] On the other hand, the retribution or fruit can be of a kind that is seemingly disproportionate to the face-value of the deed. A telling example here is the story alluded to earlier in this chapter in which the **bodhisatta** is said to have earned his 'omniscience' simply by giving almsfood to four **paccekabuddhas**. The concept of the **saccakiriya** (act of truth) would seem to integrate both types of modification: An event which appears to be magical, such as the simultaneous release of all the captive animals in Jambudīpa, can be explained in terms of the doctrine of a cultically modified version of **kamma**. The hunter invokes his attainment of **pacceka-bodhi** as a 'truth' (**sacca**) and this results in the instant liberation of vast numbers of animals.

## The Paccekabuddha's Soteriological Function

The **paccekabuddha**'s own role in the act of alms-giving - approaching the layperson, accepting the alms, and displaying powers of magic - is not to be understood as perfunctory or mechanical but rather as a deliberate expression of concern on his part for the welfare of the layperson. In short, it should be apparent that a definite salvific dimension has been assigned the **paccekabuddha** within the structures of Early Buddhist doctrine, even within the seemingly limited framework of the alms-giving procedure. The **paccekabuddha**'s own particular form of concern for the almsgiver is conveyed in the usage of the terms 'help' (P.**anuggaha**; Skt.**anugraha**) and 'compassion'(**anukampā**). We shall monitor the occurrence and significance of these two terms respectively.

**Anuggaha** (help)

**Paccekabuddhas** are seen to be motivated by concern for the welfare of laypersons: the **paccekabuddha** named Uparitṭha emerges from deep meditation with the thought: "To whom should I give help today?" '(**kassānuggahaṁ karissāmi**).[90] In the story already cited of the merchant who bestows sandals upon a **paccekabuddha**, it is described how the ascetic looks down from Mount Gandhamādana and exclaims: "I will give help to him (**karissāmi 'ssa anuggahaṁ**). When the merchant sees the **paccekabuddha** approaching he says: "Sir, help me" (**bhante mayham anuggahatthāya**). Then when he presents his shoes and parasol it is said the **paccekabuddha**, 'to help him' (**tassānuggahatthāya**), accepted the gift. The Dīvyavadāna provides us with dogmatic confirmation of the paccekabuddha's function in this respect: The **pratyekabuddha**'s 'help is the supreme mode of action of a majestic one' (See Appendix II).

**Anukampā** (compassion)

The paccekabuddha's motive for helping

others is designated by the word '**anukampā**' (compassion). In the Pali tradition **paccekabuddhas** are stated to be 'compassionate to the wretched' (**duggatānukampaka**),[92] whilst the **ekacarin** is described as 'friendly and compassionate through a mind of loving-kindness' (**mettena cittena hitānukampi**).[93] A passage in the Divyavadana remarks of a **pratyekabuddha**: 'this **ṛṣi** comes to us (for alms) out of compassion' (**ṛshir eṣo 'smākam anukampāyehāgacchati**).[94] And there is more than one Buddhist Sanskrit formula which gives emphasis to the **pratyekabuddha**'s inherent compassion: 'When there are no Buddhas,**pratyekabuddhas** arise in the world who are compassionate to the unfortunate and imperilled (**hīnadīnānukampakāh**); 'out of compassion for him (**tasyānukampārtham**)...he commenced to produce extraordinary phenomena (**prāṭihāryāṇi kartum ārabdaḥ** - See Appendix II).

Since **anukampā** is the term primarily used to describe what it is that motivates the **paccekabuddha** to 'help' the layperson, it is vital to be clear about the exact nature of the salvific enterprise here being represented. Compassion (**anukampā**) and 'worthiness of offerings' (P.**dakkhiṇeyya**; Skt.**dakṣiṇīyā**) are two outstanding characteristics of the **paccekabuddha**. We cited above just some of the occasions on which he is referred to as '**anukampā**'. Having already observed that '**dakkhiṇeyya**' is a distinctive feature of the **paccekabuddha** in the earliest sources, we note that he continues to be lauded as such throughout the later sources. He is 'worthy of offerings and a field of merit' (**dakṣiṇīyo puṇyakṣetra**); 'among gods and men the most worthy of offerings in the world' (**sadevakassa lokassa aggadakkhiṇeyya**)[96]; 'well worthy of offerings' (**sudakkhineyya**)[97], whose worthiness of offerings is unique in the world (**ekadakṣiṇīyā lokasya**)[98] It is therefore important to understand that the attributes of '**dakkhiṇeyya**' and '**anukampā**' are interconnected. '**Dakkhiṇeyya**' means that the **paccekabuddha** is a particularly auspicious fund of merit. In so far as merit assists one in this life or radically ameliorates one's conditions of existence in future rebirth then, by presenting the lay person with the opportunity of making a gift, the **paccekabuddha** gives help (**annuggaha**) to such a one. This readiness to do so is an indication of his compassion (**anukampā**).[99]

The term **anukampā** is an elaboration of the verb **kampati** which means 'to disturb', 'to agitate'. One who possesses **anukampā** is literally-speaking 'one who vibrates for or because of', 'one who is attuned to another's need'.[100] In Vedic literature, the word is used to describe the sort of protection a **deva** confers upon those who wait upon him with offerings.[101] It is used in a slightly analogous way in the Pali Canon, where it is said that by reason of their **anukampi** forest-dwelling **devatās** stimulate (**saṁvejeti**) the meditational efforts of forest-dwelling monks; presumably they do this to safeguard and protect the monks from the distractions and perils of living in the forest.[102] There are two points to note in connection with its Vedic association. Firstly, it is the term used to depict the **deva**'s response to his devotee, and so presents a direct comparison with the way the **paccekabuddha** responds to his devotee. It therefore seems that the concept has been transferred from one cultic affiliation to another, and the **paccekabuddha** has come to assume something of the salvific function normally ascribed to the **deva** in Brahmanism. We noticed earlier the strong relevance of the motif of 'light' (**div** = shining) in connection with **paccekabuddha**, and how they are said to resemble **deva** 'flame-like' forms.[103] Secondly, its principal Vedic significance is that of affording 'protection'. The one who possesses it is in a position to help others because he is a higher or superior power. **Anukampā** 'protects' others from ill-fate, especially from those beings (e.g., **yakkha, yakkhinī**) who personify ill-fate.

The notion of 'protection' seems to be uppermost in another specialised usage of the word in the Canon. In the Sigāla Sutta the Buddha deliberately takes hold of an established Vedic usage and reinterprets it according to a different set of assumptions.[104] In traditional Vedic practice the 'householder' daily invoked the six regions or directions (**disā**) of earth and sky for protection. The Buddha suggests that this custom should be replaced by a system of social responsibility and cooperation in which teachers (**ācariya**) show 'compassion' (**anukampā**) to their disciples, parents to their children, wives to their husbands, friends to one another, masters to servants and ascetics (**samaṇabrāhmaṇā**) to householders; those who are the object of this compassion, the disciples, children, etc. should reciprocate by faithfully serving and ministering to their superiors. The six groups here enumerated correspond numerically to the six **disā**, so that the parents, teacher etc. are understood to have taken over the protective function of the **disā**. A similar type of notion is found in one of the stories about **paccekabuddhas** from the Jātakas:[105] A king distinguished for his alms-giving (**mahādāna**) decides one day that he would like to bestow alms on **paccekabuddhas**, for they are 'the most worthy of offerings' (**aggadakkhiṇeyya**). Unfortunately for him **paccekabuddhas** reside in the distant and remote Himavā region. Since this region is inaccessible, the queen advises the king to perform a special rite that will bring the **paccekabuddhas** to him. The rite consists of performing **namas** and throwing seven handfuls of flowers in one of the four directions (**disā**). This is accompanied by a verbal invocation: "I praise (**vandāmi**) the worthy ones (**arahantā**) in this direction (**disā**): if there is any quality (**guṇa**) in us, show us compassion (**anukampā**) and receive our offerings." If the **paccekabuddhas** do not come it means that the rite is being performed in the wrong direction. In this case the same rite is performed in another of the four directions and so on until the right direction is eventually found. When the king comes to perform the rite in the northern direction the flowers travel to the Himavā and alight upon the heads of the five hundred **paccekabuddhas** dwelling in the Nandamūla Cave. By their power to 'discern' (āvajjati), the **paccekabuddhas** read this strange phenomenon as an invitation to visit the king. Seven of them are selected on behalf of the five hundred, and they fly to his kingdom to accept alms.

This story deserves a number of comments: Firstly, the **paccekabuddha** is identified with the notion of the regions or directions (disā). We shall examine the significance of this identification in chapter three. Secondly, the object of invocation is not the regions themselves but the **paccekabuddhas**, mirroring the new interpretation placed on region-worship in the Sigāla Sutta. Thirdly, there are obvious parallels between the rite occurring in this story and the concept of an 'act of truth' (**saccakiriya**). Both, for instance feature a verbal invocation. In this invocation an appeal is made to an inherent moral or spiritual quality (**guṇa**) possessed by the suppliant. That quality is understood to have causal power, for it is actually declared that by the power (**bala**) of our alms-giving, our virtue (**sīla**) and our truthfulness (**sacca**) we shall invite the **paccekabuddhas**. Although the term **sacca-kiriya** does not occur here, **sacca** does occur and is acknowledged to be an instrumental force. So that to all intents and purposes we here have another example of the idea of an 'act of truth'.

We have shown that **paccekabuddhas** are distinguished for their 'compassion' (**anukampā**) and therefore do have a soteriological dimension. We shall now inquire what kind of person it is to whom the **paccekabuddha**'s salvific function extends. We have already seen some of the types of people who profit from the **paccekabuddha**'s compassion. They are labourers, servants, beggars, the poverty-stricken, women members of the household, and even a dog. In addition, the Avadāna Śataka includes felons within this frame of reference: a thief and a leader of a group of bandits.[106] These examples clearly show that the **paccekabuddha** was assigned a special function with regard to votaries from the less privileged or lower social orders.

In particular, the idea of 'repentance' or the 'penitent' person is a prominent theme in stories of the encounter between laypersons and **pratyekabuddhas**, and in stories or incidents in which the attainment of **pratyekabodhi** in some future birth is the dominant theme. Since, according to the doctrine of **karma**, a person is essentially responsible for the social and economic situation they are born into, it is understandable that the theme of repentance should mostly occur within those stories in which the relevant characters are socially deprived. Their poverty or misfortune is seen as a reflection of their own past spiritual obtuseness; consequently, in order to extricate themselves from these circumstances, repentance and change of intention are necessary. An example of a story having a 'repentance' theme is to be found in the Pānīya Jātaka where an agricultural labourer, a villager, a landowner, and two village headmen each respectively repent their own bad thoughts or misdeeds and subsequently become **paccekabuddhas**.[107] In the Avadāna Śataka there are many illustrations: the merchant's wife who insults a deformed **pratyekabuddha**, repents and offers him alms-food after seeing him perform feats of magic;[108] the bandit leader who orders his men to kill a **pratyekabuddha**, but repents when the **pratyekabuddha** displays his magic powers;[109] the boatman who refuses to ferry the Buddha free of charge across the Ganges, repents when he sees the Buddha fly across.[110] We may recall the Mahāvāstu tale of the servant girl who gives a lotus to a **paccekabuddha** but takes it back again when she sees it shining in his hand. She feels 'regret' (**vipratisāra**) when she notices the **pratyekabuddha**'s hand withering and so decides to return the flower.[111] There is a tradition in Pali sources that Devadatta, after having spent a long period in hell (niraya), will at last become a **paccekabuddha** called Aṭhissara. This ultimately beneficent fate is explained by the fact that Devadatta is alleged to have repented and taken refuge (**saraṇa**) in the Buddha before he finally died.[112]

It is to be noticed that **pratyekabuddhas** and the Buddha exhibit their magic deliberately in order to elicit the repentance of the recalcitrant layperson. Magic here plays an active salvific role: 'magic converts the unspiritual person quickly', is a common refrain in the Avadāna sources (See Appendix II). If a person is regarded as unspiritual then, ipso facto, an overt demonstration of magic is considered the most effective way to touch that person's sensibilities. This seems to be the justification for the role assigned to **ṛddhi** in the Avadāna sources.

There are also some stories in which those from a higher position in the social order are shown to benefit from the compassion of the **paccekabuddha**; but these benefit in a noticeably different fashion from those who belong to a lower social rank. The stories concern mostly types of merchants, priests and kings - the three highest classes (**varṇa**). In their case it is not endemic social conditions which require amelioration but some specific misfortune. We have already cited the stories of the rich **brāhmaṇa** saved from a shipwreck and the prince protected from the **yakkhinī**. Other examples are: the king lost in the forest without water to drink - a **pratyekabuddha** shows him the right direction and guides him to water;[113] the **pratyekabuddha** who through his compassion saves an entire village from becoming the victims of a terrifying demon (**rākṣasa**).[114] In stories where a king encounters the **pratyekabuddha**, renunciation may be expected of them but never 'repentance', unlike representatives of the lower social order.

The expression **hīnādīnānukampakā** (compassionate to the unfortunate and imperilled) is regularly predicated of **pratyekabuddhas** in the Divyāvadāna and Avadāna Śataka and is also found in the Mahāyāna text, Pratyekabuddhabhūmi (see Appendix II). We are not aware of the compound **hīnādīna** occurring anywhere other than within this context, so we shall consider the meanings of **hīna** (unfortunate) and **ādīna** (imperilled) separately. It seems that these two terms correspond respectively to the two categories of person, privileged and underprivileged, that we have just been considering. **Hīna** characterises the person belonging to a lower social order and **ādīna** the person whose secure life-style is threatened. In post-Vedic literature **hīna** can mean 'weaker than, inferior to, low, vile, bad, base, bereft or deprived of'.[115] In the Pali Nikāyas, **hīna** generally describes someone who is born into circumstances beset by ill-fortune and social impoverishment.[116] We have already encountered the use of the term **ādīnava** (peril) in the Khaggavisāṇa Sutta.[117] In the Mahāvastu, **ādīnava** denotes the presence of physical danger[118] and in Pali the 'misfortune' that befalls an immoral person.[119]

The Pali sources have their counterpart to the expression '**hīnadīnānukampakaḥ** and this is the saying that **paccekabuddhas** are 'compassionate to the wretched' (**duggatānukampaka**). One who is **duggata** (wretched) is a person born into a 'wretched form of existence' (**duggati**). **Duggati** generally implies existence as a **peta**, an animal or a denizen of hell; but some forms of human existence were also regarded as **duggata**. It appears to be a doctrine of the Apadāna that a person who performed a devotional act toward a **paccekabuddha** escaped rebirth in a **duggati**: 'Having risen from his **samādhi** the **paccekabuddha** approached me for alms. On seeing the **paccekabuddha** I gave him some juice of the mango fruit....By the fruit of this deed I did not enter a **duggati** for a period of ninety-four **kappa**.'[120] And the Commentary to the Apadāna adds that the 'sayings' (**subhāsitāni**) of **paccekabuddhas** save people from the four hells (**apāyā**).[121] This doctrinal standpoint is similarly reflected in the Avadāna Śataka, where the Buddha announces that those who have performed an act of service will not enter a **duggati** in any of their remaining births.[122]

## Conclusion

We have seen that the conception of the **paccekabuddha** as a **salvific** agent extends only to the mitigation of 'worldly' (**lokiya**) misfortunes. We have observed these misfortunes to be of two kinds: those endemic to a person's social situation or way of life, and temporary or circumstantial ones. The sorts of assistance offered by the **paccekabuddha** is interpreted in terms of the conceptual framework of the Buddhist doctrine of 'merit' (**puñña**). We have sought to render an account of the metaphysical assumptions underlying that doctrine. The **paccekabuddha**'s limitations as a **salvific** agent are attributable to a combination of historical and dogmatic factors. Buddhist dogma issued a prohibition on his creating a **sāvaka** tradition, that is, against his initiating persons onto the supramundane path (**ariyamagga**). The chief purpose of this prohibition was to differentiate the **paccekabuddha** from the **sammāsambuddha**.

In the four Nikāyas there exist certain counterparts to the **hīnadīnānukampaka** and **duggatānukampaka** formulae. These formulae are reserved for the Buddha alone. Hence a parallel can be perceived, for example, between the saying 'When there are no Buddhas, **pratyekabuddhas** arise (**utpāde**) in the world who are compassionate to the unfortunate and imperilled' (see Appendix II) and the following two descriptions of the Buddha: 'A being has arisen (**uppanno**) in the world for the welfare of the many-folk, for the happiness of the many-folk, out of compassion for the world (**lokānukampaya**);[123] and, 'the Buddha, the Tathāgatha is compassionate toward all beings (**sabbabhūtānukampino**)'.[124] In comparing these two sets of formulae we can see that the **paccekabuddha**'s salvific function not only relates to a limited clientele but to a certain form of sorrow **(dukkha)**. By contrast, the Buddha's function is universal in its range and application. The limited theoretical range of the **paccekabuddha**'s salvific function can be seen to correspond directly to his practical relationship with lay-folk. In other words, the interpretation of that salvific function is based upon the way lay-folk comprehend him. That his principal soteriological significance should be for the laity is not only because Buddhist dogma debarred him from the role of **sangha**-maker but also because he had considerable religious impact upon the popular imagination. Evidently, the popularity of the **paccekabuddha** among layfolk was much to do with his willingness to use magic. If, as we are about to argue in the forthcoming chapter, **paccekabuddhas** were the pioneers and harbingers of an ascetico-religious tradition that later fragmented into sectarian divisions then the subsequent sectarian groups which utilised them, such as Buddhism and Jainism, clearly traded and capitalized on that mythical reputation in order to maximise their own designs upon the laity. It is with respect to the object of these designs that the concept of **isi** serves as an appropriate designation for the **paccekabuddha**.

**Notes**

1. **Paccekabuddhas** can give a limited form of instruction to those persons who have heeded their injunction and become '**pabbajita**'. For an analysis of what precisely this instruction comprises see

Kloppenborg pp.76-78 and Cooray p.59. Note that in those accounts where they do give some kind of instruction or guidance to novitiate '**pabbajita**', it is always to separate individuals, not on a corporate basis to groups of individuals. It is in this sense that it is inappropriate to refer to their neophytes as **sāvakas** or as members of a **bhikkhu-saṅgha**.

2. J.III.377. cp. also J.IV.114-6
3. ibid. 377
4. See, for example, those stories in which hunters and robbers either masquerade as **paccekabuddhas** or steal their robes or begging bowls in order to acquire the necessary power or protection to successfully carry out their enterprises (J.II 197-9, Ud.A.95; Dh.A.I.180ff.)
5. See Eliade pp.130-131; cf. also Kaṭha Up. II.3.16: 'an hundred and one are the arteries of the heart; one of them leads up to the crown of the head. Going upward through that, one becomes immortal' (trans. Radhakrishnan).
6. We have found a reference in Mvu III. 492ff. to the 'luminous jewel'. It there states that 'the celestial gem named luminous jewel' (**jyotirasaṁ nāma divyaṁ maṇīratnaṁ**) belongs to Śakra who, on this particular occasion, bestows it upon an ugly king. When the king ties the jewel round his head he acquires a beautiful appearance. The jewel, there fore, has to do with the concepts of 'transformation', beauty-ugliness polarity, and the region of the head. All are concepts closely associated with the figure of the **paccekabuddha**.
7. Dh.A.I.197-8; III.92; IV.200; Sn.A.I.78; Ap.A.I.187.
8. Dh.A.I.121; II.114; III.372; J.III.407;
9. D.II.88-9; Vin.I.222,230,246,294 et seq.

10. trans. Jones Vol.1.p.250. The description, 'raising the eyes no further than the length of a plough' is a specification of mendicant practice in both the Buddhist and Jain traditions. See Cakraborti p.144.
11. Mvu.III.27,171.
12. Khot.Śūrangama p.37.
13. J.V.440
14. The same term occurs at Maitrī Up.VI.34.7 in a way which suggests clear meditational parallels with the Buddhist tradition. Here it is asserted that 'deliverance of mind' (**cittaṁ mucyate**) is brought about by 'making the mind motionless' (**manaḥ kṛtvā suniścalam**).
15. Divy.88,132; Av.Śat.108,226.
16. Anav.p.8 v.18.
17. Mvu.III.27.
18. J.VI.520.
19. Jones Vol.1.p.251. See also Mvu.III.27, 414.
20. MWD. s.v., **śobhana**.
21. Mvu.III.171.
22. Mvu.I.302.
23. J.V.289.
24. J.III.379.
25. See D.II.69.
26. Maitrī Up. VI.34.4
27. Mvu.III.171.
28. Mvu.I.302.
29. J.VI.41.
30. J.III.381.
31. Pb.Ap.v.53; Mvu.I.301.
32. Mvu.I.302.
33. J.V.440.vl.
34. Mvu.III.27.
35. Mvu.I.302.
36. Mvu.414.
37. J.IV.116. See also Dh.A.III.368; IV.200.
38. J.III.434.
39. Ap.p.498 v.36.

40. J.IV.370. See also J.IV.16.
41. supra p.81.
42. Divy.88,132,312; Av.Śat.108.
43. Śvet.Up.VI.21. The term is also used in this sense in the Bhagavad Gītā.
44. 'Faith' is the standard translation for **saddhā** (Skt.śraddhā) in Buddhism. Therefore to translate pasāda (Skt. **prasāda**) as 'faith' would be somewhat confusing. It must, however, be emphasised that **pasāda** is still a faith concept. The best illustration of this is to be found in the Sampasādaniya S.(D. III.99-116). Note that at Mvu.III.63 Jones translates its antonym **aprasāda** as 'unbelief'.
45. See, for example, Vin.I.15-16; II.156, 192; D.I.110,148; II.41; M.I.397; A.IV. 186,209; Dh.368; Ud.49.
46. On the technical usage of **sāvaka** in the Canon, see BD sv. **sāvaka** and **ariya-puggala**. Becoming a **sāvaka** is synonymous with acquiring the **dharmacakkhu**, that is, with acquiring insight into the four noble truths. See, for instance, the stages of conversion in the Buddha's winning of the first **arahants** (Vin.I. 10-19).
47. See Dh.A.III.91; 367-8; IV.120; 200; Sn.A. 74,77,86,104,129; J.III.240,472; IV.16.
48. Dh.A.III.368.
49. J.I.233; Dh.A.III.368.
50. Dh.A.III.93,381; IV.200; Sn.A.104-5. The CPD defines **adhiṭṭhāna** as 'volition (of magical force)'. See also Elder's Verses I. p.130 v.38; p.279 v.1131. Later in this chapter we explore the relationship between the two ideas of 'volition' and 'magic' or 'radical transformation'. The post-Commentarial work, Abhidhammatthasaṅgaha, defines **adhiṭṭhāniddhi** as 'the

power of creating phenomena outside of one's body' (Cpd.p.61). This also seems to be its Mahāyāna conception. In the Vimalakīrti S., Vimalakīrti uses **adhiṣṭhāna** to create the 'illusions' or 'phantoms' which aid his instruction of the **śrāvaka** (p.2,116,170,206,211). Wayman (PEW Vol.XXIV pt.4. Oct.1974. p.392) writes: 'buddha were said to help chosen disciples of a progressed nature with **adhiṣṭhāna** (blessing, empowerment, or spiritual support), a kind of silent power'. We may compare the doctrine of **adhiṣṭhāna** in the Mahāyāna with **sappāṭihīrakataṁ** in the Pali Canon. In chapter one we looked at the three kinds of aids to instruction - **anusāsani, ādesanā** and **iddhi** - which each come under the nomenclature **pāṭihāriya** (extraordinary phenomenon). At D.III.121-122,125 the **dhamma** of the Buddha is said to be **sappāṭihīrakatam** ('made a thing of saving grace' transl. T.W. Rhys Davids). Therefore, both **adhisthāna** and **pāṭihāryāni** are key concepts in the understanding of Buddhist soteriology, since they represent the devices or methods through which growth in spiritual awareness and salvation is effected.

51. J.III.488,472; Dh.A.IV.201.
52. Upās.344.
53. Mvu.I.302; Av.Śat. Nos.87,88,90.
54. Av.Śat. No.89.See also Divy.133,583; Mvu. III.414.
55. Av.Śat. No.30. See also Nos.38 and 29; Mvu. I.302-3.
56. Mvu.III.27.See also Av.Śat. Nos.80 and 99.
57. Av.Śat. No 27.
58. Av.Śat. No.41.
59. Av.Śat. No.44.
60. J.IV.15-21.

61. J.I.395-400.
62. Five Chieng Sen Bronzes of the Eighteenth Century, A.Aś.VII, 1960, 2, pp.116ff. Griswold has drawn our attention to the discovery on the Laos-Burma frontier of a bronze image of a **paccekabuddha** (circa 1721) which seems to have been used to perform a special 'protective' function during a period of political disturbance and revolt.
63. See J.II.195.
64. Dh.A.III.87-93.
65. Av.Śat. No.89.
66. Dh.A.III.365-72.
67. Dh.A.I.173.
68. Dh.A.I.196-8.
69. J.V.440-1.
70. Pv.A.73ff.
71. Dh.A.I.226.
72. Av.Śat. No.80.
73. Dh.A.I.225.
74. S.A.I.349-50.
75. Pv.IV.16.
76. **patthanā** is Pali for the act of volition which produces this articulation of a wish (see J.V.39,289; Dh.A.III.369; IV.121). According to BHSD **prārthanā**, the Sanskrit equivalent of **patthanā**, hardly occurs in Buddhist Sanskrit texts. Instead the doctrinal equivalent is represented by the terms **praṇidhi** and **praṇidhāna** (see, for example, Mvu.III. 27. In the Mahāyāna **praṇidhāna** becomes the 'vow' to be a **buddha** or a **bodhisattva**.
77. See Dh.A.I.226; III.87-100; IV.120-8; 199-224; Netti.141. We read in the Comy to the Khuddaka-pāṭha (133) that 'after seeing a **buddha** and a **paccekabuddha** face to face, **arahant** status can be attained in the end.'
78. J.III.407.

79. M.II.97ff.
80. J.IV.333-42.
81. For a list of articles on the subject, see 'Duty as Truth in Ancient India', W. Norman Brown, PAPS, Vol. CXVI, 1972, p.252 fn.1. The Sanskritic equivalent, **satya-kriyā**, has not come to our notice. Nevertheless the concept of 'an act of truth' (e.g., **satyaṁkaroti**, **satyakarman**, **satyavādya**, **satyavacana**, **satyopavācana**, **satyavākya**, **satyaśrāvaṇā**, **satyamantra**, **satyādhiṣṭhāna** (cp., P. **saccādhiṭṭhāna**) **yathā vādī...tathā kārī**) is a common feature of Hindu tales and literature. See Coomaraswamy, 'Headless Magicians and an Act of Truth', JAOS Vol.64 pt.4, 1944, p.215.
82. E.W. Burlingame, 'The Act of Truth (sacca-kiriya): A Hindu spell and its employment as a psychic motif in Hindu fiction' JRAS 1917 pt.XI, p.429.
83. See W. Norman Brown op. cit., p.262.
84. J.VI.520.
85. Vin.II.194f; J.V.333ff.
86. The central importance of **ahiṁsā** in the Śramaṇa Tradition is, perhaps, mythologically indicated in the Vāmaṇa Purāṇa where, for instance, **ahiṁsā** is personified as the wife of **Dharma**, whose offspring Nara and Nārāyana taught the way to spiritual enlightenment. Cite Stutley sv **ahimsā**.
87. Maitrī Up.VI.34.3.
88. **abhisankhāra** = substratum of **kamma** (see, for example S.III.58); **sankhāra** = purposive aspiring state of mind (see, for example, M.III.99. For further information on the complex but important concept of **sankhāra**, see Johansson pp.41-53).
89. J.II.195.
90. Dh.A.IV.121. cp. also IV.200.

91. J.IV.16.
92. A.A.I.185.
93. Pb.Ap.8.
94. Divy.295.
95. Mvu.I.301; III.414.
96. Upas.344; J.IV.470.
97. Pb.Ap.53.
98. See Appendix II.
99. So, for example, the Comy (Sn.A.73-74) glosses **anukampamāno** (Sn.37) by **anudayamāno tesaṁ sukhaṁ upahattukāmo dukkhaṁ apahattukāmo** (sympathising with them by desiring to bring happiness and remove suffering).
100. See Dial. Vol.III.pp.171-172; ERE Vol.8 pp.159-160; KS I.p.132 fn.2.
101. See Dial. Vol.III.p.171.
102. S.I.198-199.
103. Compare, for instance the remark (Mvu. III.223): 'whatever village or town the brahmin Mahā-Govinda came to and stayed at, there he became as...a **deva** to the laymen' (trans. Jones).
104. D.III.188-92.
105. J.III.470ff.
106. See Av.Śat. Nos.98 and 99.
107. J.IV.114ff.
108. Av.Śat. No.80.
109. Av.Śat. No.99.
110. Av.Śat. No.27.
111. supra p.83.
112. Dh.A.I.147-8;
113. Av.Śat. No.90.
114. Divy.295.
115. MWD. p.1296.
116. See M.I.460,462; S.II.50; IV.103.
117. Sn.36,69.
118. Mvu.II.144,166; III.297.
119. D.II.85.
120. Ap. p.284. cf. also pp.288-9.
121. Ap.A.205
122. Av.Śat. Nos.22-3; 28-30.

123. M.I.21; cp. also D.III.211ff; S.II.203.
124. D.I.4,227; S.I.25.

Chapter Three
# The Paccekabuddha as Samaṇa

In the preceding chapter we noticed how Buddhist narrative literature not only furnished us with information about the popular exoteric conception of **paccekabuddhas** but also about the manner in which persons become **paccekabuddhas**. The image most commonly presented is of a 'householder' having a sudden 'awakening' experience designated **paccekabodhi**, and then directly, as it were magically, taking on the appearance of a **samaṇa**. In this chapter we shall endeavour to understand the meaning of this particular transformation motif and, in so doing decipher the significance of the **paccekabuddha**'s description as a **samaṇa**. Since we shall be discussing the figure of the **samana** on a trans-sectarian not just a Buddhist basis we shall henceforth adopt the Sanskrit rendering, **śramaṇa**, instead of the Pali in our general discussion.

Our point of departure for this discussion is a legend occurring in both the Buddhist and Jain traditions which tells the story of how four kings become **paccekabuddhas** (Pkt.**patteyabuddha**). By comparing the extant versions of this legend we hope to show that the two traditions must have derived it from an older, common source. This older, common source, we argue, represents the tradition of **paccekabuddhas** themselves. The legend therefore comprises a vital piece of testimony in the argument that **paccekabuddhas** existed historically and are to be identified with the ascetico-religious tradition out of which Buddhism and Jainism both evolved as sectarian manifestations. From here, we go on to develop the case that **paccekabuddhas** are synonymous with the earliest **śramaṇas**, themselves the originators of the Śramaṇic Movement. Further evidence in support of the theory that **paccekabuddhas** represented an antecedent tradition will be adduced by a consideration of verses from the Khaggavisāṇa Sutta as well as a consideration of passages in the four Nikāyas and the Sutta-nipāta which indicate that the Early Buddhists derived from other traditions the symbols they used to convey and illustrate the notion of Sākyamuni's uniqueness.

## The Legend of the Four Kings who become Paccekabuddhas

Buddhism and Jainism each have a metrical and a prose version of the legend that we shall henceforth designate 'the legend of the four kings who become **paccekabuddhas**'. In Buddhist sources the metrical and prose versions of the story are integrated in the same work, the Kumbhakāra Jātaka[1]. Even though the Buddhist Jātakas form part of the fifth Nikāya many of the tales in substance belong to the oldest stratum of canonical material. This is apparent from the depiction of scenes from Jātaka stories in the bas-reliefs at Sanchi, Amarāvati and Bhārhut[2]. In the Jain tradition the metrical and prose versions of this legend exist separately. The metrical version comprises stanzas forty-five to forty-seven of the eighteenth chapter of the Uttarādhyayana Sūtra, the oldest portions of which text belong to the same period and genre as the earliest Buddhist canonical material[3]. The prose version of the legend is found in

Devendra's Commentary to the Uttarādhyayana Sūtra which is a later Jain medieval work[4]. We propose to analyse the legend by comparing the prose sections with one another, prose with the metre sections, and the metre sections with each other.

## Prose Versions

Both Buddhist and Jain prose versions, relatively and in respect of their own literatures, are much later than the metrical sections. Nevertheless, they have in common the following subject-matter:

(i) The name of each king and his kingdom.

(ii) An account of each king's act of renunciation through which he becomes a **śramaṇa**.

(iii) A description of how each king attains **paccekabodhi**.

(iv) Reference to a particular 'incident' or 'event' which triggers each king's act of renunciation and **paccekabodhi**.

The prose versions differ from one another sufficiently to make it arguable that neither Buddhism nor Jainism borrowed their version directly from the other. For instance, although the kings are identical in both versions none of the incidents correspond to the same kings; and some of the incidents have no counterpart whatsoever in the other version:

**Names of the Kings**

| Buddhist | Jain |
| --- | --- |
| Nimi, King of Videha | Nami, King of Pañcāla |
| Dummukha, King of Pañcāla | Dummuha, King of Pañcāla |
| Karaṇḍu, King of Kālinga | Karakaṇḍu, King of Kālinga |
| Naggaji, King of Gandhāra | Naggai, King of Gandhāra |

**Incidents Triggering 'Renunciation' and Paccekabodhi**

| Incident | King | |
| --- | --- | --- |
| birds of prey squabbling over a piece of meat | Nimi(B) | - |
| the noise of jangling bracelets | Naggaji(B) | Nami(J) |
| the barren and the fruit-bearing tree | Karaṇḍu(B) | Naggai(J) |
| the lusting bull | Dummukha(B) | Karakaṇḍu(J) |
| the spoiling of Indra's banner. | - | Dummuha(J) |

**Metrical Versions**

The Buddhist metrical version of the legend consists of just five stanzas. In the first four stanzas respectively each king supplies his own explanation (**vyākaraṇa**) of what influenced him to become a mendicant (**bhikkhu**). The fifth and last stanza summarizes the achievement of the four kings.

90. 'I saw a mango tree within a grove
Fully-grown and with ripe-fruit.
Then I saw it damaged for the acquisition of its fruit;
On witnessing this I chose the life of a mendicant.

91. A bracelet polished by an artisan
A women wore on each arm without a sound.
But when worn together they made a noise;
On witnessing this I chose the life of a mendicant.

92. Bird fights with bird over carrion.
The single bird (with carrion) attracts many others
Who attack him to acquire the carrion;
On witnessing this I chose the life of a mendicant.

93. I saw a bull among a herd,
Possessed of strength and beauty and quivering hump.
Then I saw him attacked owing to lust;
On witnessing this I chose the life of a mendicant.

94. Karaṇḍu of Kālinga and Naggaji of Gandhāra
King Nimi of Videha and Dummukha of Pañcāla,
abandoning their kingdoms went forth without possessions.[5]

In contradistinction to the prose stories these stanzas do not say that the kings become **paccekabuddhas**. They do, however, contain the theme of the incidents (e.g. tree, bracelets, birds and bull) but without giving any indication which incident belongs to which king.

The Jain metrical version from the Uttarādhyayana Sūtra reads as follows:

45. Karakaṇḍu was king of Kālinga, Dummuha of Pañcāla,
Nami of Videha, Naggai of Gandhāra.

46. 'Nami humbled himself, being directed to do so by Sakka himself;
The king of Videha left the house and became a **śramaṇa**.

47. These bulls of kings have adopted the faith of the Jinas;
Having placed their sons on the throne, they exerted themselves as **Śramaṇas**.[6]

The above Jain metrical version resembles the Buddhist metrical version in that it too makes no mention of the kings becoming **paccekabuddhas**. It will be noticed, however, that this version differs from the Buddhist version in that it makes no reference whatsoever to any 'incidents'. Instead the kings are described as adherents of the Jain faith (v.47). A comparison of these two metrical versions reveals that stanza 94 in the Buddhist version is composed in the same **śloka** metre as stanzas 46 and 47 in the Jain version and closely resembles them. And one of the four kings, Nami, receives an additional mention (v.45) in the Jain version. We shall examine the significance of this latter observation in a moment.

Our analysis of these different versions therefore leads us to the following conclusions: Given that the Jātaka proper (metrical section) and the Uttarādhyayana Sūtra are comparatively early texts in their respective traditions then the legend, in an incipient form, must have entered both traditions at an early stage. The metrical versions are sufficiently distinct from one another to suggest they entered too early for either tradition to have borrowed the legend directly from the other. This view is shared by both Charpentier and Norman who hold that the legend must have derived from a common tradition.[7] Where the metrical versions agree, we can say this comprises the nucleus of the legend. This nucleus provides us with only the barest information: four kings who abandoned their kingdoms to become **śramaṇas**. Since neither of the metrical versions makes reference to the kings as **paccekabuddhas**, then the **paccekabuddha** ascription must it seems be regarded as a later accretion to the legend.

In the light of these observations we may go on to ask the question how it was the kings came eventually to be identified in both traditions as **paccekabuddhas**. The answer to this question must either be that one tradition borrowed from the other or that both derived this additional aspect from a common tradition. The idea that either one tradition borrowed the **paccekabuddha** motif from the other is hard to demonstrate. For it may be asked why either one tradition should want or need to derive additional aspects from a rival tradition when the core legend had already firmly established itself in their own tradition. Furthermore, a 'borrowing' hypothesis would have to take into consideration the fact that Buddhism and Jainism not only share in common the **paccekabuddha** concept, but also the complete tri-partite doctrine of which the latter is just one component: the one

(P.**sammāsambuddha**; Pkt.**titthagara**) who creates a **saṅgha** tradition; the **saṅgha** tradition itself; and the **paccekabuddha/patteyabuddha**.[8] Since this tri-partite system is so fundamental to both traditions, it is difficult to see how just one single aspect of it (viz. **paccekabuddha**) could have been borrowed independently of the other aspects. And since it is so fundamental to the structure of each, it is equally difficult to conceive that one might have derived the complete tripartite system, secondhand and in entirety, from the other. It is more plausible to assume that its co-existence in both traditions has to do with their common Sramanic origins.

Although the term **paccekabuddha/patteyabuddha** does not appear in either of the metrical versions of the legend, it is perfectly evident that the legend itself has been incorporated into the Buddhist and Jain traditions because these monarchs were regarded as spiritual paradigms. We have already seen in the Isigili Sutta that **paccekabuddhas** were presented as spiritual paradigms to the **bhikkhusaṅgha**, so it is possible here to see some functional similarity between these kings and the category of person referred to in that particular Sutta. Since the decision of the kings to renounce the world happens as a consequence of their random reflection upon natural incidents or events rather than as a result of humanly transmitted teachings, then to all intents and purposes they do not belong within an established cultus or framework of practice. For the Uttarādhyayana Sūtra their distinction simply lies in becoming śramaṇas, and in the Jātaka stanzas it similarly resides in their act of renunciation. What does emerge clearly from consideration of this basic data is the kings were considered at an early stage in both traditions to be archetypal śramaṇas and perhaps at that stage nothing more specific than this. However, with the appearance and development of more sophisticated doctrinal structures in both traditions, the problem would sooner or later arise of having to determine the exact 'spiritual-attainment' status of these legendary spiritual archetypes apropos prevailing beliefs and practices. The question would then pose itself of where they actually fitted within the framework of a 'teacher-disciple' (viz. **sammāsambuddha/titthagara-śrāvaka**) distinction. They would require to be placed into an altogether separate category in order to differentiate them from the notions of both 'teacher' and 'disciple'. Therefore the category known as **paccekabuddha/patteyabuddha** was invented. Hence, the doctrinal concept of the **paccekabuddha**, one who achieves 'spirituality' but who is neither a **titthagara/sammāsambuddha** nor a disciple of such, arose from an attempt to accommodate the tradition whose existence is testified by this legend.

In accordance with this hypothesis we shall go on to argue the case for three distinct stages in the evolution of the legend: firstly, identification of the kings as proto-śramaṇas, then as **buddhas** and, finally, as **paccekabuddhas**. The Jain figure of King Nami is of particular importance in the construction of this hypothesis. That he had added significance over and above the other kings who become **paccekabuddhas** is shown by the fact that he is assigned a separate stanza from the others and elsewhere is the subject of an entire chapter of the Uttarādhyayana Sūtra, entitled the Nami Pavajjā (Nami's going forth)[9]. In this chapter he is referred to not just as a king who forsakes his kingdom and becomes a śramaṇa but as a **sahasambuddha** (v.2), **sambuddha** (v.62) and **siddhi** (v.58); in other words, he is credited with **buddha** status. Although Alsdorf makes the point that the stanzas in which these particular predicates appear are redactorial insertions, their occurrence in the text is sufficient to show that King Nami was ranked as a **buddha** 'prior to' his classification as a **patteyabuddha** in the later commentary of Devendra.[10]

The figure of Nami is classed as a **śramaṇa** in the eighteenth chapter of the Uttarādhyayana Sūtra, as a **buddha** in the ninth chapter, and as a **patteyabuddha** in later tradition. The other term applied to King Nami in the Nami Pavajjā, **sahasambuddha**, is one which is used throughout the early canonical sources to designate the **titthagaras**, revealers of the faith and founders of the Jain community, such as Māhāvira.[11] In later canonical texts, however, the term **svayaṁbuddha** (self-become buddha) came to be the preferred designation over **sahasambuddha** for Mahāvīra and other **titthagaras**.[12] This significant development shows that Nami at one time shared the same buddhological status as the **titthagaras** but that in the intervening period between earlier and later canonical texts a new buddhological emphasis emerged signified by the adoption of the terms **svayaṁbuddha** and **patteyabuddha**. The nearest equivalent to **svayaṁbuddha** in Buddhist canonical sources is the term, **sayaṁbhū** (Skt.**svayaṁbhū**: self-become, self-existent, uncreate), which is used epithetically of both the sammāsambuddha and the **paccekabuddha** in order to mark them out from the **sāvaka** as persons who have achieved enlightenment without dependence on a teacher. But, as with **svayaṁbuddha** in Jainism, **svayaṁbhu** occurs only in the later canonical strata.[13] That **svayaṁbuddha** is likewise employed in Jainism to differentiate **buddhas** from 'followers' of

**buddhas** is confirmed by a distinction to be found in the older canonical encyclopaedic texts between it and **buddhabodhita** (those enlightened by another **buddha**), meaning 'disciples'.[14] Here too, Buddhism has a comparable term, **buddhānubuddha**.

The Jain threefold distinction of **patteya-buddha**, **svayaṁbuddha** and **buddhabodhita** seems first to appear in the later encyclopaedic period.[15] The basis for the introduction of a distinction between a **patteya-buddha** and a **svayaṁbuddha** seems to have come from the need to make a demarcation between those **buddhas** who are enlightened without an external stimulus (**nimitta**), the **svayaṁbuddha**, and those who require a stimulus, for which the word **patteyabuddha** seems to have been adopted.[16] This interpretation of '**patteyabuddha**' to mean one who arrives at enlightenment as a result of the impact of a specific stimulus, helps provide a reliable clue to the possible semantic derivation of the term itself. Norman has argued that the prefix **patteya/pacceka** could be a corruption of **paccaya** (Skt.**pratyaya**: cause, foundation), in which case the thematic association of the **paccekabuddha** prototypes, the four kings, with events or incidents which 'cause' their existential insight into the value of renunciation is highly significant.[17]

The Jain explanation for the distinction of two kinds of **buddha** proves to be more informative and illuminating than the Buddhist. The latter's explanation is more heavily doctrinal: The **sammāsambuddha** possesses 'omniscience'(**sabbaññū**), that is, the capacity to perfectly mediate **dhamma** to any person on any occasion, whilst the **pacceka-buddha** does not. The basis of this distinction is the 'teaching - non-teaching' criterion.

Therefore, in the process of the evolution of the legend of the four kings the identity of the kings appears to pass through three stages, culminating in their assimilation to the concept of **paccekabuddha**. In its oldest form the legend comprises a 'myth' portraying the proto-**śramaṇas**, the figures who instigated the Śramaṇa Movement. The original myth conveys the following essential information: proto-**śramaṇas** are **kṣatriyas**; 'renunciation' (**pravrajyā**) is the significant cultural innovation; the significant religious innovation is the contemplative rather than rite-centred approach to reality, where moral, spiritual and religious truth are mirrored in Nature and so become accessible through reflection on the natural world. The basis is therefore laid for the development of contemplative and meditational modes of spirituality.

This original myth depicts a state of affairs in which the prototype concept of a **buddha** or 'holy-man' is still in its formative stages. The cultus of the individual **buddha** had not yet emerged. It was a period in which the principal emphasis was upon renunciation of society and upon 'contemplative' modes of experience. Established forms of systematic training, teaching and group-organisation had not yet evolved, for renunciation was still a maverick phenomenon. This was the era of the original **munis**. In the next evolutionary stage the number of renouncers increased until they became an accepted social phenomenon: doctrinal emphases emerged; groups (**saṅgha** and **gaṇa**) grew up around individual holy-men, and each of these groups consolidated into a 'cultus' or 'sect' with its own system of instruction and training. Eventually the Śramaṇa Movement evolved to a point where each 'cultus' became intent on affirming its own supremacy. In order to reinforce these claims to supremacy each introduced a code of restrictive practice signalling the departure from the tradition of a plurality of **buddhas** and away from the ideology of self-realisation that had so far characterised its development. This was the third and final stage in the formation of a buddhology.

Thus the legend of the four kings who become **paccekabuddhas** has provided vital evidence in helping us to decipher the origin of the **paccekabuddha** concept. Firstly, it has shown how the concept is used to refer back to the first **śramaṇas** who were regarded by the Buddhists and Jains to be an integral part of their own tradition. Secondly, we have seen how the term **paccekabuddha** functioned as a doctrinal concept denoting that these 'early śramaṇas' were worthy of being called **buddhas**. Thirdly, we have noted that the actual term **paccekabuddha** is applied to these **śramaṇa** figures only in later recensions of the legend. This suggests that the term **paccekabuddha** was superimposed on these figures at some belated stage. We have sought to account for this in terms of certain developments characterising the Śramaṇa Movement itself such as its splintering into rival groups where matters of doctrine and dogma became matters of increasing concern.

The particular problem that has exercised scholars such as Pavolini Norman, Sakurabe, Fujita et al, as to whether **paccekabuddhas** were an offshoot of either the Buddhist or Jain 'cultus', or were themselves some alien or foreign 'cultus' incorporated into these traditions, is a problem that dissolves when it is realized that the branch of ascetics which the term **paccekabuddha** denotes refers to the background tradition out of which Buddhism and Jainism both developed. At the very outset these figures were considered **buddhas**, not 'aliens' or 'outsiders', and therefore comprised the raw material out of which a systematic buddhology eventually came to be fashioned. Given the premises on which historical Buddhism was based, it sooner or later became necessary to introduce a principle of discontinuity with predecessors or forerunners. For to admit that 'enlightenment on one's own' was still possible after the advent of Sākyamuni would be to undermine his role as integral founder and focal centre of the **saṅgha**. In the case of Jainism the doctrinal situation was a little different. Jainism had allowed and continues to allow the possibility of salvation for persons who exist outside the confines of Jain faith and practice. This helps to explain why it is not so much the fact of the enlightenment of **patteyabuddhas** that was of interest to them as the manner of that enlightenment.

It is not crucial to our argument to ascertain whether there was a time-lapse between the demise of **paccekabuddhas** and the advent of Sākyamuni but simply to indicate that the tradition antedated him. The doctrinal assertion that **paccekabuddhas** and **sammāsambuddhas** cannot co-exist (**supra** Introduction) is not one found in either the early or main-Nikāya periods but located in the more scholastic genre of the later and post-Nikāya texts. Nevertheless, in chapter one we saw that the rudimentary distinction of **paccekabuddha** and **sammāsambuddha** had already entered Buddhist vocabulary as early as the main-Nikāya period. That the distinction was not an original hallmark of Buddhism, however, is shown by the fact that **buddha** was at first a pluralistic concept, as we also have shown in chapter one. Although we cannot be precise about when the **paccekabuddha-sammāsambuddha** distinction entered into Buddhism, it is evidently motivated by the intention to place the figure of Sākyamuni into a category on his own.

The idea that paccekabuddhas constituted

the pre-sectarian phase of the Śramaṇa Movement explains why they reputedly gave 'explanations' (**vyākaraṇa**) of the cause of their enlightenment together with 'moral advice' (**ovāda**) but did not in a formal sense establish criteria and techniques of instruction. The appearance of such criteria and techniques were both the cause and the consequence of sectarian impulses. In due course the Śramaṇa Movement underwent a transition from individualism to corporate institution. That which began as a form of disaffection among individuals , acquired in time the force of a concerted movement where persons concentrated themselves into groups and these groups in turn, began to differentiate themselves from one another. In the previous chapter we saw that Buddhist narrative literature depicts **paccekabuddhas** as householders who 'renounce' the world and then reside together in a religious coterie on the mythical mountain of Gandhamādana. Their conception is never allowed to develop beyond this rudimentary stage to a point where they can be said to possess 'sectarian' characteristics. A vital piece of evidence in piecing together the puzzle of their true identity comes from the observation that in Jātaka tales featuring accounts of persons becoming **paccekabuddhas**, **paccekabodhi** itself is always depicted as coinciding with a person's decision to renounce the household life, that is, with the decision to become a 'renouncer'. In brief, becoming a **paccekabuddha** is represented as synonymous with becoming a **pabbajita** or **samaṇa**, thereby illustrating that the conception of the **paccekabuddha** is somehow indissolubly bound up with the notion of the **śramaṇa**. This observation is corroborated by the statement in post-Canonical passages that among the two categories of enlightened person, **sammāsambuddha** and **paccekabuddha**, only the latter can achieve enlightenment as a 'householder', that is without first having become a **pabbajita**.[19]

The theory of **paccekabuddhas** as the ascetic forerunners of Buddhism is sufficient to explain why buddhology has come to consist of a bipartite (**sammāsambuddha** and **paccekabuddha**) not a tripartite (**sammāsambuddha**, **paccekabuddha** and **sāvakabuddha**) distinction, given the fact that it was the **sāvakasangha** who were the principal authors, keepers and transmitting agency of the doctrine. Since Buddhism's survival and advancement centred on the concept of the **sangha** then, at face value, one would have expected the **satthar** (teacher) and the **sāvaka** (i.e., arahant) to comprise the two kinds of **buddha**, or at least one would have supposed the **sāvaka** to be made superior to the **paccekabuddha**. It is highly telling that in the corpus of literature compiled and composed by a **sāvaka** tradition we find the **paccekabuddha** to be superior to the **sāvaka** in respect of **bodhi** status and as a source of merit. For the **paccekabuddha** to be elevated in this manner shows that he must have constituted a paradigm prior to the time when the **sāvaka** tradition acquired momentum. This is to suggest that his 'historical' precedence guaranteed his 'doctrinal' precedence over the **sāvaka**. The **sāvaka** received tertiary ranking because his status was wholly-derived from the **satthar**: he was an offspring, a son of the Buddha (Buddhaputta)[20] not 'self-become' (**sayaṁbhū**) like the **sammāsambuddha** and **paccekabuddha**.

Since the **paccekabuddha** has retained his superiority to the **sāvaka**, it became accepted doctrine that 'householders' might adopt the aspiration to become a **paccekabodhi** at some future rebirth; the realisation of **paccekabodhi** in one's same life-time was, of course, inappropriate during the era of a **sāsana**. On the other hand, aspiration for **paccekabodhi** to be realised in a future life did not constitute a threat to the institution of the **bhikkhusaṅgha** because the goals that already could be realised through becoming a **bhikkhu** meant enlightenment came sooner than by this latter aspiration.[21] Therefore, when fenced around with these regulations the notion of **paccekabodhi** could be made to serve the interests of the 'cultus' by furnishing another form of incentive for a layman to belong to: the incentive of future enlightenment as a **paccekabuddha**.

## Buddhism and Jainism - Common Traditions

The argument that **paccekabuddhas** represent the tradition of early **śramaṇas** out of which Jainism and Buddhism evolved as 'sectarian' projections, is indirectly corroborated by the resemblances of Buddhism and Jainism on a number of fronts. These resemblances are so strong and numerous that they cannot sufficiently be explained by a 'borrowing' hypothesis and therefore, we submit, are better explained by reference to the supposition of a common ancestry. If our interpretation of the identity of the **paccekabuddha** is correct, then the solution to the problem of this identity serves as the important missing link in support of the theory of the common derivation of these two Hindu heterodoxies.

In the introduction to his translation of the Ācārāṅga and Kalpa Sūtras, Hermann Jacobi has perceptively indicated some of the major family resemblances between Buddhism and Jainism in the areas of history, doctrine and practice. To this list we shall add some of our own observations regarding fundamental similarities on certain key points. Our purpose in so doing, however, is merely to suggest avenues that might at some future time be pursued in more depth and detail, as well as to show that the similarities are sufficiently striking as to warrant some kind of explanatory hypothesis regarding their relationship and interaction, such as the one offered in the above **paccekabuddha** theory. The points of resemblance are:

1. Both are **śramaṇa** traditions - having the same 'lay-monachist' structure - and both are **nāstika** in their attitude to the Vedas.

2. They share the same core doctrinal concepts. As rival sects one would expect their interpretation or accentuation of these concepts to vary slightly, as it does: e.g., **ahiṁsā**,**karma**,**saṁsāra**,**mokṣa** (liberation),**nirvāṇa**,**pāpa** and **puṅya**, etc.

3. The Buddha and Vardhamādana (i.e.,Mahāvira) belonged allegedly to the **ksatriya** class: the former to the Śākyas, the latter to the Jñātikas.[22] The Dīgha Nikāya asserts that only a **kṣatriya** not a **brāhmaṇa** can become a **sammāsambuddha** in the present aeon.[23] All the Jain **titthagaras** are **kṣatriya** by birth.[24] Buddhism and Jainism both maintained the doctrine of cosmic progress and decay which gives the entire raison d'etre to the conception of the **sammāsambuddha/ titthagara**, the one who periodically restores, revives or discovers and makes known the truth to others.[35]

4. At respective stages of their doctrinal development the number of Jain **titthagaras** and the number of **sammāsambuddhas** acknowledged by each tradition to have existed prior

to Gotama and Mahāvīra coincide at twenty-four.[26]

5. There are common appellations for saints and sainthood: **jina, muni, sambuddha, arahant, mahāvīra, sugata, tathāgata, buddha.**[27]

6. Freedom from the **āśravas** (P.**āsava**) constitutes 'liberation' in both traditions.[28]

7. They share the triple formula of **rāga, dosa, moha** (passion, greed and delusion).[29]

8. They have the same number of basic moral precepts: the 5 **sīlas** and the 5 **mahāvrātas**.

9. They originated in the same geographical region: principally ancient Māgadha and Videha.[30]

10. They celebrate a regular assembly of the monks (P.**uposatha**; Pkt.**posaha**).[31]

11. There are many similarities in the legend of Vardhamādana and Sākyamuni. For example, Jainism and Buddhism both hold the doctrine that the embryo of a **cakravartin** or an **arahant** enters its mother in the form of an elephant or bull.[32]

12. The Jains employ the term **tri-ratna** which functions as their counterpart of the Buddhist ti-ratana **(Buddha, dhamma** and **saṅgha**): 'right faith' or 'discernment' (Skt.**samyak-darśana**) in the Jina's doctrine; 'right knowledge' **(samyak-jñāna)** of the doctrine; 'right conduct' (**samyak-caritrya**). We may notice here that whilst the Buddhist formula centres upon three entities, the Jain formula consists of three imperatives.

13. The Buddhist denial of the metaphysical

substantiality of the objects of perception, known as the concept of **suññatā** in the Pali Nikāyas and the doctrine of **śūṇyavāda** in Mahāyāna, has its counterpart in the Jain doctrine of the indeterminacy of empirical reality (**syādvāda**) [33]

14. The Jains subscribe to the doctrines of impermanence (**anitya**) and unsatisfactoriness (**dukkha**) though not to no-self (**an-ātman**). They do, however, see the **jīva** (soul) as ontologically separate from the **a-jīva** (body),and liberation consists integrally in disengaging the two, just as, in Buddhism, liberation is consonant with the realisation of **anattā** (no self) in the **khandhas**. The difference is therefore not so much one of objective, which in both cases is expressed in terms of the concept 'self', as in the variation of interpretation placed on the concepts involved.[34]

15. The 3 **guptis** are the Jain equivalent of the 3 **moneyyas** of the Buddhists: restraint of 'mind' 'speech' and 'body'.[35]

16. Buddhism and Jainism each possess a **caitya** (shrine) tradition.[36]

17. The Jain collection of sacred books is called **gaṇipiḍaga** and the Buddhist Canon **tipiṭaka**.[37]

18. Both are 'contemplative' (**dhyāna**) traditions, and the realisation of their spiritual goals consists ultimately in a form of gnosis (**prajñā**) or 'cognition' (**kevala-ñāṇa**). Their difference consists largely in the fact that Jainism has a more physicalist ontology (e.g., with reference to **karma** and the 'self') and in accordance with this stresses physical austerity (**tapas**); whilst Buddhism,

holding a less physicalist view, subscribes to a 'middle way' doctrine.[38]

## The Mythical Identity of the Four Kings

We now propose to examine further data which relate to or can shed light on the identity of any of the monarchs from the legend of the four kings who become **paccekabuddhas**. It appears that three of the kings - Karaṇḍu, Dummukha and Naggaji - receive no significant mention elsewhere in either Brahmanic or Śramanic literature.[39] However, King Nimi or King Nami is quite a different proposition. We have already noted that he receives special mention separately from the three other kings in the Uttarādhyayana Sūtra version of the legend and, in addition, is the subject of an entire chapter in the same work. Elswhere in Jain canonical literature, Nami is mentioned in the Sūttagame and the Aupapātika Sūtras.[40] It is also worthy of note that two of the twenty-four Jain **titthagara** have similar-sounding names - Ariṣṭanemi and Nimi.[41] In Buddhist literature mention of King Nimi, Nami's equivalent, is not confined to the Kumbhakāra Jātaka story of the kings who become **paccekabuddhas**. He is the subject of another Jātaka story and receives frequent mention in other canonical sources too. In addition there are other kings of the dynasty of Videha who figure prominently in the Buddha's discourses. In Brahmanical literature there are references to Videhan kings with the same patronymic. These are evidently Brahmanical counterparts of the same mythical personages.[42]

In view, therefore, of Nimi's apparent significance we shall analyse and compare the relevant material relating to him in the various traditions with a view to shedding light on the earliest formative concept of a **paccekabuddha**. We refer to this material as the 'Nimi' complex of legends.[43]. Broadly speaking we class material as belonging to this complex if it features either the name Nimi or a variant of it, or if it refers to some king of Videha who renounces his kingdom. In terms of this classification the relevant figures and the sources in which they are located are listed below and will be discussed individually in the order we have given them. It will be noticed that Janaka is a name which occurs frequently in the list; this is because Janaka (lit.progenitor) happens to be the patronymic for King of Videha.

1. Nami (Utty.IX.and XVIII.45-7).

2. Nimi (Kumbhakāra J. : III.377ff.).

3. Nimi (Makhādeva S. : M.II.78-82; Nimi J. : VI.96ff. Makhādeva J. : I.139; Miln.115,291; Cp.1.6; Cp.A.42ff.; Kh.A.128; Dip.III.36).

4. Nemi (Isigili S. : M.III.70).

5. Nami Sāpya (Rg.V.I.53.7; VI.20.6; X.48.9).

6. Nami Sāpya (Pañc.Brh.XXV.10.17).

7. Nimi (Mbh.XII.8600).

8. Makhādeva (M.II.74ff.; J.I.137-9; VI.95-96).

9. Mahājanaka (Mahājanaka J. : VI.39ff.).

10. Janaka the **pravrajita** (Mbh.XII.571ff.).

11. Janaka the virtuous ruler (Mbh.II.137-8; XIV.2483).

12. Janaka who sings the song (**gītā**) of Mithilā burning (Mbh.XII.529; 6641; 9917).

13. Janaka the liberated householder (Mbh.IX.19-21).

14. Janaka (patron of Yājñavalkya) (Śat.Brh.XI; Bṛhad.Up.IV).

Nami (1)

As we have already indicated, one of the chapters of the Uttarādhyayana Sūtra is entitled Nami's Renunciation (**Nami Pavvajjā**). This chapter comprises sixty-two verses which feature a dialogue between King Nami and Sakka, King of the Gods. We shall summarise this dialogue and analyse certain features of the text, bearing in mind that this particular Nami was at some time also designated a **patteyabuddha**. The opening verses set the scene for the dialogue by informing us that King Nami of Mithilā, Videha has become a **sahasambuddha** and renounced his throne in order to lead the life of a **śramaṇa**. He is then approached by Sakka who is disguised as a **brāhmaṇa**. Sakka accuses him of abandoning his responsibilities as a **kṣatriya**, namely as a conqueror, a ruler and a patron of the sacrifice. It is appropriate that Sakka should disguise himself as a **brāhmaṇa** for **brāhmaṇas** are the traditional opponents of **kṣatriya** renunciation. Brahmanic literature evinces approval of renunciation only for kings who are no longer effective rulers in their own kingdom.[44] Nami answers these criticisms by presenting an altogether different interpretation of the kṣatriya's responsibilities. He explains that his decision to become a **śramaṇa** does not mean he abandons his **kṣatriya** values but that he interprets them differently. He takes the traditional functions of the **kṣatriya** that Sakka cites - constructing forts (v.18) and palaces (v.24), punishing criminals (v.28), conquest (v.32), offering sacrifices (v.38) and amassing wealth (v.46) - and imbues them with a radical new moral and spiritual interpretation. Hence he speaks of the fortress of faith (**saddhā** - v.20), of being guarded by the three **guptis** (**tigutta** - v.20), of the weapons of virtue (vv.21-22),of the conquest of self (vv.34-36), of **tapas** without offering sacrifice (v.40), and of fulfilment through austerity (**tavam** - v.49) rather than by amassing wealth.

What motivates Nami to become a **śramaṇa**? The answer is to be found in the nature of the **kṣatriya**'s relationship to the **brāhmaṇa**. In its traditional conception the **kṣatriya**'s role and function within society is dictated by the religious theory and practice of the **brāhmaṇa** class. Through 'renunciation', that is, through abdicating his rulership and becoming a mendicant, the **kṣatriya** throws-off the persona prescribed for him by the **brāhmaṇa** and establishes a fresh identity of his own-making. As 'renouncer' he is now 'self-become' and no more the creation of the **brāhmaṇa**. Far from shedding his **kṣatriya** identity by renouncing life as a householder, Nami succeeds in assuming his true **kṣatriya** identity. This is the conclusion reached by the Nami Pavajjā.

After Nami has succeeded in refuting Sakka's criticisms, the king of the gods concedes defeat, removes his **brāhmaṇa** disguise and reveals his true identity. From this point onward his criticism alters to praise. Now he extols Nami with kṣatriyan superlatives: 'he who has conquered anger, vanquished pride, banished delusion and subdued greed, he who is the supreme (**uttamo** - v.58) among men'. Finally, as he takes leave of Nami, he bows at his feet which are said to be marked with the **cakka** (wheel) and **aṁkusa** (hook), emblems of the universal monarch (cakravartin). That Nami should receive this adulation and homage from the patron deity of the **kṣatriyas**, is itself due acknowledgment that he is a true **kṣatriya** after all.[45]

Having provided a brief summary of the major theme of this version of the Nami legend we now propose to examine some features of the text itself. The first five verses of the chapter serve as a preface to the dialogue which takes up most of the chapter. They introduce us to Nami and his achievements. In them he is declared to be a **sahasambuddha** who placed his son on the throne and 'retired from the world' (**abhinikkamī** - v.2).[46] It is said that he first became enlightened and then retired from the world (v.3). He, therefore, became enlightened as a householder not as a **śramaṇa**, an interpretation which squares with the representation of the **paccekabuddha** in Buddhist narratives as one who attains enlightenment as a householder. In verse four it says that after renouncing his kingship he resorts to a solitary (**eganta**) place; there is no mention or suggestion that he joins an 'order' or 'community' (**gaṇa**). His representation here, therefore, is very much like the figure of the **ekacarin** depicted in the Khaggavisāṇa Sutta. In due course he is described as a 'royal seer' (**rāyarisi** - v.5, 6,8,62) the significance of which we shall have reason to discuss later in this chapter. It is next related that the news of Nami's renunciation creates an 'uproar' (**kolāhala** - v.5,7) in the city of Mithilā. Buddhist tradition informs us that there are five occasions on which an 'uproar' (**kolāhala**) takes place.

Two of them are when a **buddha** or a **cakkavatti** (Skt.**cakravartin**) is predicted.[47] When Nami is requested by Sakka to explain the uproar in Mithilā (v.7), Nami compares the traditional function of the king and ruler to a 'sacred tree' (**caityavṛkṣa**) whose leaves, fruits and flowers are a refuge (**saraṇa**) at all times to many (v.9). But, he says, when the elements shake and damage the tree, its inhabitants, the birds, panic with fright. Nami is here utilizing an archetypal symbol, the **caitya** tree which was held in such veneration in Ancient India that not even a single leaf should be destroyed. This is because it was believed to be the resort of supernatural beings such as **devas**, **yakṣas** and **nāgas**.[48] This imagery is chosen to represent Nami's renunciation because it conveys the degree of gravity associated with the act of renunciation in terms of upsetting the divinely sanctioned norms of society, notably, the sacred duty of kingship. We also note with interest that the same image of the leafless, damaged, barren tree figures as one of the incidents in the legend of the four kings, occurs twice as a metaphor in the Khaggavisāṇa Sutta and appears as well in the legend of King Mahājanaka.

In the section which justifies Nami's decision to become a renouncer, there is one particular verse which above all others enshrines śramaṇic values.

> 'There is much blessing for the **muni**,
> the houseless monk.
> Who is free from all ties and knows himself
> to be solitary.'[49]

This verse celebrates the figure of the **muni** as one who is emancipated from the constraints of society, and is a verse that quite clearly belongs to the same thematic stock as those of the Khaggavisāṇa Sutta and the moneyya suttas.

Verse fourteen is another key verse since it occurs elsewhere in connection with the figures Janaka (12) and Mahājanaka (10), and happens also to be one of the **samaṇabhadra-gāthā** which are imputed to be utterances of **paccekabuddhas** (see Appendix III). It therefore links up all these mythical personages with one another and with the town of Mithilā. This verse reads

> 'Happy are we, happy live we who call
> nothing our own;
> When Mithila burns, nothing of mine burns.'

The Nami Pavajjā concludes with an epilogue (vv.56-62) praising the king. Sakka declares Nami to have attained perfect liberation (**mutti uttama** - v.57), to be enlightened (**sambuddha** - v.62) and to be one who will acquire **siddhi** (v.58) after death.

Finally, the name of this mythical king warrants some comment. Nami means 'one who brings into subjection'.[50] Hence in verse thirty two it says that to 'bring into subjection' (**nānamanti**) other kings is the hallmark of a true **kṣatriya**. In the Jain prose version of the legend of the four kings it says that Nami acquired his name because his adversaries 'humbled' themselves before him (**paḍivakkha rāyāṇo tassa rāino nam-iyā**).[51] Similarly, Nami Sāpya, the figure in the Ṛg Veda who is an ally of Indra and slays the demon Namuci (infra p.150), takes his name from **namya** meaning 'one who makes the foe bow down'. Pāṇini, the grammarian, observed that Mithilā, the place where Nami ruled, originally meant 'the country where enemies are crushed' [52] All these interpretations indicate that Nami functioned as some sort of eponymous hero, a symbol of the powerful **kṣatriya**. However, we have seen how the Jain tradition has transformed the legend of this epic warrior from one who was distinctive for conquering others into one distinctive for conquering his self: 'Nami humbled himself' (**namī namehi appāṇaṁ**).[53] King Nami, the archetypal **kṣatriya** who became archetypal 'renouncer', is the mythical embodiment of the beginnings of the institution of renunciation.

Nimi (2)

This figure is the Buddhist equivalent of the king the Jains refer to as Nami in the legend of the four kings who become **paccekabuddhas**. As a **paccekabuddha** he is not mentioned elsewhere, although he may be the same as Nimi (3) and Mahājanaka (10).

Nimi (3)

This king is a Buddhist figure whose main story is told in the Nimi Jataka, though he is mentioned elsewhere too. He is distinguished on four counts: Firstly, he is renowned for his great acts of **yañña** (sacrifice) and **dāna** (giving). He is also described as a conqueror (**arindama**), a royal seer (**rājīsi**) and a universal sovereign (**cakkavatti**). Secondly, he is the last in the line of a dynasty of Kings of Mithilā, all of whom become renouncers (**pabbajita**). In the Majjhima Nikāya it tells us that the king who founded and gave his name to this dynasty of renouncers is named Makhādeva. According to the Jātakas, Nimi is a later rebirth of Makhadeva himself, so that the same person in different rebirths founded and ended the dynasty of kings who became **pabbajitas**. Thirdly, the Nimi Jātaka equates King Nimi with the **bodhisatta** and does not represent him as a **paccekabuddha**. Fourthly, his story bears a close resemblance to the theme of the Nami Pavajjā: like Nami, King Nimi has an encounter with Sakka, King of the Gods, in connection with the theme of renunciation. On one occasion when he is pondering whether it might not be more preferable to live as a renouncer oneself than to supply alms (**dāna**) to renouncers, he is visited by Sakka. Sakka decides to take him on a Dantesque tour of the particular sphere of the non-human cosmos over which he himself presides: the heaven of the thirty-three gods (**tāvatiṁsa-devaloka**) and the many hells (**niraya**). Whilst showing Nimi this panorama he explains that the only way to avoid rebirth in these realms is to become a monk (**brahmacariya**) instead of a householder. At the climax of the tour, Sakka invites Nimi to remain with him in the **tāvatiṁsadevaloka** but Nimi declines and returns to the world of humankind once more. At a later stage in his life, Nimi heeds Sakka's warning and decides to become a renouncer. It is on this account that Nimi has become renowned in Buddhist tradition as the king who 'entered the **tāvatiṁsadevaloka** in a human body'.[54]

It would seem that the story of Nimi mythologically depicts some form of yogic or meditational attainment (viz. **jhāna**) in which the character of Nimi verifies for himself higher and lower states of existence corresponding to the traditional cosmology of the non-human worlds of the **devaloka**s and the **niraya**s. The object of the story is to make plain that his experience of these states left him realising that rebirth in the **devaloka**s, resulting from the religious practice of almsgiving (the merit earned from alms-giving would entitle him to rebirth as a god), is nevertheless inferior to living as a **brahma**-

**cariya**.

The striking similarity in the myths of Nimi and Nami lies not only in the fact that both kings become renouncers but in the fact also that each has an encounter with the god Sakka. In each story Sakka has a dual role: In the Nami story, as a **brāhmaṇa** he is critical of the king's renunciation but, as himself, he praises the renunciation; in the Nimi story he teaches the king that **brahmacariya** is superior to life as a householder but, ironically, invites him to remain in the place where virtuous householders are reborn, the **tāvatiṁsa-devaloka**. Sakka's ambiguous role signifies how seemingly drastic and momentous in social terms was the change in the **kṣatriya**'s status on becoming a renouncer. That Sakka, the patron deity of the **kṣatriyas**,ultimately sanctions 'renunciation' is shown by the fact that in the Jain metric version of the legend of the four kings it says he 'directs' (coio) Nami to become a **śramaṇa**,[55] and in the Nimi story it says that he acknowledges the superior salvific value in becoming a **brahma-cariya**.

Nami (4)

One of the **paccekabuddhas** listed in the Isigili Sutta has the name Nami. There is no way of knowing whether it is the same figure as the **paccekabuddha** Nimi (2) or Nami (1).

Nami Sāpya (5)

This figure is mentioned on three separate occasions in the Rg Veda:

(i) 'Thou Indra, with thy friend **(sakhyā)** Nami Sāpya, Slewest from far away the guileful

Namuci'

(ii) 'Namī Sāpya...joined me (Indra) as a friend (**sakhyā**) of old (**bhūt**) in search of kine'

(iii) 'He (Indra) guarded (**prāvan**) Nami, Sayya's son in slumber and sated him with food, success and riches'[56]

From these verses we discover that Nami Sapya is a friend or ally (**sakhā**) of Indra,[57] the Vedic form of Sakka, and he assisted Indra in slaying the **asura** Namuci. Therefore we may safely infer that he is some kind of **kṣatriya**. A further clue to his identity is provided by the occurrence of a parallel expression in a verse from the Aitareya Brāhmaṇa: 'Indra is the comrade of the wanderer' (**indram iccarataḥ sakhā**). We quote the verse in full:

> "Manifold is the prosperity of him who is weary",
> So have we heard, O Rohita;
> Evil is he who stayeth among men,
> Indra is the comrade of the wanderer.'[58]

> **nānā śrāmtāya śrīrastīti**
> **rohita suśrum̐**
> **pāpo nṛṣdvaro jana**
> **indram iccarataḥ sakhā**[59]

These are the words of Indra who adopts a human form and urges Rohita, a **kṣatriya** and son of King Hariścandra, to become a 'wanderer' (**carato**) in the forest (**araṅya**). The parallels with the legend of Nami (1) are obvious enough: we have just seen that Sakka (=Indra) directed Nami to leave household existence and become a **śramaṇa**. The usage of **śrāmtāya** is semantically significant since the concept of the **śramaṇa** is nascent in the idea of one who is weary (**śrāmta**) of the company of men (**jana**).

Should we therefore interpret the recurrent expression 'friend of Indra' to mean that Nami Sāpya was a 'wanderer' (**iccarata**) and therefore a **śramaṇa**? The evidence provided by this Aitareya Brāhmaṇa passage is suggestive, but when taken in isolation is by no means conclusive. We have found additional corroborative evidence in another Ṛg Vedic passage, evidence which ties in with the allusion to Namuci's slaughter. This is the occurrence of the phrase 'Indra is the friend of **munis**' (**munīnāṁ sakhā**).[60] This phrase linking Indra with the **muni** could prove to be the key to our interpretation of the identity of Nami Sāpya. In the Buddhist canonical tradition it is qua **muni** that the Buddha overcomes Māra, another name for whom is Namuci: 'You are **buddha**, you are teacher, you are the **muni** that conquers Māra' (**tuvaṁ buddho, tuvaṁ satthā, tuvaṁ Mārābhibbhū muni**).[61] Namuci (lit.**na muci**: not releasing) in Vedic literature is an **asura** or **dasa** who initially makes a compact with Indra but whom Indra later slays. In Buddhist literature, Namuci is an **asura** with a large army and another name for Māra - presumably because he is an archetypal adversary and symbolises an intractable opponent. Vṛtra is the primal demon[62] and by slaying him, Indra acquires 'sovereignty' (**rājyam**).[63] By the same token, the Buddha's conquest of Māra affords him the right to be a **dharma-rājā**.[64] Thus the Buddha's conquest of Māra and his winning of immortality is a repetition of the Indra-Namuci myth. One of the expressions used in this connection, 'cutting off' (**cheti**) Māra's bond (**Mārabandhānam**),[65] seems to have derived from the myth of Indra's conquest of Vṛtra. In the story of Indra's compact with Namuci, Indra agrees not to slay his adversary by day or by night; he therefore slays him at dawn.[66] It is not without some irony that we therefore discover the Buddha routs the forces of Māra and realises enlightenment at dawn, the point of transition between night and day.[67] Not surprisingly, perhaps, Jacobi informs us that there is a version of the story of Namuci in Jain literature too in which Namuci is defeated by the Jain monks.[68] It therefore seems that some kind of link can be established between the concepts 'friend of Indra' (viz. Nami Sāpya), '**muni**' or 'wanderer' (**iccarata**), and the 'slaying of Namuci'. We have established that both Nami Sāpya and the **muni** are friends of Indra and both also are conquerors of Namuci (or Māra). On this basis it is possible to conjecture that Nami Sāpya was either a **muni** or a synonym for the **muni** generally, or their patron. Nami Sāpya's **kṣatriya** status is quite clearly signified by his being the friend of Indra and by helping Indra slaughter Namuci. The Ṛg Veda shows that the **muni** too has certain **kṣatriya** associations: He is linked with Vāyu and Rudra in the Keśin hymn and, elsewhere, **maruts** are compared to the **muni** - all these being deities of the **kṣatriya** function.[69]

## Namin Sāpya (6)

The Pañcaviṁsa Brāhmaṇa mentions a Namin Sāpya and describes him as a King of Videha who 'went straightway to the world of heaven' in consequence of making an offering (**dakṣiṇā**) of one thousand cows.[70] The significance of this reference is made clear by other passages in this and other Brāhmaṇas. For instance, elsewhere in the same Brāhmaṇa it says '"The world of heaven is as far removed from this (earthly) world" they say, "as a thousand cows standing the one above the other". Therefore, they say: "He who sacrifices with a sacrifice of which a thousand **dakṣinā** are given, reaches these worlds"'.[71] According to the Kauśītaki Brāhmaṇa, the gift of a thousand cows is the complete gift which cannot be surpassed: "by all may I obtain all".[72] The Pañcaviṁsa Brāhmaṇa adds: 'This is the highest sacrifice: the thousand is the highest (number). He who knows this comes to the highest end'.[73] In Upaniṣadic literature Janaka, the patronymic for a King of Videha, is a byword for one who makes a **dakṣiṇā** of 'one thousand' cows;[74] this must refer back to the figure known by the name Namin Sāpya in the Pañcaviṁsa Brāhmaṇa. Thus in Brahmanic religion he represents the paradigm for their concept of the royal seer (**rājarṣi**), one who through extensive sacrifices reaches heaven.

The resemblance between this myth and the Buddhist story of Nimi (3) is more than apparent. Namin Sāpya going straightway to heaven may be compared with Nimi entering the **devaloka** in his human body.[75] These would seem to constitute different versions of the same archetypal myth. However, the interpretations placed on this myth are crucially different. Whereas for Brahmanic religion the King of Videha's '**daksiṇā**' of a thousand cows represented consummation of the highest conceivable religious goal that the **brāhmaṇa** 'cultus' provides for the **kṣatriyas**, by contrast, the same event signified for the Śramana tradition the exhaustion of a particular approach to religious matters and became, for them, the crucial turning point or denouement in the development of religious conceptions. The legend therefore held a significance of a very different kind for each tradition. Evidence of the precise nature of that difference is to be found in the variant Brahmanic

and Śramanic interpretations of the meaning of
the term **rājaṛṣi**: a king who performs
extensive sacrifices, on the one hand, and on
the other a king who renounces the world. In
chapter one we saw how in Canonical Buddhism
the term **rājīsi** could be used in either of
these two senses. Since the notion of the
**rājaṛṣi** represented a normative concept in
both Brāhmaṇa and Śramaṇa traditions, the clue
to the antithesis between the two traditions
must reside somewhere in its conception. This
conception must at some time or other have
undergone a radical reinterpretation. In so
far as the **rājaṛṣi** represented the ultimate
attainment possible within the **brāhmaṇa**
'cultus', the rejection of that attainment by
the opponents of Brahmanic religion inevitably
entailed the repudiation of everything that
the 'cultus' stood for. That rejection therefore gave birth to the very concept of 'renunciation' itself: emancipation from the grip of
the **brāhmaṇa** 'cultus' could only be achieved
by ceasing to be a householder altogether.
Society had to be abandoned because the
**brāhmaṇas** and Brahmanic religion held such
hegemony that it was impossible to exist within society without allegiance to their values.
The Brahmanic concept of the **rājaṛṣi** served
as a kind of virility symbol for the hold and
influence of their 'cultus' upon society at
large. In so far as the **kṣatriyas** conformed
to the requirements of that 'cultus' the
**brāhmaṇas** had succeeded in winning over as
their ally the most important and powerful
section of society. Therefore , in order to
best undermine Brahmanic religion, its critics
focussed their attack upon their most potent
symbol, and endeavoured to give it a meaning
that more directly challenged and questioned
its former significance.

Nimi (7)

The Sānti Parvan section of the Mahābhārata makes reference to a certain Nimi who gave away his kingdom to **brāhmaṇas** in order to obtain heaven.[76] If this is another allusion to the myth of Namin Sāpya (6) then here we have a formulation of the myth sufficiently ambiguous to be compatible with both its Śramaṇic and Brahmanic interpretations. In the act of a king making a gift of his most essential asset to the **brāhmaṇas** we have the idea of the highest expression of **dakṣiṇā**. On the other hand, the same act entails if not implies renunciation since the king has surrendered up the kingdom over which he rules.

Makhādeva (8)

King Makhādeva of Mithilā, Videha, is first mentioned in the Makhādeva Sutta of the Majjhima Nikāya.[77] Other versions of his legend are to be found in the Makhādeva and Nimi Jātakas.[78] In connection with our discussion of Nimi (3), we observed that Makhadeva founded the custom (P.**vatta**; Skt.**vrata**) of renunciation (**pabbajjā**) among the kings of Videha and (according to the Jātaka versions only) returned, eighty-four thousand generations later, in the form of Nimi (3) to bring an end to the custom in that particular dynasty. Apart from having the distinction of being the progenitor of renunciation, Makhādeva is also depicted to be the originator of the practice of the **brahmavihāra** meditations. These meditations are represented as the principal religious accomplishment of the tradition of renunciation in its earliest phase. The **brahma-vihāras** are therefore shown to be seminally linked with the history of the renunciation tradition.

In chapter four we shall discuss this association further and examine the role of the **brahmavihāras** as a direct religious counterpart to Brahmanic sacrifice.

Mahājanaka (9)

There are a number of reasons why the Jātaka tale of King Mahājanaka should figure significantly in our discussion.[79] Firstly, some of the episodes describe events which mirror imagery used in the Khaggavisāṇa Sutta. Secondly, though Mahājanaka is supposed to be the **bodhisatta** (a former birth of the Buddha), he happens to possess many of the characteristics which are elsewhere associated with **paccekabuddhas**. In view, therefore, of the pronounced emphasis on **paccekabuddha** motifs we propose to show that this particular Jātaka provides a typical example of how a legend has been tampered with and, in this case, assimilated within the framework of a **bodhisatta** birth story. Hence the form of the Mahājanaka Jātaka serves as an individual illustration of the sorts of general confusion surrounding legends of these kings of Mithilā, a confusion largely attributable to the different sectarian interpretations and dogmatic emphases placed on them. We shall proceed by summarising the account of Mahājanaka's **pabbajjā**, pointing out certain anomalies or inconsistencies in the story as it stands and showing how these are best explained through the hypothesis that a **bodhisatta** frame-story has been superimposed upon an older legend or legendary material. We shall then go on to argue that this older material related to a proto-**śramaṇa** figure.

'Renunciation' is the principle theme of this legend, the same as the Namipavajjā. On a certain occasion Mahājanaka decides to visit his mango orchard in order to sample its fruit. Later, he goes a second time to his orchard, only to discover that his subjects have stripped one of the trees of all its fruit and left it badly damaged. Close by it he sees that there is a barren tree which has not been touched; this tree remains as it has always been, majestic and unsullied. Disturbed (**saṁvegam paṭilabhitvā**)[80] by this striking contrast between the two trees,King Mahājanaka perceives a moral in the incident: kingship is like the fruit-bearing tree - others are intent upon seizing the kingdom and its wealth; but the renouncer (**pabbajita**) resembles the barren tree - he has no possessions to be stolen and therefore will remain unharmed. Mahājanaka's observations lead him to renounce life as an householder.

The term **saṁvega**, used here to describe the impact which the scene in the orchard has upon the king, is of some importance. It is a word that occurs within the vocabulary of Buddhism and Jainism, having a comparable doctrinal meaning in both. The term denotes the rudimentary emotional experience that brings about disillusionment with the world and material things, so making it possible for the process to begin of non-attachment and disregard (P.**nibbidā**; Skt.**nirveda**) of worldly objects.[81] Buddhist sources tell us that Mogallāna's and Sāriputta's conversion to Buddhism came about as a consequence of their experience of **saṁvega**;[82] that the Buddha experienced a form of **saṁvega** in the story of his encounter with the four signs (**nimitta**) - sickness, aging, death and renunciation - causing him to abandon household existence;[83] and that **paccekabuddhas** 'hold on to the image which disturbs' (**upaṭṭhita-saṁveganimittam gahetvā**) and thereby attain **paccekabodhi**.[84] In terms of attempting to classify the types of experience that lead to

**saṁvega**, it seems they are all characterised by awareness of the fundamental truth of the impermanence (**anicca**) of all things. The classical example or paradigm for this form of awareness is King Makhādeva himself, since according to tradition he started the momentous custom of renunciation on the basis of discovering on his head a grey hair, symbol of aging and decay.[85] So we can see that **saṁvega** is the human faculty or sensibility that provides the practical justification for the Buddhist teaching of the three marks of existence (**tilakkhaṇa**). Consequently, it is not surprising that **saṁvega** is stressed to be the efficient cause of **paccekabodhi**. In belonging outside the dispensation of a Buddha's teaching, prospective **paccekabuddhas** did not have a body of doctrine to resort to, only the resources of their own experience and perception of reality. In respect of bringing about spiritual transformation **saṁvega** is clearly the key concept which underlies renunciation and the realization of **paccekabodhi**.

The conceptions of **hiṁsā** (harming) and **dukkha** (suffering) are dominant themes within the Mahājanaka Jātaka. For example, the fruit-bearing tree comes to harm whereas the barren tree stays unharmed. The circumstances of a fruit-laden tree and a kingdom resemble one another in that both are susceptible to plunder.[86] Such plunder brings with it **dukkha**. Therefore **hiṁsā** and **dukkha** are the inevitable outcome of living in society. We have seen that these concepts, which provide the impetus towards renunciation, are major doctrinal characteristics which the Śramana traditions of Buddhism and Jainism have in common. In view of these observations on Mahājanaka's renunciation, it can be seen why the ethical concept of ahiṁsā (or **avihiṁsā**) is framed as the negation (**a-hiṁsā**) of a vice rather than as an affirmation of a positive characteristic. Such a formulation indicates that the concept originated as a critique of existing mores; hence it ties in with the concept of renouncing society.

To return to the story of the Mahājanaka Jātaka we find that, after having become a renouncer, the king encounters a **tapasa** or Brahmanic ascetic named Migājina. Migājina proceeds to ask Mahājanaka about the circumstances of his renunciation:

> 'They, say, O Lord of the Chariots (**rathesabha**), that one does not become a **samaṇa** and conquer **dukkha** of one's own volition (**paccakha**) but according to a proper procedure (**vijja**) and practice (**kappa**). Who therefore is your master (**bhagavā**) and instructor (**satthā**)?'

Mahājanaka's reply comprises a statement which can be read as a classical definition of the proto-**śramaṇa**'s or **paccekabuddha**'s essential ideological standpoint:

> 'The fruit-bearing and the barren tree were together my instructors' (**sattharo**).[87]

This reply indicates that for Mahājanaka the impetus towards renunciation does not derive from any human or cultural institution but from contemplating the natural world. That is to say, the source of religious inspiration is not 'tradition' (**śrūti**), as the Brahmanic ascetic would suppose, but 'reflection'.

According to the Jātaka story we are told that prior to his disillusioning experience in the orchard Mahājanaka befriends and 'waits upon' (**upaṭṭhāti**) **paccekabuddhas**, supplying them with alms; in return the **paccekabuddhas** provide him with instruction (**ovāda**). After the orchard experience Mahājanaka does not immediately become a **pabbaj-**

**ita**, but for three months pines for the company of **paccekabuddhas** and longs to become like one of them. In due course he decides to renounce his kingdom and become a **pabbajita**. Thereupon he sets out on a long journey to the Himavā pursued by his chief queen, Sīvalī, and many of his subjects who together hope to persuade him to return. Sīvalī catches up with him and tries by many arguments to persuade him of the error of his decision. Her attempt fails and he travels onto the Himavā region where he dwells for the remainder of his life. At one point during his journey to the Himavā Mahājanaka encounters a young woman wearing two bracelets on one arm. He notices that they jangle together and make a noise. He notices that when she puts them on separate arms they become silent because they can no longer jangle together. Mahājanaka sees in this an illustration (**paccaya**)[88] of how it is better for people to become separate and solitary like the bracelets on different arms[89]. This same image is used as a metaphor in the Khaggavisāṇa Sutta [90] and is also the meditational topic (**ārammaṇa**) by which King Naggaji in the Kumbhakāra Jātaka attains **paccekabodhi**.[91] Further illustrations occur in the Mahājanaka Jātaka which are not found in the Khaggavisāṇa Sutta but which are nevertheless reminiscent of its solitary wanderer (**ekacarin**) theme. So, for example, Mahājanaka comes across a fletcher at work and notices that the man verifies the straightness of the arrow shaft by looking along it with just one eye. This is another illustration of the value placed on singularity. Likewise, on another occasion, the king cuts a reed and uses it to demonstrate to his Chief Queen that once a person has cut himself off from his family he can return to them no more.

The Jātaka version of the story of King

Mahājanaka, however, contains a number of significant anomalies. Firstly there is the sudden and unexplained disappearance of **paccekabuddhas** from the story subsequent to the time when Mahājanaka has the orchard experience. The earlier part of the story indicated that **paccekabuddhas** were his regular acquaintances (his wife even mistakes him for a visiting **paccekabuddha** when she passes him on the stairway as he departs from his palace.[92] But shortly after his orchard experience we learn that he pines for their company and then, subsequent to his renunciation, no longer encounters **paccekabuddhas** anymore or expresses any desire to do so. The turning point for their omission from the story appears to be the incident in the orchard. Why should this be so? The reason would seem to be that it would be considered doctrinally incongruous for Mahājanaka to share the company of **paccekabuddhas** after becoming a **pabbajita** since he is supposed to be the **bodhisatta**. In sharing their company it might be anticipated that he would aspire like them to **paccekabodhi**[93]. Such an aspiration would be wholly inappropriate for the **bodhisatta**, as his energies are entirely directed towards the eventual realisation of **sammāsambodhi**. It would be similarly incongruous for him to be seen in the company of **paccekabuddhas** and yet at the same time to be following an inferior path (leading only to rebirth in, for instance, the **brahmaloka**) to the path of the **paccekabuddha** (leading to **nibbāna**). On the other hand, it is not incongruous for him to share their company as a 'householder' for **paccekabuddhas**, as we have seen, teach householders no more than the advantages of 'renunciation'. We may therefore surmise that the redactors thought it better to omit the **paccekabuddha** beyond the stage of Mahājanaka's orchard experience rather than be faced with these doctrinal difficulties.

The second anomaly concerns the nature of the orchard experience. In other Jātaka stories this type of experience leads directly to the attainment of **paccekabodhi**. In the Jātaka prose narrative of the story of the four kings who become **paccekabuddhas**, King Karaṇḍu has an identical experience to Mahājanaka but, in his case, it results directly in **paccekabodhi**[94]. We suggest that these anomalies would not exist if **paccekabuddhas** were absented from the story altogether and if Mahājanaka himself were represented not as the **bodhisatta** but just as a 'householder' who becomes a **paccekabuddha** or proto-**śramaṇa**. In endeavouring to adapt a traditional folk-legend to a Jātaka framework, we maintain the redactors substituted the **bodhisatta** for this archetypal figure and (probably) introduced subsidiary roles for **paccekabuddhas** as a way of compensating for having deprived the hero of his essential **paccekabuddha** status. We are inclined to the conclusion, therefore, that Mahājanaka was originally identified as a **paccekabuddha**.

Janaka (10)

This particular Janaka is mentioned within the Mahābhārata in the context of a debate on the duties of kingship[95]. In order to dissuade Yudhiṣṭhira from renouncing his kingship, his brother Arjuna tells him of an 'old legend' (**pura-itihāsa**) which the people recite about a certain King Janaka of Videha and his queen: once upon a time King Janaka had abandoned his kingdom and become a shaven-headed monk (**muṇḍaka bhikṣu**). Stricken with grief by the king's renunciation (**pravrajyā**), the queen searched in various solitary places for her husband. When she found him she confronted him with various reasons why it was a mistake for him to forsake his kingship and she urges him to return to his former life. Quite clearly this legend is a Brahmanical version of the Buddhist story of Mahājanaka and his verbal confrontation with Queen Sīvalī. One distinctive difference between the two versions, however, is that the Brahmanical one consists entirely of a monologue delivered by the queen, who functions as the spokesperson for Brahmanical opposition to **kṣatriya** renunciation; Janaka is made to remain silent in order that only the one orthodox viewpoint should be expressed. In the Buddhist version, however, Mahājanaka is the primary speaker and argues 'the case for' renunciation. This difference illustrates how the same legend has been adapted to fit different sectarian interests.

Janaka (11)

The Mahābhārata also has isolated references to a Janaka who is a virtuous ruler and a Janaka who attains success by making gifts[96]. These attributes are distinctive features of Nimi (3).

Janaka (12)

There are separate references in the Mahābhārata to a King Janaka of a former age who celebrated his own act of renunciation by composing a now famous stanza about himself and Mithilā.[97] We have already noted that this same stanza is repeatedly found throughout the Nimi complex of legends. Since the stanza both alludes specifically to Mithilā, and summarises the fundamental Śramanic viewpoint - that true freedom is to be free of possessions, no matter how precious or dear - it indicates a seminal connection between the Śramaṇa Movement and the region of Videha.

**Janaka** (13)

There is also a reference in the Mahābhārata to a King Janaka who is an example of someone who has attained liberation (**mokṣa**) as a householder.[98] The Buddhacarita similarly mentions a Janaka, King of the Videhas, as figuring among those kings who were householders 'well-skilled in attaining the merit which leads to final bliss'.[99] It may be recalled how Nami becomes a **buddha** as a householder, and Namin Sāpya reaches heaven through performing the duties of a **kṣatriya qua** householder.

Janaka (14)

The earliest extant reference to a king by the name of Janaka occurs in the eleventh **kānda** of the Śatapatha Brāhmaṇa. This Janaka is described as a universal monarch (**samrāt**) and the patron of Yajñavalkya. He would therefore seem to be identical with that Janaka who features prominently in the Bṛhadāraṅyaka Upaniṣad as the patron of Yajñavalkya.[100] In the Brāhmaṇa he is depicted as one who reinterprets and challenges the traditional assumptions of the priestly 'cultus'. As such, he would seem to reconcile in himself those images of Namin Sāpya (5) and Nimi (3) whose stories, we argue, are different sectarian versions of the same myth. That this Janaka is identical with Namin Sāpya would seem to follow from the evidence of a passage in the Bṛhadāraṅyaka Upaniṣad, where the name Janaka is synonymous with the concept of a gift of a 'thousand' cows.[101]

The passages relating to Janaka in the Śatapatha Brāhmaṇa deserve some attention. It is said, for instance, that Janaka quests among **brāhmaṇa** for knowledge of the offering to Mitra (**mitravinda** **iṣṭi**). He eventually acquires that knowledge from Yajñavalkya.[102] This particular 'offering' (**iṣṭi**) may constitute a Brahmanic counterpart of the Buddhist **brahma-vihāra** meditations for, like them, it provides a soteriological and protective function: it ensures that a king 'conquers repeated death' and achieves 'a full lifespan'.[103] Loving kindness (**metta**), the first of the **brahmavihāra** meditations, is a cognate of Mitra, the name of the Vedic deity associated with the conception of **ahiṁsā** as the basis for an ethical code. Of Mitra, the Śatapatha Brāhmaṇa says, 'he never injures the animate or the inanimate, and hence is the friend of all'.[104] Again, the reference to Janaka's search for the significance of the rite relating to Mitra may represent the Brahmanic counterpart of the Buddhist affirmation that a King of Videha,Makhādeva, originated the custom of renunciation together with the practice of the **brahma-vihāra** meditations. In the next chapter we shall be endeavouring to show how the practice of renunciation, **ahiṁsā** and the **brahma-vihāras** are historically interconnected.

The Śatapatha Brāhmaṇa also informs us that Yajñavalkya himself learns about the ultimate meaning of the Vedic fire rite (**agnihotra**) from Janaka.[105] From the time of this disclosure their roles are reversed and Yajnavalkya the sage becomes the tutee of the king. Janaka's interpretation of the fire offering entails its de-ritualisation: he claims that it can still be performed when ritual objects are not available.[106] Elsewhere in the same

**kānda**, Yajñavalkya applies this method in a verbal disputation with a **brāhmaṇa**. He argues the case that the entire Vedic pantheon can be reduced to the function of 'breath' (**prāṇa**).[107] Such is the impact of this disclosure that upon hearing it his opponent drops dead. Though it is not explicitly acknowledged, Yajñavalkya is tantamount to being guilty of brahmanicide for having caused the death of his antagonist, a theme which we will pursue in the next chapter. In the Bṛhadāraṇyaka Upaniṣad a similar episode occurs but with some interesting variations. On this occasion Yajñavalkya claims that 'mind' (**manas**) is the essential principle (**brahman**) of the **yajña**, that it is 'infinite' (**anantam**) and constitutes liberation (**mukti**).[108] Not only is there an etymological link between **manas** and **muni** but in chapter one we saw how the concept and figure of the muni is associated in Buddhist sources and elsewhere with the power of 'discerning' and 'knowing' - functions of the **manas** faculty.

According to the Bṛhadāraṇyaka Upaniṣad Yajnavalkya concludes a discourse on 'awakening' (**budho**) by announcing that Janaka is one who has realized that goal.[109] Janaka responds by making a gift of the Kingdom of Videha to Yajñavalkya and declaring himself to be his servant. Having initially promised Yajñavalkya a 'thousand' cows in return for instruction, Janaka finally surrenders everything he possesses. We may notice too that Janaka achieves this summum bonum whilst still occupying the role of a householder. Directly after the proclamation of his 'awakening' Janaka announces his act of renunciation. This pattern of events resembles the accounts of how persons become **paccekabuddhas** in the Jātaka tales, where the concepts of 'awakening' and 'renunciation' are viewed as integral to one another; but it also provides striking parallels with the story of Nami in the Uttarādhyayana Sūtra.

## Conclusion on the Nimi Complex of Legends

Among the passages and stories relating to the fourteen different figures which we have just discussed we have seen that some evidently comprise different versions of the same legend and that others have some theme or themes in common which justify their inclusion within the same complex of legends. In the course of our discussion we have tried to indicate that apparent differences can often be attributed to various sectarian interpretations and emphases. We have also drawn attention to some of the detailed concepts and themes within a specific legend where we have regarded it as shedding light on the identity of the **paccekabuddha** and his connections with the origin of the Śramaṇa Movement. As a result of this comparative analysis we are now able to draw together the main threads into a series of points that summarize the basic Nimi myth:

i. The myth centres upon a monarch (or dynasty of monarchs) of Mithilā, the capital of the ancient region of Videha.

ii. This monarch is very distinguished and powerful, signified by titles such as **cakravartin, samrāt, rājarṣi**.

iii. He belongs within the **brāhmaṇa** 'cultus' and fulfils its obligations par excellence (viz. the **daksiṇā** of one thousand cows).

iv. He obtains a form of 'insight' which, on the one hand is synonymous with realising the limitations of the **brāhmaṇa** 'cultus' as traditionally understood and which, on the other hand, entails the concept of complete renunciation.

v. His 'renunciation' threatens the existing status quo and is referenced by verbal confrontation between himself and Sakka, the traditional patron deity of the **kṣatriyas**, between himself and his queen, as well as by a general state of 'uproar' in Mithilā itself.

It becomes apparent from this summary that the Nimi myth depicts the origins of 'renunciation', with Nimi himself corresponding to the figure of the proto-**śramaṇa**. We have seen that the real clue to this interpretation lies in the particular sequence of events: the **kṣatriya** from Videha who belongs within the **brāhmaṇa** 'cultus', sees the limitations of that 'cultus' and abandons it altogether. On the basis of the construction we have here placed upon the Nimi complex of myths, the fundamental impetus behind the Śramaṇa Movement was disaffection with the priestly 'cultus' and its monopolistic trends. This disillusionment may well be indicated by that aspect of the verbal root √**śram** which means 'to become weary' (i.e., disillusioned) as much as with the sense commonly associated with **śramaṇa**, 'to exert, to toil, to perform acts of austerity'.

## Conclusion to the Legend of the Four Kings

Our researches into the identity of the tradition referred to by the legend of the four kings who become **paccekabuddhas** has taken us no further than establishing the mythological significance of just one of them. Therefore, in view of the comparative obscurity of the remaining kings and the special significance assigned to Nimi, it behoves us to furnish an explanation of how the legend of the four kings who become **paccekabuddhas** originated. Since it appears to belong exclusively to the Buddhist and Jain traditions it probably originated as a modified or amplified Śramanic version of the Nimi myth, with the intended purpose of giving the concept of 'renunciation' a significance beyond that of just the region of Videha. The four kings represent suzerains of four distinct regions of Northern India (Videha, Pañcāla, Kāliṅga and Gandhāra) and therefore testify to the presence of the śramaṇa custom throughout the main cultural centres of the time. The number four would here signify 'universality', as in Indian cosmography it denotes the quarters (**diśā**) of the world.[110] Our knowledge of the identities of the other kings is insufficient to establish whether there is any historical basis to this legend or whether it was purely a contrivance to further the cause of the Śramaṇa Movement.

## **Kṣatriya** and Renunciation themes in Pali Sources

Our basic argument so far in this chapter has been that the figure of the **paccekabuddha** is to be identified with the first **śramaṇas**, the pioneers of 'renunciation', who were kings or **kṣatriyas**. We now propose to supply corroborative evidence for this basic argument by drawing attention to the prevalence of either 'kingship' imagery or **kṣatriya** concepts in the representation within the Pali sources of the **ecakarin** figure and the

**paccekabuddha**. This will involve us in looking at material comprising: verses from the Khaggavisāṇa Sutta; tales of **paccekabuddhas** in the Commentary to the Khaggavisāṇa Sutta; the legendary tale of the five hundred **paccekabuddhas** mentioned in the Isigili Sutta; verses known as the 'stanzas illustrating the blessings of the **samaṇa**' (**samaṇabhadragāthā**); and the myth of the 'origins of kingship', as related in the Agañña Sutta of the Dīgha Nikāya.

**The Khaggavisāṇa Sutta**

**The King as Ruler (Sn 35: daṇḍa)**

The first stanza of the Khaggavisāṇa Sutta opens with a reference to the **daṇḍa** (rod/ stick/ weapon)

> 'Having laid down the rod against all creatures
> Not hurting even one of them.'
>
> (**sabbesu bhūtesu nidhāya daṇḍaṁ**
> **aviheṭhayaṁ aññataram pi tesaṁ**)

It is no accident that the theme of the **daṇḍa** should come at the beginning of a Sutta whose main thesis is 'renunciation'; for the first fruit or advantage of becoming a **samaṇa**, according to the Sāmaññaphala Sutta, is abstention from harming others.[111] The instrument of the **daṇḍa** can signify 'oppression', 'punishment' or 'justice' and has become for this reason a symbol par excellence of regal power.[112] The Laws of Manu say 'let the king always uplift his rod'[113] and in the Mahābhārata it states that 'the use of the rod is the function of the king'.[114] The **daṇḍa** came to symbolise the king's rulership because both Hindu and Buddhist lore held that kingship arose as a punitive institution, charged with the responsibility of imposing law and order. As supreme secular authority, the king alone possessed the necessary power to establish stability in society. He acted as protector of 'rights' and the 'status quo' by dint of punishing those who offended against them. The term **daṇḍanīti** came to be the word for the science of government or polity in Ancient India. Since the utterances of **pacceka-buddhas** in the Jātaka tales are invariably addressed to kings then the 'verses' of the Khaggavisāṇa Sutta may also have constituted utterances addressed to kings.

**The King as Conqueror (Sn 42: cātuddisā)**

'He is a man of the four regions and not hostile,
Being contented with whatever happens;
A fearless overcomer of dangers,
One should wander alone like a rhinoceros.'

**(cātuddiso appaṭigho ca hoti**
**santussamāno itarītarena**
**parissayānam sahitā acchambhī**
**eko care khaggavisāṇakappo.)**

The phrase **cātuddiso...hoti** (He is a man of the four regions) can be read as an epithet either for a 'king' or for one who cultivates the **brahmavihāra** meditations.[115] In chapter four we shall show that the particular formulation given to the **brahmavihāras** is closely analogous to the formulation of certain sacrificial rituals performed by the king: both employ the spatial concepts of the 'regions' and both are methods of surmounting dangers. For example, in the Aitareya Brāhmaṇa it says of the Punarābhiṣeka Ceremony performed at the **rājasūya** sacrifice that the king is 'free from harm and injury, unoppressed, protected on every side; by the form of the threefold knowledge he wanders (**saṁcarati**) through all the quarters (**diśā**), finding support (**pratiṣṭhā**) in the world of Indra'.[116] This description might apply as much to a **muni** and adept of the **brahmavihāras** as to a monarch. In chapter one we saw that the muni is a wanderer who acquires sovereignty over the world by means of the threefold knowledge; and the **brahmavihāras** ward the adept against harm and injury. We may note also the use of the term **sahitar** (overcomer) in the same verse. This is a martial term, meaning 'one who conquers' or 'defeats'.[117] As the king - literally or by ritual - conquers the **cātuddisā**, and so establishes his sovereignty and secures his own protection, the one who cultivates the **brahma-vihāras** conquers by the power of meditation the **cātuddisā**, etc.

In the opening section of the Khaggavisāṇa Sutta (Sn.42) there is an implied reference to the **brahma-vihāras**, and towards the end of the same Sutta (Sn.73) all four are listed:

'Constantly cultivating loving-kindness, equanimity, compassion release and sympathy;
Unobstructed by the whole world,
One should wander alone like a rhinoceros.

**(mettaṁ upekhaṁ karuṇaṁ vimuttiṁ**
**āsevamāno muditañ ca kāle**
**sabbena lokena avirujjhamāno**
**eko care khaggavisāṇakappo.)**

The term **loka** (viz. **sabba loka**) used here can mean either the 'spatial' world or the 'inhabitants' of that world. In this sense loka is the semantic equivalent of the English term 'world' which also has this double sense. In this passage both meanings are involved: the **ekacarin** can move spatially throughout the world because the inhabitants do not 'obstruct' or 'oppose' (**avirujjhati**) him. The brahma-vihāras conduce toward physical freedom because they placate the 'beings' who might constitute that 'obstruction'.[118]

## The King as Renouncer (Sn 46)

The convention of **kṣatriya** renunciation is directly evidenced in one of the Khaggavisāṇa Sutta verses:

> 'If one cannot find a friend who is a preceptor,
> A wise companion whom it is beneficial to abide with,
> As a king abandoning his kingdom
> One should wander alone like a rhinoceros.'
>
> **(No ce labhetha nipakaṁ sahayaṁ**
> **saddhiṁcaraṁ sādhuvihāri dhīram**
> **rājā va ratthaṁ vijitam pahāya**
> **eko care khaggavisāṇakappo.)**

This verse occurs several times in the Pali Canon and in the Buddhist Sanskrit tradition which is an indication that it was a widely-known and generally accepted stanza.[119] It also has the reference to the king abandoning his throne.

## The Paccekabuddha as King (Sn 72: **rājā migānaṁ**)

'like the strong-jawed lion, by might
king of the animals, overcoming as he wanders,
One should resort to remote areas;
One should wander alone like a rhinoceros.'

(**Sīho yathā dāṭhabalī pasayha
rājā migānaṁ abhibhuyyacārī
sevetha pantāni senāsanāni
eko care khaggavisāṇa kappo.**)

The **ekacarin** is here compared to the lion, king of the animals (**rājā migānaṁ**). His identification with the lion symbolises the ascetic's mastery over the dangers inherent in the terrestrial world. The lion epitomises 'fearlessness'. For example, in the preceding verse (Sn 71), the **ekacarin** is compared to the lion because the lion 'does not tremble at sounds' (**saddesu asantasanto**). Elsewhere in the Sutta-nipāta (546) the lion is said to have 'abandoned fear and terror' (**pahīna-bhayabherava**). The comparison with the lion follows from the fact that both ascetic and animal inhabit similar terrain: 'remote areas' (**pantāni senāsanāni**), the forests and the four regions (**cātuddisā**).[120] The **paccekabuddha** himself is compared to the lion in the Paccekabuddhāpadāna and the Niddesa.[121]

Lion imagery is also used to represent the Buddha. The 'lion-roar' (**sīhanāda**), for example, is used as a metaphor for the Buddha's act of preaching:

'He, the most excellent of all beings, best of persons,
Bull among men, the most excellent of all creatures,

> Will turn the wheel (of **dhamma**) in the forest named after the isis (**isivhaya vane**)
> Like the roaring lion, the strong lord of animals.'[122]

As the lion's roar demonstrates its ascendancy over the other forest creatures so the Buddha's act of teaching, his turning the wheel of the **dhamma**, indicates his pre-eminence among those who lay claim to religious and spiritual authority, the **aññatitthiyas** (wanderers of other views) and **parappavādas** (those who hold alien doctrines).[123] He is stated to utter the lion's roar 'in the assemblies (**parisā**) where men congregate';[124] he leaves his lair, like the lion, surveys the four regions (**cātuddisā**) and roars three times.[125] It is said that he is **sammāsambuddha** because he 'rightly' (**sammā**) roars the lion's roar. The metaphor of the lion's roar does not occur in conjunction with **paccekabuddhas** since they do not teach **dhamma**.

## Rājāhaṁsa

Another regal motif occurring in Buddhist narratives is that of the comparison of **paccekabuddhas** with the **haṁsa** (goose).[126] In Buddhist folklore the **haṁsa** is regarded as the king of the birds. [127] In the Dhammapada it states that 'geese travel on the path of the sun through the air by magic (**iddhi**)'.[128] In **paccekabuddha** stories this same image of the goose in flight is often used to illustrate the **paccekabuddha**'s own powers of levitation; so, for instance, one story tells how levitating **paccekabuddhas** are mistaken for a flock of birds by onlooking lay-persons.[129] The figure of the **muni** too seems to have connections with the concept of **haṁsa**: in the Sutta-nipāta it says that the householder is to the **muni** as the peacock is to the goose - the latter surpasses the former in 'swiftness' (**java**).[130] Interestingly, the same word is used as a superlative for **manas** (mind) in the Ṛg Veda: 'mind is the swiftest (**javiṣṭham**) of birds',[131] once again showing the seminal connection between **muni** and **manas**.

## Janinda

In a verse from the Paccekabbuddhāpadāna a third type of regal epithet, **janindā** (lord or ruler of men), is applied to the **paccekabuddha**.[132] Inda (Skt.Indra) is another title of Sakka, who is said to be **dev'indā** (king of the gods).[133]

In summary, the three hierarchies of kingship - animal, bird and human - signify different but complementary kinds of power. The **paccekabuddha**'s identification with the lion, the king of the beasts, signifies his supremacy at the mundane level of earthly existence; his identification with the king of the swans indicates his supremacy at the supra-wordly level; and his identification with the lord of men his supremacy on a spiritual level. These correspond respectively to power over 'danger' (**bhaya**), to 'magical power' (**iddhānubhāva**) or power over empirical forms, and realizing the highest form of spirituality by achieving the status of 'supreme person' (**uttamaporisa**).[134]

## Tales of Paccekabuddhas in the Commentary to the Khaggavisāṇa Sutta

In the Introduction we noted that each verse

of the Khaggavisāṇa Sutta was considered by Buddhist tradition to comprise a **vyākaraṇa** (explanation) or **udāna** (utterance) of an individual **paccekabuddha**, depicting the vital factor in his own attainment of **paccekabodhi**. The Pali Commentaries to the Khaggavisāṇa Sutta contain narratives telling how each **paccekabuddha** came to be enlightened. In each and every narrative the prospective **paccekabuddha** is represented as a king of Bārānasī. This poses the question of how and why the later Pali tradition came to identify the authors of the Khaggavisāṇa Sutta with monarchs of Bārānasī. We have already identified the origins of the **paccekabuddha** tradition with the 'renouncing **kṣatriya**' of Videha epitomized in the mythical figure of King Nimi. A renouncing **kṣatriya** or 'king' therefore served as the initial prototype for the **paccekabuddha** concept. Bearing this in mind, we approach the above question by considering the Buddhist tradition's own genealogies of the Buddha. In the Singhalese Chronicles, the Mahāvaṁsa and the Dīpavaṁsa, there are genealogical lists which inform us that the great dynasty of Videha to which Nimi belonged was superseded by another dynasty centred at Bārānasī.[135] This latter was the last major dynasty before the rise of the Sākya dynasty, the one to which the Buddha himself belonged. Since this is the only Bārānasī dynasty mentioned in these genealogies then it seems not unreasonable to suppose that the tradition which represented the authors of the Khaggavisāṇa verses as kings of Bārānasī had in mind this particular dynasty. Although the genealogies are no use for dating, owing to their exaggerated and stereotyped numeration, they do at least inform us of what were believed to be the great dynasties of the past and provide some idea of their chronological sequence. We find, for example, that the sequence of dynasties here corresponds with the dynastic setting featured in the Jātaka recension of stories about **paccekabuddhas**. These stories are set either during the period of the Videha dynasty of Makhādeva or during the Bārānasī dynasty of King Brahmadatta. A quite significant observation relating to these stories is that the ones set during the Videha dynasty depict kings as the only persons to become **paccekabuddhas**, whereas the ones set within the Baranasi dynasty do not mention kings becoming **paccekabuddhas**.[136] Furthermore, **paccekabuddhas** in the latter era are represented as giving instruction (**ovāda**) to kings, whereas **paccekabuddhas** of the former era are not associated with instruction at all.[137]

This genealogical and narrative information reinforces the hypothesis that the Śramaṇa Movement originated in Videha. The shift of spiritual ancestry from the Videha to the Bārānasī dynasties here signifies the spread of the movement to the Kingdom of Kāsi. According to Thakur there is some historical evidence that Kāsi took over hegemony from Videha.[138] The Kāsi phase in the evolution of the Śramaṇa Tradition is indicated by persons other than kings becoming **paccekabuddhas** and by **paccekabuddhas** themselves acquiring an identity as religious teachers. In the light of these observations the Baranasi period seems to have evidenced an evolutionary transition in the renunciation tradition - from its beginnings as an unilaterally-inspired phenomenon to a coordinated movement - laying the foundations eventually for the development of sectarian differences.

The authors of the commentaries to the Khaggavisāṇa Sutta probably located within the Bārānasī era those who composed its verses because Bārānasī was the place where the Buddha had set the wheel of the **dhamma** rolling, being the place where to all intents and purposes the Sākyamuni 'cultus' began. The transition from the dispensation of the **paccekabuddha** to that of the **sammāsambuddha** was effected by the Buddha's initial act of teaching at Bārānasī in that it marked the first step in founding a religious community. That the authors of the Khaggavisāṇa verses should have been represented as kings of Bārānasī can be explained simply as the persistence of the archetypal myth that **śramaṇas** were 'renouncing kings'. Our inquiry regarding the identities of the authors of the Khaggavisāṇa verses has therefore brought to light evidence of a secondary stage in the evolution of the Śramaṇa Movement.

## The Legend of the 'Five Hundred' Paccekabuddhas

Both the Pali texts and the Mahāvastu record a tradition of 'five hundred' **paccekabuddhas**.[139] No precise significance need be attached to this number since it is a literary stereotype denoting a sizeable collection of people.[140] The story of the birth and enlightenment of these five hundred ascetics is also found in the Mahāvastu and the Pali Commentaries.[141] Their legend is quite evidently not original but a fabrication of a number of themes or motifs that have traditionally come to be associated with the figure of the **paccekabuddha**. It is said that the 'five hundred' are offspring of one mother whose name, is Padumavatī, (lotus flower). In Buddhism the lotus flower is an archetypal symbol of 'transcendence'; in Brahmanic ritual the lotus leaf symbolises the womb.[142] In the Pali sources, Padumavatī gives birth to just one child, a boy called Mahāpaduma (Great Lotus Flower), but then other boys emerge from her 'after-birth moisture' (**yonisaṅsedaja**). The explanation for this peculiar birth motif may be found within the canonical sources themselves which refer to four different types of life-production or generation: the egg, the womb, 'spontaneous uprising' and 'moisture' (**saṅsedaja**).[143] **Saṅsedaja** means 'putrifying substances'; it therefore seems probable that the author of this story had in mind a 'pool of dirty water' when he used the term since this is one kind of matrix it signifies.[144] Hence the motif of emerging from the 'afterbirth moisture' symbolises the **paccekabuddhas** as 'lotuses' rising, unsullied, out of the polluted water. This traditional Buddhist image of 'purity' and 'transcendence' is used of the **ekacarin** and the **muni**. Later Buddhist iconography represents **paccekabuddha** and **sammāsambuddha** as seated on the lotus.[145]

The lotus flower figures in the story of their enlightenment too. When they are sixteen years old they visit their father's lake. Here they contemplate the lotuses blossoming and dying in the water and, as a result, discern the notion of 'impermanence' and attain to the 'knowledge of **paccekabodhiñāṇa**'. Afterwards each of them sits cross-legged in the middle of a lotus. At sunrise (nb. the time of day when the Buddha's own enlightenment occurred), they become transformed into '**samaṇas**' and fly away to Mount Gandhamādana.

Another archetypal feature to be noticed is their kṣatriyan identity: they are represented as the sons of King Brahmadatta and Queen Padumavatī of Bārānasī. Therefore they too are linked with the Bārānasī dynasty, in the same way as the **paccekabuddhas** who uttered the verses of the Khaggavisāṇa Sutta. There is evidently some ulterior motive for identifying the'five hundred' **paccekabuddhas** with

Bārānasī since the Isigili Sutta, the earlier of the two traditions, identifies them instead with the area of Rājagaha. We shall endeavour in a moment to unravel this particular incongruity.

There are two further points to be noted concerning the legend: Firstly, according to Jātaka sources, the mother of the **paccekabuddhas**, Padumavatī, is a former rebirth of Uppalavaṇṇā, one of the Buddha's two chief female-disciples. She is distinguished for her powers of **iddhi** like her chief male-disciple counterpart, Mogallāna.[146] The powers which Uppalavaṇṇā possesses are a distinctive feature of **paccekabuddhas**, as we noted in chapter two. Secondly, there is a curious typological resemblance between one aspect of the story of the 'five hundred' **paccekabuddhas** and a facet of the legend of the Buddha himself. According to tradition, Siddhattha fathered only one flesh-born child, the boy Rāhula, but in a 'religious' sense Siddhattha is also said to be the father of the **bhikkhusaṅgha** and of **arahants**. These are referred to as **samaṇa Sākyaputtiyā** (sons of the renouncer of the Sākyas)[147] and **puttā-orasā** (sons of the breast).[148] In the legend of the five hundred **paccekabuddhas**, Mahāpadma, who is first-born among them , forms the counterpart of Rāhula, the sole flesh-born child, whilst the remaining number, the 'moistureborn' ones form the counterpart of the Buddha's own disciples.

Consequently, the legend of the birth and enlightenment of the 'five hundred' **paccekabuddhas** demonstrates that the Buddhist tradition largely apprehended the figure of the **paccekabuddha** through a series of archetypes or fixed images - viz., five hundred, royalty, lotus, Gandhamādana. This would seem to imply that the concept of the **paccekabuddha** no longer referred to a living tradition but rather to a past tradition sufficiently remote for its significance to have become predominantly symbolical and mythical.

## The Verses on the Blessings of Being a 'Śramaṇa'

In the Buddhist narrative tradition there exists a collection of verses, entitled the **'samaṇa bhadragāthā'** (Skt.**śramaṇabhadragāthā**) which set forth the benefits of being a **'śramaṇa'** (See Appendix.III). There are two extant versions, one in Pali, the other occurring in the Mahāvastu.[149]The seminal themes and non-sectarian character of these verses suggest that they belong to a relatively early stage in the evolution of the Śramaṇa Tradition. In the narrative context in which they occur they happen to be linked with the Videha-Bārānasī dynasties. The Pali tradition ascribes the authorship of these verses to a **paccekabuddha** called Sonaka.[150] and some of the verses clearly imply that a tradition of renunciation existed among kings.

## The Myth of the 'Origins of Kingship' in the Agañña Sutta

Finally, as part of the evidence linking the concept of the **paccekabuddha** or prototype **śramaṇa** with kingship we examine the myth of the 'origins of kingship' occurring within the Agañña Sutta of the Dīgha Nikāya.[151] **Paccekabuddhas** or **samaṇas** are not mentioned here but it becomes apparent that the functions of the king in the secular world and the **samaṇa** in the spiritual sphere are directly analogous. We can also compare this interpretation of kingship origins with the Nami Pavvajjā section of the Uttarādhyayana Sūtra which is also concerned with the role and relationship in society.

In our previous discussion of the Nami Pavvajjā we saw that it defends and justifies the view that the king should renounce his kingdom and become an ascetic. The Agañña Sutta, by contrast, emphasizes the obligations and duties the king has towards his subjects as their ruler. The office of kingship is not censored, as in the Nami Pavvajjā, but evaluated positively. The different perspectives of the Nami Pavvajjā and the Agañña Sutta are an indication that they are the product of two different time periods: the proto-**śramaṇa** period on the one hand and the post-Buddhist era on the other. The proto-**śramaṇa** ideal is that kingship should be abandoned because it merely reinforces bankrupt Brahmanic values. In due course, however, kingship acquired a new respectability among the **śramaṇa**, and by the advent of the Sākyamuni era the notion had been re-evaluated in accordance with Sramanic societal objectives.

The Agañña Sutta teaches that kingship first arose in response to the need to provide a check to the growing immorality and anarchy in society. The people **(mahājana)** come to a decision that it is time to put a stop to the alarming growth rate of immorality in society. So they select from among the populace the person having the most perfect form (**abhirūpa**), appearance (**dassanīya**), grace (**pāsādika**) and power (**mahesakkha**) and confer on him the power of kingship. Herein the first king comes to acquire the title **Mahāsammata** (the Great Chosen One). It is to be noticed that a person is not made a monarch by appeal to 'divine right' or 'divine appointment' as in the Brahmanic interpretation,[152] but the right to the office is awarded by contract (**quid** pro **quo**) from the people. The conditions of this contract between king and people are such that

The king is expected to

a. be indignant (**khīyati**) rightly (**sammā**).
b. condemn or censure (**garahati**) rightly.
c. banish or exile (**pabbajeti**) rightly.

The people are expected to

a. hand over to the king a share (**bhāga**) of their rice (i.e., produce).

This interpretation of how kingship arose is then followed by definitions of the terms **khattiya** and **rājā**: **khattiya** is said to mean 'lord of the fields' (**khettānaṁ pati**); **rājā** to mean 'he delights others by means of the **dhamma**' (**dhammena pare rañjeti**).

The terms and concepts here chosen for the interpretation and representation of monarchic function have striking parallels with those used to describe the function of the **śramaṇa** in society. For example, the principle of a contract between king and people (**mahājana**) also obtains between the **paccekabuddha** (qua **śramaṇa**) and the **mahājana**: just as the citizen is required to give a share of his rice to the king in return for protection, so when the donor gives a portion (**bhāga**) of his rice as food to the **paccekabuddha** he acquires merit (**puñña**) which serves to 'protect' him. In Early Buddhist imagery merit-earning is compared to sowing a seed in a field (**khetta**) so that it will grow into a plant and yield fruit (**phala**). According to the Agañña Sutta the **khattiya** is a 'lord of the fields' (**khettānaṁ pati**). There is a sense in which this same expression may also depict the soteriological status of **buddha**:

as the 'supreme intermediaries' through which the spiritual growth or transformation of others takes place, they can be seen as 'lords' or 'mediators' of the governing principles in the universe. The notion of 'buddha-fields'(P.**buddhakhetta**; Skt.**buddhakṣetra**), where the right conditions exist for the ripening of merit, is a doctrinal feature of later Hīnayāna and of Mahāyāna Buddhism.

As in the Agañña Sutta, kings (rājāno) are said to delight others by upholding **dhamma**, **samaṇa** correspondingly delight others by teaching **dhamma**. One of the principle meanings of the root verb √**raj** from which **rañj-eti** and **rājā** are derived is 'to shine'. We saw that **paccekabuddhas** transmit their religious power non-verbally by emitting, as it were, an aura of light. As the right physical appearance or form is a necessary qualification for kingship, so the appearance and form of the **paccekabuddha** is a decisive factor in the response of the prospective donor. Indeed, the term **pāsādika** is found to be used of both **paccekabuddhas** and kings.[153]

According to the Agañña Sutta the monarch is expected always to do things 'rightly' (sammā); Sākyamuni himself is distinguished as a **sammāsambuddha**, a title which betokens his sovereignty. Another listed responsibility of the king is that he must 'banish' or 'exile' (pabbajeti) the harmful elements within society. The term **pabbajeti** is the causative form of the verb **pabbajati** describing the process of a householder becoming a **bhikkhu** or **samaṇa**. The king therefore exiles and censors others,whereas the **samaṇa** is one who has censored his own former way of life and exiled himself from it,as exemplified by the story of Nami. What the king imposes on others, the **samaṇa** imposes on himself. This marks an important directional change from external to internal constraints, from coercion of others to introspection and self-awareness. It is this awakening of the **kṣatriya**'s moral sensibilities to the notion of **hiṁsā** (injury) which heralded the onset of the Śramaṇa Movement.

**Nimi in the Four Nikāyas and the Sutta-nipāta**

Earlier in this chapter we noted the existence of a core of myth which testifies to the beginnings of the tradition of renunciation (**pravrajyā**), and which is common to the literature of a number of sectarian traditions - Brahmanic, Jain and Buddhist. We also saw that the common denominator in the different versions of this myth is the figure of Nimi, King of Videha, whom we argued became the prototype for the concept of the **paccekabuddha**. We now propose to draw to a conclusion the argument that Nimi formed the prototype for the **paccekabuddha** concept by examining the form given to the Nimi myth in the first four Nikāyas of the Pali Canon. The very fact that a rendering of the myth is to be found in the four Nikāyas is an indication that some sort of historical continuity or contiguity existed between Buddhism and the **paccekabuddha** tradition. Even more importantly, the way in which the myth happens to be utilised and adapted provides evidence of an attempt by the authors of the Nikāyas to erect a Sākyamuni 'cultus'.

The Nimi myth is present in the Nikāyas in three forms: in the story of Daḷhanemi; in the doctrine of 'the great man' (**mahāpurisa**); and in the use of 'kingship' concepts to represent the soteriological significance of the Buddha. Before examining these topics we need to make one preliminary observation. The **paccekabuddha** is not mentioned explicitly in any of the passages we shall be considering. There are grounds for arguing that the **paccekabuddha** tradition is nevertheless being tacitly acknowledged when we explore the uses of symbolism and particular synonyms in the relevant passages. The lack of an explicit reference to the **paccekabuddha** might be thought a weakness in our argument; on the contrary, it serves to strengthen the contention that the differentiation of **buddhas** into two types was a transitional phenomenon developing out of the tendency of the Śramaṇa Tradition to ramify into separate groups having their own distinctive points of emphasis. We therefore maintain that the material we are considering is too early for explicit dogmatic judgments to be found, but that distinctions are beginning to express themselves in symbolical form.

## The Story of Daḷhanemi

The story of King Daḷhanemi is told in the Cakkavatti-sīhanāda Sutta of the Dīgha Nikāya.[154] We have not seen fit to incorporate it within the Nimi complex of legends - unlike the Makhādeva story which is also found in the four Nikāyas - for the simple reason that, unlike the Makhādeva tale, it is not a **jātaka** genre story. Instead, Daḷhanemi is patently a mythical figure utilised as a symbol to represent Sakyamuni's role in his capacity as a **sammāsambuddha**.

The Sutta tells how the Buddha teaches his **bhikkhu** the story of Daḷhanemi to illustrate the need to preserve the 'tradition' founded by himself. King Daḷhanemi possesses the status of a **cakkavatti** (Skt.**cakravartin**: universal sovereign). This status is symbolised by the presence of a wheel in the sky above the palace: the **dibbaṁ cakka-ratanaṁ** (heavenly jewel wheel). As long as the **dibbaṁ cakkaratanaṁ** is visible to the king, his sovereignty is secure. If it begins to eclipse (**osakkhita**) [155] and wane, it is a warning to the king that he is growing old and approaching death, and therefore should relinquish his throne to the eldest son and become a **pabbajita**. When the **dibbaṁ cakkaratanaṁ** starts to do this in his own reign, Daḷhanemi immediately heeds its warning and becomes a **pabbajita**. He is now for the first time referred to as a **rājīsi**. Here we may recall that the 'renouncing' kings Nimi (3) and Nami (1) were referred to also as **rāja-ṛṣi**. Seven days after Daḷhanemi's **pabbajjā** the **dibbaṁ cakka-ratanaṁ** vanishes completely. Its total disappearance signifies that, in the transition from one generation of ruler to another, the achievements of the outgoing king are susceptible to undoing. These achievements are safeguarded, however, if the successor to the throne consults his father, now a **rājīsi**, for advice on how to rule the newly-inherited kingdom. If he does so, the **dibbaṁ cakkaratanaṁ** will once more appear, and the new monarch will assume the same **cakkavatti** status as his predecessor. The newly-manifest image of the **dibbaṁ cakka-ratanaṁ** will move in all four directions of the compass (**cātuddisā**), and the king with his army will follow and consolidate his sovereignty in these regions. If at the time of accession each new monarch consults his predecessor (i.e., the **rājīsi**) on how to rule, then the tradition of the **cakkavatti** will prove to be a long established one. However, if any new monarch fails to do this, his power will decline and the political and moral dissolution of society will set in. If this occurs anarchy and injustice will prevail throughout the world over many generations.

There are several reasons for supposing that

the story of Daḷhanemi is an adapted version of the Nimi myth. In the first place, there is an obvious similarity between the names Daḷhanemi (strong-felly) and Nimi: In the Nimi Jātaka, for instance, King Nimi is referred to as **nemikumāra** (Prince Nemi).[156] Secondly, Daḷhanemi figures in indefinite past time (**bhūta-pubba**) as a mythical personage and represents, like Nimi, the paradigm 'renouncing' king. The central theme of the story - the need for the new monarch to heed the counsel of the late monarch - represents a modified version of the Brahmanic doctrine of the **kṣatriya**'s dependence on the **brāhmaṇa** [157]. The new king acquires the capacity to become a **cakkavatti** only by obedience to the counsel of the **rājīsi**; similarly, in the Brahmanical Rājasūya Sacrifice, the attributes of kingship are not the inherent possession of the royal prince but are conferred by the superintendent of the rites, the **brāhmaṇa**.[158] Both traditions therefore subscribe to the doctrine of the dependance of 'temporal' power (**kṣatra**) on 'spiritual' power - conceived of as **brahman** in Brahmanism and **dhamma** (the counsel of the **śramaṇa**) in Buddhism.

It is to be noticed too that the **dibbaṁ cakka-ratanaṁ**, symbol of the king's office, resembles the wooden ceremonial wheel used in the Brahmanic kingship rites. In these rites the wheel is firstly mounted or elevated on a post, spatially the highest component of the ritual; by analogy the **cakka-ratana** is set in the heaven (**dibbaṁ**). This signifies that all lower, mundane levels of 'power' exist only by sanction of a higher authority. Secondly, the wheel is turned clockwise by the king through one hundred and eighty degrees and this signifies his mastery or conquest of the quarters of the earth. By comparison, the **dibbaṁ cakka-ratanaṁ** revolves in a clockwise direction through the four points of the compass, signifying the monarch's universal sovereignty. In addition the **dibbaṁ cakka-ratanaṁ** traverses the sky in the four directions, symbolising flight. The power of flight is not only a characteristic of **paccekabuddha** but in Indian folklore signifies the divinity of kings.[159]

At face value the **dibbaṁ cakka-ratanaṁ** would seem to be a symbol for the moon.[160] It is located in the sky (**dibbaṁ**), waxes and wanes (nb. the time-span of seven days equals a quarter-phase of the moon), and is 'luminous' (after traversing the four regions it is said to return to the royal capital and remain above the judgment hall 'illuminating' [**upa-sobhayati**] the inner apartments of the king. Thus the **dibbaṁ cakka-ratanaṁ** is a symbol of the spiritual and moral awareness of the king. The moon represents an important symbol in the context of kingship renunciation. We have already seen, for example, that both the **muni** and the **paccekabuddha** are likened to the 'moon's orb freed from Rāhu'; and in a certain Jātaka story a King of Videha decides to 'go forth' when he sees Rāhu covering the light of the moon.[161] In Buddhist sources, therefore, the full-moon symbolises the '**śramaṇa**'s emancipation from all ties'.[162] The use of moon-imagery also indicates the seminal link between **ksatriya** and **sramana**. In Vedic tradition the **asura**, Svarbhānu (later Rāhu), is said to cause eclipses and Indra is said to combat him.[163] Hence a full-moon was the sign of Indra in supremacy; furthermore the Indra worship festival reaches its climax on the fifteenth of the month at the time of the full-moon.[164] In Buddhist myth, Indra is supplanted by the Buddha as the one who thwarts Rāhu's attempts to swallow the moon.[165] The Buddha's assumption of Indra's traditional function denotes that 'renunciation', the act of becoming a śramaṇa, is no longer a sufficient goal in itself - one must in addition follow the teaching of Sākyamuni.[166]

The stories of both Makhādeva and Daḷhanemi have been incorporated into the Buddhist Canon in order to illustrate the vital importance of preserving 'tradition'. The two figures represent important counterparts - Makhādeva signifying the era of the pre-Buddhist, and Daḷhanemi the post-Buddhist, dispensation. By virtue of his own act of renunciation (**pabbajjā**) each monarch instigates a tradition: Makhadeva, the tradition of **pabbajjā** (and the **brahma-vihāra** meditations), and Daḷhanemi, the tradition of the **dhamma-rājā** and **cakkavatti** (the universal sovereign who rules by the principles of justice). The dynasty of Makhādeva symbolises the continuity of the older tradition in the pre-Sākyamuni era, and the dynasty of Daḷhanemi the Buddha's **dhamma** in the post-Sākyamuni era. Each story is intended to illustrate that it only needs one single generation to depart from the established tradition for that tradition to become irretrievably damaged. The consequences are far greater, however, in the post-Sākyamuni era, because the Buddha's **dhamma** has universal implications; the welfare of the entire world is considered to depend on it. This is an extremely important point to note, for the claim to 'universal' significance constitutes the fundamental affirmation or credo of the Sākyamuni 'cultus'. That is why Daḷhanemi is portrayed as a **cakkavatti** and why the myth is centred upon the theme of the **cakkavatti**.

It is immediately apparent that in this story the figure of King Daḷhanemi is supposed to symbolize the Buddha and that Daḷhanemi's own descendants are meant to represent the **saṅgha**. The declared purpose of the discourse constituting the Cakkavatti-sīhanāda Sutta is to convince the **bhikkhu-saṅgha** that they must not lose sight of the value of the teaching that has been imparted to them but must endeavour to observe and preserve it for future generations. The tale of Dalhanemi is a cautionary one told to illustrate what can happen when the **dhamma** is not cherished by a given generation: Society falls into decline, immorality and suffering abound and social anarchy results. The Sutta's underlying assumption is that the existence of the **dhamma** is perpetually under threat owing to the death of individuals who maintain it; such deaths are an inescapable fact of existence. So, for example, even the Buddha himself must eventually die and no longer influence and control the fate of the **dhamma**. The **saṅgha** should understand this and, having reconciled themselves to the fact of the Buddha's death, accept that the responsibility for the maintenance of the **dhamma** now devolves upon them.

A further clue in deciphering the myth lies in the notion of **pabbajjā**. When Daḷhanemi sees the **dibbaṁ cakka-ratanaṁ** waning he decides to become a **pabbajita**; in a similar fashion, Prince Siddhattha renounces the world when he encounters the 'four signs' (**cattāri nimittāni**) of old age, sickness, death and the **samaṇa**.[167] Daḷhanemi's renunciation makes it possible for the **dibbaṁ cakka-ratanaṁ** to remain; similarly, the Buddha's renunciation ensures that there will be a **sammāsambuddha** to initiate the teaching of the **dhamma** as well as a **saṅgha** to perpetuate it throughout the generations.

The concept of the **rājīsi**, the king who has become a renouncer and who knows the **dhamma** (the principles of correct rule) is the key concept in the preservation of the values which maintain the existence and prosperity of society. The original significance of this particular use of the term **rājīsi** derives from the Nimi myth. In his capacity as a mighty king with the power to use force Nimi is the archetype of 'original' man, the Brahmanic **rājarṣi**. Forsaking this role for an existence characterised instead by **avihiṁsā** (refraining from injury), he becomes the original **śramaṇa**, the archetype of spiritual man, the Śramanic **rājarṣi**. As the Brahmanic **rājarṣi** maintains the sacrifice which upholds reality, the Śramanic **rājarṣi** maintains the **dhamma** for the same reason.

Therefore, the essential Nimi myth which depicts the origins of the Śramaṇa Movement has been re-adapted by the Buddhists in the form of the Daḷhanemi myth to illustrate their own values and dilemmas at a later stage in the evolution of the Śramaṇa Tradition. At one time the significant factor in the preservation of values had been the custom of **pabbajjā** exemplified by the **paccekabuddha**. Now the **bhikkhu-saṅgha** inherits that role. In the post-Sākyamuni era the dynasty of the **isi-saṅgha** supersedes the **paccekabuddha** or **isayo** dynasty. By the same token the episode of the four signs (**cattāri nimmitāni**) that we have just referred to in connection with the Buddha's own decision to renounce the world represents a re-enactment within the 'cultus' of the archetypal myth of the renouncing kṣatriya: king, sign, renunciation. One is even tempted to argue that the numerical correspondence of these 'four' signs with the 'four' kings who became **paccekabuddhas** and their signs is more than just coincidence. In other words, the episode of the four signs in the legend of the Buddha replicates the legend of the four paradigm proto-śramaṇas.[168]

## The Doctrine of the 'Mahāpurisa'

We have just seen that the Cakkavatti-sīhanāda Sutta provides evidence of how the Buddha's function as a founder of a tradition can be conveyed in terms of an existing paradigm: As Nimi/Makhādeva founded the dispensation of **pabbajjā** and the tradition of the śramaṇa; Sākyamuni founds the dispensation of the **dhamma** and the tradition of the **saṅgha**.

The Nikāya doctrine of the **mahāpurisa** (Skt. **mahāpuruṣa**) also comprises an important piece of evidence in support of the thesis that **paccekabuddhas** are to be identified as the historical antecedents of Buddhism.[169] According to this doctrine, a **khattiya** (Skt.kṣatriya) born with 'thirty-two' signs (**lakkhaṇāni**) on his body is destined to become either a **cakkavatti** or a **sammāsambuddha**.[170] The importance of the **mahāpurisa** doctrine is that it furnishes us with a definition of the **sammāsambuddha**. It defines the **sammāsambuddha** in terms of two basic categories:

a. Kingship. The **sammāsambuddha** is a **cakkavatti**-designate. A **mahāpurisa** is confronted by two options when he reaches the age of consent : he may remain as a monarch and eventually acquire the stature of a **cakkavatti**; or he may abandon the heirdom and become a renouncer.

b. Renunciation. A **mahāpurisa** will become a **sammāsambuddha**, if, and only if, he forsakes his heritage as a secular monarch and becomes a renouncer.

It is to be noticed that there is no mention of the experience of bodhi in this definition. The omission is highly significant for it indicates that the conception of a **sammāsambuddha** is primarily soteriological not buddhological. This means he is defined functionally, that is, in respect of others, not solely in terms of his own type of spiritual or meditational accomplishment. This particular definition also makes it apparent that the idea of the archetypal renouncing monarch (viz.,Nimi) formed the original 'blueprint' for the concept of a **buddha**. The interpretation given to the idea of **buddha** in the **mahāpurisa** doctrine is seen to correspond to the representation of **paccekabodhi** in the legend of the four kings and in other Jātaka tales - as the conviction that 'household-life' must be abandoned for **pabbajjā**. In view of the absence of any mention of a **bodhi** experience in the **mahāpurisa** formulation of the concept of a **sammāsambuddha**, we must infer that the representation of the Buddha's **bodhi** as a unique,unprecedented experience - the standard interpretation of Nikāya doctrine - is a form of superimposition on the part of the 'cultus'. This commits us to the interpretation that Sākyamuni's distinctiveness resided not in any claim to exercise a monopoly over the ability to experience **bodhi** without reliance on a teacher or corpus of teaching but rather in his characterisation as a **bhagavan** (lord) and 'teacher' (**satthar**).

## The Choice of Kingship Predicates to Represent the Soteriological Function of the Buddha

We have just seen that in the **mahāpurisa** formula the **sammāsambuddha** is defined as one who chooses 'renunciation' instead of 'kingship'. Thus the one and only factor which differentiates the 'secular king' from the **sammāsambuddha** is 'renunciation' - 'renunciation' becomes the crucial transmuting agent. In choosing to be a 'renouncer' the heir-apparent does not cease to be a 'king', rather he becomes a 'transformed' king - as we saw to be the case in the Nami Pavvajjā. The meaning of the symbolism is clear: by killing the 'secular' king (that is, by self-conquest) the 'spiritual' king is brought to life.Therefore, the legendary motif depicting Siddhattha to be a **khattiya** prince who renounces his future entitlement to the throne is simply an applied existing archetype. His 'renouncing king' identity assimilates him to the principle ideological standpoint of the **śramaṇa**: world-renunciation.

In the time which elapsed between the beginnings of the Śramaṇa Movement and the advent of the Sākyamuni 'cultus' one noteworthy development in the concept of kingship was the appearance of the concept of the **samrāj**[171] or **cakkavatti**, the monarch who by his superior 'might' and 'power' conquers the entire world, subjugating all other kings under his own authority. The figure of Sākyamuni is assimilated to the image of the **cakkavatti** because the title of **cakkavatti** conveys the 'universal' significance and 'world-transforming' character of his person and teaching. This idea receives its most eloquent canonical expression in the Sela Sutta:

Sela (a Brahman):

'"You (i.e. the Buddha) are worthy to be a king, a **cakkavatti**, a lord of the chariot
A conqueror of the four quarters, a lord of the Jambu grove.
Khattiyas and hostile kings become your

subjects;
Rule Gotama, king of kings, lord of man."

"I am a king, Sela", said the Lord
"An incomparable **dhamma-rājā**,
I turn the wheel with the dhamma, the wheel that cannot be turned back".'[172]

It was not considered injudicious to represent the Buddha by an inherently 'martial' symbol such as the **cakkavatti** since it was a concept that had been tempered and refined by the complementary notion of the **dhamma-rājā**: 'a king who conquers by **dhamma**, not by the **daṇḍa**...one who protects the people'.[173] We have, for instance, observed in the Buddhist theory of kingship and the Daḷhanemi myth that a king's right to rule depends not on his 'might' but on his capacity to rule according to principles of 'justice' (**dhamma**); if he does not rule justly then he loses the right to be king. Buddhism therefore absorbs the notion of 'power' entirely into the notion of 'ethical justice', so that the former cannot thrive without the latter.[174]

Significantly, the cakkavatti title distinguishes the figure of Sākyamuni from his antecedents, the **paccekabuddhas**. It defines the all-sufficiency and sovereignty of his teaching and, therefore, by implication, the beginning of a new era or dispensation (signified by the affirmation that the wheel 'cannot be turned back'), in which his 'cultus' provides the definitive path to **bodhi**.[175] We recall, however, that the Buddhist figure Nimi (3) and the Jain figure, Nami (1), are also classed as **cakkavatti**. This leads us to notice another subtle distinction between the Nimi and Sakyamuni myths: In the former case, the **kṣatriya** already has acceded to the throne and is therefore a king at the time he decides upon renunciation. In the wording of the **mahāpurisa** doctrine, however, it is the prince or heir-apparent, the one who has not yet succeeded to his rightful heritage as **cakkavatti**, who becomes a 'renouncer'. Whereas Nimi is depicted as a literal king, the attribution of 'kingship to Sākyamuni is primarily of symbolic significance. The same distinction applies to the Buddhicised notion of **rājīsi**. The term **rājīsi** is applied literally to Nimi and Nami but only symbolically to Sākyamuni because it denotes a 'renouncing king'; the **bodhisatta** is still a prince when he renounces the world. The precise wording of the doctrine of the **mahāpurisa** is therefore prudential and serves to differentiate the figure of the **sammāsambuddha** from the **paccekabuddha** by making the former a **cakkavatti**-designate, not an actual incumbent of that office. The nature of this distinction leads us to infer that the doctrine of the **mahāpurisa** as formulated in the Nikāyas was deliberately framed to accommodate Sākyamuni within, and to differentiate him from, an antecedent tradition in which the paradigm of spirituality was the 'renouncing **kṣatriya**'.

## The Cakkavatti and the Paṭi-Rājās

Since the 'secular' image of the **cakkavatti** is used to convey the soteriological significance of the figure of Sākyamuni (**qua sammāsambuddha**), and the **paccekabuddha** is acknowledged to be the buddhological counterpart of Sākyamuni, then one should expect to find in the elaboration of the **cakkavatti** conception some motif or image that corresponds to the **paccekabuddha**. And this we do find. We have seen that the Nikāyas define the **cakkavatti** as a king who acquires universal dominion by conquering all other kings and absorbing them within his empire. He can therefore be said to be a figure who asserts his superiority in a land of many kings, absorbing them within a single, monolithic system. If Sākyamuni corresponds to the royal sovereign in the analogy then it could be argued that paccekabuddhas correspond to the conquered or lesser kings (paṭi-rājā), in which case the use of this particular symbol within Buddhism serves to show how the figure of Sākyamuni relates to the **paccekabuddha** tradition.[176] The following Table, based on Pali and Buddhist Sanskrit sources, shows how the distinction between the **sammāsambuddha** and **paccekabuddha** functions on the analogy of the **cakkavatti** versus the **paṭi-rājās**.

| | cakkavatti myth | paccekabuddha status |
|---|---|---|
| a. | The **cakkavatti** is a universal sovereign He is the sole king (**eka rājā**). There cannot be two **cakkavattis** at the same time (A.I.28; D.II. 173; III. 62; M.III 65, 173). | **paccekabuddhas** cannot coexist with a **sammāssambuddha**, that is they cannot occupy the same **'field' (khetta).** This dogma is represented in mythological form: **paccekabuddhas** are forewarned by **devas** of the impending birth of a **sammāsambuddha.** Consequently all those **paccekabuddhas** still alive when the birth of Buddha is imminent immediately enter **parinibbāna** (Skt. **parinirvāṇa**) (Mvu.I.196-7, 357-9; Lal.13-14; Sn.A 128-9). |

| | |
|---|---|
| b. The Buddha (**qua cakkavatti**) sets the wheel of the **dhamma** rolling at Isipatana(Vin I.11)/ **Isivhaye vane** (the forest called after the **isis** - Sn.684) | In the Avadāna versions (**supra**) those **pacceka-buddhas** remaining when the Buddha's birth is announced are residing at Rsipatana. This locality is the place where the Buddha begins the foundation of his kingdom and and the place where correspondingly the **pacceka-buddhas** relinquish theirs |
| c. The **cakkavatti** conquers the four quarters (**cāturanto vijitāvī**);the **paṭi-rājās** reside in the quarters (D.III 62; Sn 552-4; M.III 173). | The **ekacarin/pacceka-buddha** resides in the quarters. In the archetypal myth there are four kings; each king reigns in a different quarter of N. India |
| d. The **paṭi-rājās** are not forced into submission but voluntarily submit to the **cakkavatti**'s sovereignty. | The **paccekabuddhas** acknowledge the superiority of the **sammāsambuddha** and willingly comply with the **deva**'s command to 'leave the field of the Buddha, who bears the marks of excellence'(that is, who is a **mahāpurusa** Mvu. I.357). |
| e. The **cakkavatti** is **janapadātthavariya-patta**(one who protects the people).That responsibility is no longer divided among many kings (D.III 16; III 146; A.III 149). | The **paccekabuddha** is conceived as a source of protection for the **mahājana**. In the dispensation of the Buddha they are superseded by the **ti-sarana. Buddha dhamma** and **saṅgha**). |
| f. The **cakkavatti** has | The Buddha's disciples are |

| | |
|---|---|
| a thousand sons who assist his conquest (D.II 16; III 59). | the sons of the Buddha. **Sāriputta** is known as his 'general' (**senāpati** - Sn. 556-7) and the **saṅgha** is titled **cātuddisāsaṅgha** (the **saṅgha** of the four regions). |

We wish to expand upon two particular features in particular of the above correspondences: the term **paṭi-rājā** and the name Isipatana. Not only does there exist a thematic resemblance of paccekabuddhas to 'lesser kings' but also linguistic affinities between the terms **paṭi-rājā** and **paccekabuddha**. Our first observation is that an oft-occurring synonym for **cakkavatti** is **eka rājā**.[177] So, for instance, the term **pratyeka-rājā** is found in a passage of the Mahavastu with an analogous meaning to the usage of **paṭi-raja** in Pali. In this passage the **bodhisattva** addresses Māra with the words: **'sayyathāpi nāma rājā cakravartī pṛthu pratyekarājāno tena hi te pāpīmaṁ saṁnirjinṣyāmi'** ("As the **cakravartin** Pṛthu vanquished the regional kings, I will vanquish you, wicked one").[178] The term **pratyeka-rājā** is used here to denote those lesser kings who are an obstacle to the **cakravartin**'s sovereignty (viz., **eka-rājā**). To our knowledge, the equivalent form, **pacceka-rājā** is not found in Pali. The nearest semantic equivalent is **paṭi-rājā** (lit., against a king; cp., **pratyeka-rājā** lit., 'against one king'). But the occurrence of **pratyeka** as a prefix to **raja** as well as to **buddha** is interesting in view of the typological associations between the **pacceka-buddha** and the **paṭi-rājā**. Since, however, the usage is isolated to the Mahāvastu we can do no more than note its occurrence.

Another important and problematic term is Isipatana, the name of the place where the

Buddha preached his first sermon. We have tried to show that the emergence of a dual buddhology of **paccekabuddha** and **sammāsambuddha** was occasioned by the Śramaṇa Tradition's evolution from a maverick phenomenon to an organised movement having individual teachers with their own groups of followers and disseminating their own particular message or philosophy. The introduction of the **paccekabuddha-sammāsambuddha** distinction constituted a de facto recognition of these two phases or eras in the tradition. The imagery of the Buddha 'turning the wheel of the **dhamma** at Isipatana' forms an important motif within this process of transition as it is intended to convey the idea of a tradition entering upon a new, unprecedented dispensation. The image of 'turning the wheel' derives from the concept of the **cakravartin** (**cakra** + **√vṛt**: wheel + to revolve/move). The 'turning wheel' therefore symbolises universal achievement.[179] The same image is used to symbolise the Buddha's assumption of the role of teacher (**satthar**) and the inauguration of the era of his teaching (**sāsana**). The act denoted by the expression 'turning the wheel of the **dhamma**' earned the Buddha the right to be called a **sammāsambuddha**; that is to say, it is the act which essentially underwrites the distinction of **sammāsambuddha** and **paccekabuddha**. The event which marks the act of the Buddha turning the wheel of the **dhamma** is the preaching of the first sermon, which for that reason is known as the **dhamma-cakka-pavatana** sermon. This sermon was delivered at Bārāṇasī. According to commentarial tradition, Bārāṇasī is also the place associated with the legendary 'five hundred' **paccekabuddhas** among whom were the authors of the Khaggavisāṇa verses. In chapter one we saw, however, that the Majjhima Nikāya connects **paccekabuddhas** principally with the mountain of Isigili, near Rājagaha in the region of Magadha, the region where according to tradition the Buddha attained his enlightenment. Canonical sources maintain he preached his first sermon at Bārāṇasī rather than in Magadha because an 'unclean **dhamma**' (**dhammo asuddho**) had overtaken Magadha.[180] This implies that the region had already become a stronghold of some other 'cultus'. In fact there is some historical evidence to suggest that during the period of Buddhism's inception conflict ('cultic' or 'political') existed between the two areas, which might explain why the Buddha and the **paccekabuddhas** have significant connections with both regions.[181]

Buddhist tradition makes it quite clear that the Buddha preached his first sermon at a place associated with a ṛṣi tradition: **Isivhaya vane** (Sn.684), **isipatana** (Vin.I.8), **Ṛṣipatana**(Mvu.III.328; Lal.297); **Ṛṣivadana** (Mvu.III.333,334).[182] To site this place as the location of the Buddha's first sermon was quite evidently a symbolic way of stressing the final 'demise' of a **paccekabuddha** tradition. The Mahāvastu interprets the ṛṣis in the place-name to refer to **pratyekabuddhas**. Taking the word **Ṛṣipatana** to mean the 'fall of the ṛṣis' (i.e., **pratyekabuddhas**), it proceeds to describe how the last remaining **pratyekabuddhas** in the world, confronted by the prospect of Sakyamuni's birth, attain their **parinirvāṇa**: rising into the air,their bodies conflagrating and their bones falling to earth.[183] Although the Lalitavistara has the variant, **Ṛṣipattana**, it similarly construes this to mean 'town' or 'dwelling of the **rsis**',that is,of the **pratyekabuddhas**.Moreover, Przyluski has shown that **pattana** is derived from a word which originally denoted a city where a **cakravartin** is enthroned (that is, an imperial city).[184] This information proves very significant in the light of our own observations that the concept of a **sammāsambuddha** is derived from that of the **cakravartin** and that Sākyamuni effectively assumed his identity as **sammāsambuddha (Skt.samyaksaṁbuddha)** at **Ṛsipatana.** Thus we might conclude that tradition had Sākyamuni preach his first sermon at **Ṛsipatana** because it had the connotations of an 'imperial city'. This ploy signified Sākyamuni's elevation to the status of 'Cakravartin Lord Buddha', that is, his enthronement as a 'spiritual' **cakravartin** (universal sovereign). Correspondingly, it marked the final ending of the reign of **paṭirājās (paccekabuddhas)**, the heterogenous tradition of the past.

By way of summarising this section we shall refer to the impact which the **cakravartin** archetype and the legend of the four kings who become **paccekabuddhas** had upon the formulation of the legend of the Buddha's life.

Conception

The motif of the elephant entering the mother's side as a symbol of conception pertains also to the **cakkavatti.**

Birth

At birth, the **bodhisatta** is found to possess the thirty-two major marks of the **mahāpurisa,** signifying his **cakkavatti** qua **sammāsambuddha** status.

Renunciation

The number of 'signs' **(nimittāni)** which influence the **bodhisatta's** renunciation of the world corresponds to the number of 'renouncers' in the legend of the four kings who become **paccekabuddhas.**

Enlightenment

We have noticed how the **sammāsambuddha** is

not defined in terms of the uniqueness of the Buddha's **bodhi** but by reference to the figure of a prospective **cakkavatti** who renounces the world.

Teaching

The image used to denote the significance of the Buddha's (act of) teaching ('turning the wheel') derives from the concept of the **cakkavatti**.

Death

Devotees honour the Buddha's death by the erection of **thūpas**. We noted in chapter one that this honour is reserved also for **paccekabuddhas**, **sāvakas** and **cakkavattis**. Originally, **thūpas** must have been the 'tombs' or 'burial mounds' of kings.[185] They may even have entered as a cultic factor into Buddhism and Jainism via the **paccekabuddha** tradition by dint of the fact that these proto-**śramaṇas** were themselves 'renouncing' kings.

## Conclusion

By examining the Nimi complex of myth we have come to the conclusion that the figure of the **paccekabuddha** can be identified with the proto-**śramaṇa** whose original conception was as a 'renouncing king'. Further evidence for the historical continuity of the Buddhist tradition with the proto-**śramaṇa/paccekabuddha** is to be seen in the Buddhist adoption of the 'renouncing king' as the archetype for their own figurehead, Sākyamuni. At the same time, the addition of the **cakkavatti** motif to Sākyamuni's representation as king indicates precisely how his followers wished to define and differentiate their own particular 'cultus' in regard to antecedent and concomitant traditions. Consequently, the origins of the Buddhist doctrine of a 'dual' buddhology can be attributed to dogmatic factors. The Buddhist **saṅgha** sought to win followers and initiates by fitting Buddha within a mythical and doctrinal framework which depicted his uniqueness and his universal significance.

**Notes:**

1. J.III.377ff.
2. On the dating of these early Buddhist monuments, see Garrett-Jones p.3.
3. See Introduction pp.xxix-xxx
4. This work, circa 11th cent. CE, has been translated into German by Hermann Jacobi, Ausg.Erz.pp.34-55. Other Jain versions of the prose tale of one of the four kings, Nami, are found in Bhāvadevasuri's Parśvanātha Caritra (transl.Bloomfield pp.130-136), circa 12th.cent.CE, and in the Kathākośa (transl.Tawney pp.18-28), circa 15th cent.CE. Because the Jain prose versions are so late we have discounted the various sub-plots which occur within the tales as strictly irrelevant to our inquiry and have taken cognisance of the main frame-story only. The sub-plots have themselves been analysed by Charpentier(2). Three of Devendra's stories of the four kings conclude with stanzas in **triṣṭubh** metre which is normally found only in early Jain texts, so these stanzas are certainly citations from an older text. Nevertheless, they make no mention of the kings as **patteya-buddhas**.

5. Jataka Stories, Vol.3 p.231. The Pali reads

Amb'āham addaṁ vanamantarasmiṁ
nīlobhāsam phalinaṁ saṁvirūlhaṁ,
tam addasaṁ phalahetū vibhaggaṁ,
tam disvā bhikkhācariyam carāmi.

Selaṁ sumaṭṭaṁ naravīranitthitaṁ
nārī yugam dhārayi appasaddaṁ,
dutiyañ ca āgamma ahosi saddo,
taṁ disvā bhikkhācariyaṁ carāmi.

Dijā dijaṁ kuṇapam āharantam
ekaṁ samāṇaṁ bahukā samecca
āhārahetū paripātayiṁsu
taṁ disvā bhikkhacariyaṁ carāmi.

Usabh'āham addaṁ yūthassa majjhe
calakkakuṁ vaṇṇabalūpapannaṁ,
tam addasaṁ kāmahetū vitunnaṁ,
taṁ disvā bhikkhācariyaṁ carāmi.

Karaṇḍu nāma Kalingānaṁ Gandārārañ ca Naggaji
Nimirājā Videhānaṁ Pañcālānañ ca Dummukho, ete raṭṭhāni hitvāna pabbajiṁsu akiñcanā. (J.III.380-1.vv.90-4).

6. karakaṇḍū kālingesu paṁcālesu ya dummuho
namī rāyā videhesu gandhāresu ya naggai

namī namei appāṇaṁ sakkhaṁ sakkeṇa coio
caiuṇa gehaṁ vaidehī sāmaṇṇe pajjuvaṭṭhio

eae narindavasabhā nikkhantā jinasāsaṇe
putte rajje thaveuṇaṁ sāmaṇṇe pajjuvaṭṭhiya. (Utt.XVIII.vv.45-47)

7. See Charpentier p.41 fn.1 and Norman p.93.
8. The idea of the **sañgha** in Jainism is similar to that of Buddhism but its nature or composition is slightly different. In Buddhism the **sañgha** is synony-

mous with the order of monks and is often referred to as the **bhikkhu-saṅgha** for this reason. The Buddhist laity does not constitute part of the **saṅgha**. In Jainism (Śvetāmbara sect), the **saṅgha** is fourfold: male and female laity plus monks and nuns. Monks and nuns are those who 'renounce' the household life and are known as **munis**. Householders are of two kinds: **śrāvakas**, those who are simply faith adherents; **śramaṇopāsakas**, those who undertake twelve lesser vows of asceticism. See Schubring p.297.

9. op. cit. ch.IX.
10. In his Article 'Namipavvajjā' (Indological Studies in Honour of W. Norman Brown, American oriental Series 47, pp.8-17) Alsdorf observes that stanzas 1-5,36 (first **pāda** only),55,59-60 are composed in **ārya** metre and the remainder of the text in **śloka**. Since **ārya** is a later form of metre than **śloka** he concludes that stanzas 1-5 and 54-60 are redactor's additions to an old gnomic poem.
11. Norman (op. cit. p.103 fn.17,18) cites the following passages:
'**samaṇe bhagavaṁ Mahāvīre āigare tittha-are sahasambuddhe**' - Aupapātika S. 16.-38.
Vyahāpannatti I.1.5 - Suttāgame I.384.
'**arahantāṇam bhagavantāṇaṁ āigarāṇaṁ titthagarāṇaṁ sahasambuddhāṇaṁ**' - Aupapātika S.20.
12. Norman (p.104 fn.21) cites Samavāya 2 (= Suttāgame I.316).
13. The paccekabuddha is referred to as **sayambhū** at Pb.Ap.51; Miln.105; Sn.A. 64; Kh.A.229; Vism.234; Upās.344; Mvu.I. 197,338 (**svayambhū**); and the **sammā-sambuddha** at Ud.49; Bu.XIV.1(= J.I.39); Pb.Ap.58; Miln.214,227,236 (**sayambhū... Tathāgato, anacariyako**: self-become is

the tathāgata, without a teacher); Mvu.I. 434 (**svayambhū**).

14. Ṭhāṇamga II.1.104 (Suttāgame I.189); Pannavaṇā S. I.77 (Suttāgame II.289). On the Jain canonical encyclopaedic texts, see Schubring pp.87-88,114-115; Gopalan pp.31-32,36; Winternitz pp.441-442,472-473.
15. According to Schubring (p.23) the term **patteyabuddha** first occurs in the Viyāhapannatti (895a) and in later passages of the Samavayanga (123a) and Nandī S. (203a). They are here mentioned without any form of definition. **Patteyabuddhas** first figure in Jain narratives in the Āvassaya, a Mūla Sūtra.
16. Stevenson p.171.
17. Norman pp.94-100
18. Pug.73
19. Sn.A.48,51; Upās.344.
20. Ud.55; A.IV.202; Vin.I.44; S.III.83.
21. 'The canonical texts enumerate the virtues and advantages of the religious life and proclaim the superiority of the religious life over that of the lay life (Dīgha, I. p.47-86; Majjhima, I.p.91); Madhyama, T.26, ch.36, p.659 b-c; Suttanipāta, v.60 seq. Hsien yu ching, T.707, p.813 c-815 a). If it is admitted that an upāsaka, living at home, can attain the first three fruits of the religious life (Majjhima, I,p.467; 490-491), it is doubtful whether he can reach Nirvāṇa without having first put on the religious robe (Majjhima, I,p.483; Saṁyutta, V, p.410; Kathāvatthu, I,p.267; Milindapañha, p.264-265). One thing is certain, that a monk attains holiness more surely and quickly than a layman (Tsa pao tsang ching; T 203, No.111,ch.9,p.492 c sq.).' - Vimalakīrti p.76 fn.71.
22. Jacobi, I.A. Vol.IX. p.159.

23. D.II.3.
24. Buhler p.51.
25. Schubring pp.15ff.
26. Jacobi, SBE.XXII. pp.xxxiv-xxxv; Minor Anthologies pp.XIXff.
27. Jacobi, op. cit. pp.xix-xx.
28. ERE.Vol.7. pp.469-70; Erghardt p.3.
29. Utt.XXXII.v.7.
30. Buhler p.ix; Jacobi, SBE.XXII. pp.x-xii, 256; Stevenson pp.41-42. The Jains subscribe to the conception of an abode which functions very much like the Mahayana **buddha-kṣetra** in that it is a place inhabited by titthagaras, where beings can be ripened for **mokṣa** unhindered. The name of this ideal abode, interestingly, is **Mahāvideha**. See SBE. XXII.p.194; Stevenson pp.113,170,216,256-272.
31. Jacobi, SBE.XLV. p.23.fn.2.
32. Compare Jacobi, SBE.XXII. p.246 with J.I. 150; Lal.43ff. See also Renou pp.115ff; Jacobi, op. cit. p.xvii.
33. Barth p.148; Hiriyanna pp.163-6,208.
34. Jacobi, SBE.XLV. p.83 fn.2, p.84 fn.4; Gopalan p.173. On the realisation of the selflessness of the **khanda**, see Vin.I. 13-14.
35. Gopalan p.180.
36. V.R. Ramachandra Dikshitar, 'Origin and Early History of Caityas', IHQ. Vol.XIV pt.3, 1938, p.448.
37. cf. W.B.Bollee, 'Buddhists and Buddhism in the Earlier Literature of the Śvetāmbara Jains' - Buddhist Studies in Honour of I.B. Horner, edit. L.Cousins, A. Kunst and K.R.Norman, D.Reidel, 1974, p.34.
38. The Jains performed physical austerities (**tapas**) in order to stop **karma**. They were known as **nigraṇṭha** (P.**nigaṇṭha**), meaning 'without the bonds' (of **karma**). See also Schubring p.327; ERE.

Vol.7. p.471.

39. Karaṇḍu/Karakaṇḍu of Kālinga.

We have found no allusions to this figure outside the context of the **paccekabuddha** legend.

Dummukha/Dummuha of Pañcāla.

a. The Ait.Brh. (VIII.23) mentions a Dummukha Pañcāla, a king who 'went round the earth conquering on every side' (transl.Keith). He is probably the same mythical personage as in the four kings legend. Note that he is represented as a 'universal sovereign', though not technically as a **cakravartin** as Charpentier says (p.36 fn.3), since that term is not found within the Brāhmaṇas.

b. A Dummukha is mentioned as being one of the foremost **kṣatriyas** present at Yudhiṣṭhira's initiation ceremony (Mbh.II.116)

c. In Manu (VII.41) there is a Sumukha and a Nemi who are said to have perished for their lack of humility.

d. Hopkins (Epic p.177) cites a Summukha who is a **rsi** of the south. The **ṛṣi** Narada is also said to have a colleague by the name (Mbh. II.145). The Divy. (211,217) mentions an irascible ṛṣi called Durmukha who realised the 5 **abhijñas**.

Naggaji/Naggai of Gandhāra

a. A Nagnajit of Gandhāra, is said to have given his own peculiar interpretation of an aspect of ritual. But since he was a **kṣatriya** his interpretation was rejected as invalid by the brāhmaṇa fraternity (Sat.Brh.VIII.I.4.10). A Nagnajit of Gandhāra is also mentioned at Ait.Brh.VII.34.

b. A Nagnajit occurs in the legend of Kṛṣṇa:

a. Kṛṣṇa carried off the daughter of the king of the Gandhāras at a **svayam-vara**, and princes were yoked to his car (Dowson p.162).

b. Kṛṣṇa 'speedily smashed the Gandhāras and conquered all the sons of Nagnajit' (Mbh. trans. Roy.vol.IV. 120; cf. also Harivaṁsa 4970).

c. A Nagnajit was the disciple of Prahlād (Mbh.I.2455, see Hopkins, Epic, sv Prahlāda).

In terms of the four kings as a collective group, there is one passage in the Mbh (VII.120) that might be of some importance: 'thou didst...O Karṇa vanquish the Kamvojas, having proceeded to Rājpura'. Many kings amongst whom Nagnajit was the foremost, while staying in Girivrāja, as also Amvaṣṭhas, the Videhas and the Gandhārvas, were all vanquished by thee' (Roy. Vol.VI. p.8). Not only are the Videhas (viz.Nimi) here brought together with Nagnajit here as seemingly allies or confederates, but the place of their defeat is Girivrāja (Rājgir), an area traditionally associated with **paccekabuddhas**.

40. Charpentier (2) p.99.

41. It is arguable that Nami and the 22nd and 21st Jain **titthagaras**, Ariṣṭanemi and Nimi, originally referred to the same legendary figure. Charpentier, for one, assumes that Nami and the 21st **titthagara** have the same identity. Reasons that can be adduced to support their common identity are

a. The Kalpa Sutta refers to Nimi and

Nami.

b. Both **titthagaras** are sometimes referred to as Neminātha.

c. Ariṣṭanemi was the **titthagara** immediately preceding Pārśvanātha, who is considered to be historical (circa 800 BCE). This places him sequentially (though not of course in terms of Jain canonical timescales) in the era depicted by the Nimi complex of legends.

d. In the Mahājanaka Jātaka the father of Mahājanaka (a putative Nimi) is called Ariṭṭhajanaka. The name Ariṣṭanemi could therefore have arisen as a consequence of compounding the identities of Nami and his alleged father.

e. The Buddhist Nimi is referred to as **nemi kumāra** (J.VI.96. cf. also vl.96.28; 97.9; 98.10).

In view of what we are about to argue, namely, that the notion of the Buddha is based upon the format of the Nimi myth, it is quite understandable that a tradition should have existed in which this figure should himself have become classified as a **titthagara**. Similarly, the existence of such a tradition is compatible with the thesis that there was originally a single buddhology.

42. This complex of legends belongs to a literary genre known as **itihāsa** ('so indeed it was') and **ākhyāna** ('the telling of a previous event').

Charpentier op. cit. p.120 remarks on the multiple versions of the Nimi saga: 'Freilich sind die konige von Mithilā kaum zu den beruhmfesten heroen der indischen sagenpoesie gezalt worden, aber aus episoden, die wahrscheinlich nich von der lebensgeschichte eined mannes herruhren, hat die volkssage einen einzigen grossen helden geschaffen, einen typus dess herrscherhauses, von dem die alte geschichte sagt, dass seine meisten mitglieder 'durch ihre religiose kenntnisse hervorragend' waren'.

43. The name Videha first occurs in the Śat. Brh. (cf. XI.6.2.5; XI.4.4.13; XIV.6. 12.2. See also Tait.Brh.3.10.9.9). The Śat.Brh. (I.4.1) says that the name Videgha Māthava came from the Vedic conquerer of the region. The Kingdom of Videha is first mentioned in the Yajurveda (VI.II.298). On the geographical location and territorial extensions of the Ancient Kingdom of Videha see Thakur pp.10-11,20-22,27-8; SBE.XII. p.xlii.

44. 'It has been laid down that renunciation should only be adopted by kings in times of distress, when overtaken by old age or defeated by an enemy. Those (who have laid this down) do not applaud renunciation as the duty (kṛta) of the **kṣatriya**' - Mbh.XII.10.17-18. Similarly in the story of Janaka, his wife declares: 'they that are desirous of happiness but are very poor and indigent and abandoned by friends may adopt renunciation' - Mbh. transl. Roy Vol.VIII. p.34).

45. 'Indra is the **Kṣatra**, and the Rājanya is the **kṣatra**' (Śat.Brh.V.1.1.11. trans. Eggeling, SBE.XLI. p.3.

46. Compare the use of the same verb, **abhinikkamati**, in the Khaggavisāṇa Sutta (Sn.64).

47. Kh.A.120.

48. Stutley sv **caitya**.

49. Utt.IX.16. In v.60 Nami is described as **munivaro** (best of munis), an epithet used for the Buddha also.

50. MWD p.528.

51. Erz.Ausg. p.46.

52. Thakur p.7.
53. Utt.IX.61; XVIII.45.
54. Miln.115,291; Kh.A.128.
55. Utt.XVIII.46.
56. See, respectively, Rg.V. I.53.7; X.48.9; VI.20.6.
57. **sakhā** could as well be translated 'companion' or 'confidante' and signifies an equal. See J.Gonda, 'Mitra and mitra: the idea of 'friendship in Ancient India', I.T. Pt.1. pp.82-83.
58. Ait.Brh.(2) p.303.
59. Ait.Brh.(1) VII.15.
60. Rg.V.(1) VII.17.14.
61. Ṣn.547,571.
62. Śat.Brh.XI.15.5.7; XII.7.3.4.
63. Rg.V. V.18.12.
64. Vin.I.8.
65. Dh.350.
66. See M.Bloomfield, 'The Story of Indra and Namuci', JAOS XV. pt.1. 1893.
67. Mvu.I.229-30.
68. SBE.XLV. p.86.fn.1.
69. Rg.V. X.136.7; VII.56.8.
70. Pañc.Brh.XXV.10.17.
71. ibiḍ. XVI.8.6.
72. Kauś.Brh.XXV.14.
73. Pañc.Brh.XVI.9.2.
74. Kauśitaki.Up.4.1.
We notice that Dh 106 refers to the concept of making an offering (**yajetha**) with a thousand (**sahassena**):

**Māse māse sahassena yo yajetha sataṁ samaṁ**
**ekañ ca bhāvitattānaṁ muhuttam api pūjaye,**
**sā yeva pūjanā seyyo yañ ce vassasataṁ hutaṁ**

'Though, month after month, with a thousand,
One should make an offering for hundred

years;
Yet if only for a moment one would honour a (saint) who has perfected himself
That honour is, indeed, better than a century of sacrifice - trans. Narada.

Māra _qua_ Namuci also refers to the 'thousandfold gift' (**sahassa bhāga**) when addressing the Buddha. See Sn.427. According to the Brāhmaṇadhammika Sutta (Sn.308), in former times the **rājā**, lord of the chariots (**rathesabha**), was induced (**saññatta**) by the **brāhmaṇa** to slaughter hundreds of thousands of cows in sacrificial rites.

75. It should be noted that Nimi (3) and Namin Sāpya (6) are not the only figures in either Buddhist or Brahmanical tradition said to have entered heaven bodily. In the Padmapurāṇa, Yayāti visits heaven (see Dowson p.377); and in the Mbh, Yayāti is classed as a **rājarṣi**. Yudhiṣṭhira, of the Mbh, also goes bodily to Indra's heaven. The passages in Miln. (115,291) which cite King Nimi as entering the **tāvatiṁsadeva-loka**, also cite three other kings: Sādhīna, Guttila and Mandhātā (Mandhātri, is a **rājarṣi** in the Brahmanical texts. See Roy Vol.VIII. p.13,25). Sādhīna's legend is told at J.IV.355-360 and basically follows the same pattern as Nimi's story: because of his great virtue, Sādhīna is invited to become a **pabbajita** on his return to the world of men. Hence, of course, he is reborn in the **tavatiṁsa-deva loka** not in the **brahma loka** like Nimi. On Guttila and Mandhātā, see sv DPPN.
76. Mbh.XII.8600.
77. M.II.74ff.
78. J.I.137-9; VI.95-96.
79. J.VI.39ff.

80. J.VI.44.
81. Compare Utt.XXIX.1-2 (cf. also Jacobi, SBE XLV.pp.161-2) with Sn.935, A.I.36 and Sn.A.115. On **nibbidā**, see Dh 277-9.
82. Thag.A.III.93.
83. J.I.28.
84. Upas.344. Pb.Ap.3: (**paccekabuddhas** are those) who attain **paccekabodhi** 'by means of **saṁvega**' (**Ten 'eva saṁvega-mukhena**). cp. also Sn.A.115.
85. J.I.138.
86. One of the samaṇabhadragāthas reads 'When the kingdom is ransacked nothing of his is plundered'.
87. J.VI.60-1.
88. ibid. p.65
89. The Bhārhut Stūpa depicts Mahājanaka with his wife, Sivalī, (see Cunningham, 'Stūpa of Bhārhut', London 1879, plate XLIV.2. p.95). Inscribed above the relief are the words 'Janaka **rājā** Sivalī **devī**'. The legend of Mahājanaka seems also to be depicted in some of the relief carving on the great stūpas at Amarāvatī (See Fergusson, 'Tree and Serpent Worship', plate LXXXVI. pp.227f.). There are two scenes - pre- and post-renunciation - one depicting a king in his chariot riding by two **pīpal** (nb. not **amba** as in the Jātaka story) trees, one bearing fruit, the other barren; the other shows an ascetic surrounded by women (Mahājanaka's wives). It is to be observed that the woman standing directly in front of the ascetic is wearing only one bracelet on each of her arms; all the remaining women depicted have several. It seems that the episode of the 'single' bracelet is here being portrayed.
90. Sn.48-9.
91. J.III.380 v.91.
92. J.VI.52-3.

93. This happens, for example, in the story of Susima's **paccekabodhi** (Kh.A.198).
94. J.III.376-7.
95. Mbh.XII.571ff.
96. Mbh.III.1378; XIV.2483.
97. Mbh.XII.529; 6641,9917.
98. Mbh.XI.19-21.
99. SBE.XLIX.p.95.
100. op. cit. ch.IV.
101. op. cit. II.1.1. cf. also Kauśitaki Up.IV.1.
102. XI.4.3.20.
103. Gonda (3) p.80.
104. Śat.Brh.V.3.2.7.
105. XI.6.2.10.
106. XI.3.1.1-4.
107. XI.6.3.1-11.
108. op. cit. III.1.
109. Bṛhad.Up.IV.4.
110. At Divy.61. 'four' kings are named in a similar manner to the four kings who become **paccekabuddhas**, three of them coming from the same regions:
'**Pingalaś ca Kalingeṣu Mithilāyāṁ ca Pāṇḍukaḥ**
**Elāpatraś ca Gandhāre Śankho Vārānasī-pure**
Likewise, Nami is mentioned in the Suttāgame (SBE.XLV. p.268) along with three others - Rāmagupta, Bāhuka, and Tārāgaṇa - making a total of four. Leumann (WZKM. Vol.6, 1892, p.55) first put forward the thesis that the idea of four **paccekabuddhas** in number may have come from the conception of the four **diśa**: Die Vierer Conception ist augenscheinlich von den view haupt und vier Neben richt ungen der Windrose ausgegangen'. The archetypal notion of the four **paccekabuddhas** may have served as the prototype for the title '**saṅgha** of the four quarters' (Vin.I.305; II.147; D.I.145).

111. D.I.63.
112. On **daṇḍa** as a kingship concept, see L. Dumont, 'The Conception of Kingship in Ancient India', Contributions to Indian Sociology Vol.VI. Dec.1962 pp.64-65,67-68; Gonda (3) p.18,22f.; Mbh. Roy Vol. VIII. pp.25-26.
113. Manu VII.102.
114. Mbh. Roy Vol.I.11.17.
115. See the commentarial gloss at Sn.A.88.
116. Ait.Brh.VII.11.
117. **sahitar** der. from **sahati** which can either have an active meaning - 'to conquer, defeat, overcome - or a passive meaning - 'to bear, endure' (PED). This ambiguity of usage indicates that in the non-secular situation of asceticism, 'to bear' or 'endure' is a way of 'conquest'. **Padac (parissayānam sahitā acchambhī)** has a parallel in **gātha** 45c (**abhibhuyya sabbāni parissayāni**: conquering all dangers). **Abhibhavati** is another martial term, as is shown in its usage later in the Khaggavisāṇa Sutta: like the strong-jawed lion, by might king of the animals, overcoming as he wanders' (**sīho yathā dāṭhabalī pasayha rājā migānaṁ abhibhuyyacarī** - 72).
118. We draw attention to the fact that **avirujjhati** comes from the verbal root **√rudh** which is also the root of the verb **ūparodhati** (to impede, hinder), and the absence of **ūparodhati** is among two of the eight blessings (**bhadra**) characterising the **samaṇa**. The root **√rudh** has also a very similar meaning to the root **√vṛ**. The arch-enemy of Indra, the patron deity of the **kṣatriya**, is Vṛtra the **asura** (P. Vatra - J.V.153; S.I.147) which means 'he who 'obstructs, restrains, covers'. We have noted that the identities of Vṛtra

and Namuci are compounded, and that Nami Sāpya (5) helps 'slay' or 'remove' the obstacle of Namuci 'from far away'. In view of what we have said about the common identities of Nami Sāpya and the **muni**, the myth of 'slaying' Namuci from far away could be referring to the action of the **brahma-vihāras** which remove 'obstacles' without physical contact, that is meditationally or at a distance. (In another part of Sn [the Pasūra S.] **avirujjhati** occurs in the context of the theme of kingship. The philosophical disputant (**diṭṭhigatika** lit.'one who goes or resorts to a view') is compared to a warrior (**sūra**) whose appetite has been quenched at the king's table and is therefore eager to meet an adversary (**paṭisūra** - 831). By contrast, there are those who wander 'without an army' (**visenikatvā** - 832-3), that is, who 'do not oppose (or counter) one view with another' (**diṭṭhīhi diṭṭhiṁ avirujjhamānā** - 833), who do not exalt in the idea of a contest. We have noted that the **muni** is known for not having a 'view'; and at Sn.55 the **ekacarin** is said to have 'transcended the discordant effect of having a view' (**diṭṭhīvisūkāni upātivatto**).

119. Dh.329. E.W. Hopkins ('The Social and Military Position of the Ruling Caste in Ancient India, as represented by Sanskrit Epic', JAOS Vol.13.) writes (p.93): 'That the act (of 'renunciation') was really common is shown by the fact that it is the first thing of which a king weary of reigning thinks.' A regular reflection to be found in the Commentarial tales illustrating the Khaggavisāṇa stanzas (see Sn.A.60,72,82) is: 'Thereupon he thought: 'Which is best, kingship or the

**dhamma**' of the **samaṇa**? Happiness (**sukha**) resulting from kingship is small (**paritta**) and has many perils (**ādīnava**); happiness resulting from the **dhamma** of the **samaṇa** is great and has many good consequences'.

120. At Sn.p.107 we find the rather interesting reference to the concept of a **buddha** in the plural: **durāsada hi te bhagavanto sihā va ekacarā** (These **bhagavans** are difficult of access, wandering alone like lions). This, if any passage in the Pali sources, suggests that Gotama belonged to a category of persons who were distinguished as **ekacara** (or **muni**).
121. Pb.Ap.v.52; Nd II.71.
122. Sn.684 (cp. also Sn.562,1015).
123. A.II.238; M.I.63.
124. D.I.175; A.V.32.
125. A.III.21.
126. **haṁsa** is usually translated as 'swan' by English translators of Pali texts. However, according to J.Ph.Vogel, 'The Goose in Indian Literature and Art', E.J. Brill, 1962, p.74, **haṁsa** always designates the goose and nothing else.
127. See J.II.353.
128. Dh.175.
129. A.A.I.354.,
130. Sn.221.
131. Rg.V. VI.9.5.
According to Vogel (op. cit. pp.30-31) the goose was a symbol for non-attachment and psychic power. In the Tait. Brh (3. 10.9) a certain sage is described as become a golden swan, gone to heaven and obtained union with the sun (cite Macdonell p.168). We may compare this attainment with the form of Buddhist **iddhi** in which the adept is said to travel cross-legged in the sky, like the

birds on wing and to touch and feel both the sun and moon with his hand (D.I.78). Hopkins, Epic, p.19 writes that the **haṁsa**'s high flight and loneliness makes it an emblem of the pure soul and of God. The goose also emigrates to the Himavā and lives at Lake Mānasa (MWD p.810) we may compare the **paccekabuddha** whose mythical home is Mount Gandhamādana and Lake Anottata in the Himavā (Ap.A. 162; A.A.I.173; IV.109; J.III.257. etc.).

132. Pb.Ap.v.54.
133. See, for instance, J.III.392.
134. cf. Dh 97.
135. See Mvṁsa II.1ff; Dvṁsa III.14-37.
136. Compare J.III.476ff with J.III.238ff; 451-3; IV.114-6; V.247-9.
137. J.I.395-6; 470; III.241-5; 307; V.252-5.
138. On the decline of the famous ancient Videha dynasty, see Thakur pp.59ff. He remarks (p. 61): 'There is reason to believe that Kāśi people had a hand in the overthrow of the Videhan dynasty, for, already in the time of the Great Janaka (Kṛti Janaka) Ajātaśatru of Kāśi showed his jealousy of Janaka's fame.... The Mahbhārata also refers to a great battle between King Janaka of Mithilā and King Pratardana of Kāśi.' Thakur is here alluding to the Upaniṣadic passage (Bṛhad.Up.II.1ff.; Kauśitaki Up.IV.1ff.) in which Ajātaśatru of Kāśi is seen to emulate Janaka by offering a **brāhmaṇa** one thousand cows in return for knowledge of **brāhman**. The integration or close contact of the two kingdoms is implied by the usage of the expression, **kāśi-videhesu** in the Kauśitaki.Up. version.
139. M.III.68; Mvu.I.357.
140. See, for example, D.I.1; M.III.277; Vin.II.76; Mvu.III.67,360,429.
141. Mvu.I.357; III.153-72; A.A.I.174-6; 345-

56; Thig.A.182-190.
142. Śat.Brh.VI.4.1.7.
143. D.III.230; M.I.73.
144. M.I.73.
145. MMK.II.40.3ff.
146. See DPPN sv Uppalavaṇṇa.
147. Ud.55; A.IV.202; Vin.I.44.
148. S.III.83.
149. J.V.252-3; Mvu.III.452-3.
150. In the Mvu 'Śronaka is represented as a **ṛṣi bāhirika** (cf. Jones 1. .p.236 n.2) who has acquired the 4 **dhyānas**, the 5 **abhijñas** and who is **mahānubhāve** and **mahārddhika**. This disparity between the Pali and Sanskrit versions concerning the identity of Sonaka can be accounted for as follows:
    i. In both versions Sonaka is the son of a **brāhmaṇapurohita** (brahmanical advisor to the king).
    ii. The Mvu identifies him with a **brāhma-ṛṣi** rather than as a **paccekabuddha** probably because of
        a. his Brahmanic origins (supra i).
        b. the assimilation of the concept of the **paccekabuddha** to the Brahmanic notion of **ṛṣi** .
151. D.III.92-3.
152. See A.L. Basham,'The Wonder that was India', Fontana edition, 1971, p.82; E.W.Hopkins, The Divinity of Kings, JAOS Vol.51, 1931, pp.313- 314; Gonda (3) pp.48-49.
153. The god Varuṇa is the archetype of **prasannatā** (clarity, serenity, graciousness) cf. Hopkins, The Divinity of Kings, op. cit. p.312. Sn.A.(123) cites a charming adage: 'people are naturally entranced **(atitta)** by the sight of a **buddha**, a full-moon, an ocean and a king.'
154. D.III.58ff.
155. Not as T.W.Rhys Davids (Dial. pt.III. p.59) translates: 'to sink'. **Osakkati** = 'to

retract, withdraw, retreat' (PED). A cognate of one of the terms used to describe the eclipse of the **dibbaṁ cakka-ratanaṁ**, **osakkita** (moved back), occurs in a Comy (Vv.A.432) to describe the period of decline (**osakkana-kāla**) between the time of the stability of the **sāsana** (**sāsanaṭhita-kāla**) and its final disappearance (**antaradhāna**). In the theme of the waning of the **dibbaṁ cakka-ratanaṁ** we therefore seem to have a symbolic allusion to the doctrine of cycles of cosmic growth and decay.

156. J.VI.96.
157. 'It is not enough that the king should employ Brahmans for the public ritual, he must also have a permanent, personal relationship with one particular Brahman, his **purohita** (Ait.Brh.VIII.24), so that the **purohita** presides as **hotr** or **brahman** priest i.e. as sacrificer or controller, to royal sacrifices. Moreover, the king depends on him for all the actions of his life, for these would not succeed without him. The **purohita** is to the king as thought is to will, as Mitra is to Varuṇa (Śat.Brh.IV.1.4.1.et seq.). The relationship is as close as a marriage - Dumont: 'The Conception of Kingship in Ancient India', op. cit. p.51.
158. Bṛhad.Up.I.4.11.
159. See A.M. Hocart: 'Flying through the Air', IA, April 1923, pp.80-82.
160. Support for the argument that the **dibbaṁ-cakka-ratanaṁ** signifies the 'moon' rather than the 'sun' is supplied in Waddell's Article, 'Jewel' (Buddhist), ERE Vol.7. p.544.
161. J.III.363ff.
162. See Sn.498 a-b (cp. J.I.183):

    **ye vītarāgā susamāhitindriyā**
    **cando va Rāhu-gahaṇā pamuttā**
    (Those who are without passions, whose

faculties are well composed who are like the moon freed from Rāhu's grasp)

163. Rg.V. V.40.6.
164. cf. Hopkins, 'Epic' pp.125-126; Erz.Ausg. p.40.
165. S.I.50ff.
166. In deciding to teach the **dhamma**, the Buddha is identified with the figure of Brahmā. Since it is Brahmā who persuades him to teach in the first instance (Vin I.5ff.) the **dhammacakka** is sometimes also referred to as the **brahma-cakka** (A.II.24; III.9, 417; V.33; M.I.69).
167. A.I.145-146; J.I.59ff.cp. also the legend of Vipassī Buddha: D.II.21ff. and M.I.163/ 240/ II.212.
168. The apparent connection of the Buddha with (the) four **paccekabuddhas** is not just reflected in the number of 'images' or 'signs' (**nimmita**) which provoke his 'renunciation', but seems to have some basis in the Jātaka stories. According to the Kummāsapiṇḍa J. (III.406ff.), the **bodhisatta**'s almsgift to four **paccekabuddhas** is said to be the cause (paccaya) of his very 'omniscience' (sabbaññutañāṇa), that is, of his eventually attaining **sammāsambuddha** status.
169. Both Horner (MLS. Vol.II. p.317.fn.4) and Woodward (KS. Vol.V. p.137) maintain that the doctrine of the **mahāpurisa** was originally Brahmanic. This interpretation receives support from the Sela S. (Sn pp.102 ff.) where the **brāhmaṇa** Sela states that the thirty- two signs of a mahāpurisa are found in his own tradition of **mantas** (Skt.**mantra**), and from the Miln. (235-236) in later tradition. Horner, in fact, points out that there are two versions of the **mahāpurisa** doctrine in the Nikāyas, Brahmanic and Buddhist.
170. D.III.142ff; also D.I.89; II.16.
171. The meaning of **samrāj** is akin to that of

**cakravartin** - i.e., great king or universal sovereign - but is mentioned in earlier texts than the latter. In the Rg.V. it is an epithet of, for instance, Mitra-Varuṇa (V.63.2-3; 68.2) the Viśvadevas (X.63.5) Agni (I.27.1; VI.7.1) and Indra (IV.19.2). To our knowledge, it is not posited of anyone other than **devas** until the period of the Brāhmaṇas (Ait.Brh.VIII.14; Śat.Brh.IX. 3.4.8), and then became closely bound-up conceptually with the performance of the **rājasūya** ritual. We may compare the formation sam-rāj with sam-buddha' By contrast, the earliest usage of the term **cakravartin** seems to be in the Buddhist texts or the Maitrī Up.(I.4). **Cakravartins** feature also within Jain hagiology (see Utt.XVIII.34ff.).

172. Sn 552-4.
173. D.II.16; III.46; A.III.149.
174. According to A.II.109 the **dhamma** is king (**raja**) even of the **cakkavatti**; the **cakkavatti** is said to be dependent (**nissāya**) on the **dhamma**.
175. According to the Matsya Purāṇa the birth of a cakravartin heralds a new age, in which he embodies the **dharma** (cite Stutley p.58). This is a very similar understanding of the significance of the concept within the Cakkavatti-sīhanāda S. The identification of the Buddha with the **cakkavatti** is therefore indicative of the belief that he heralded a new dispensation.
176. The notion of 'lesser' or 'rival kings' has its counterpart in Brahmanic ritual. See J.C.Heesterman, 'Brahmin, Ritual and Renouncer', WZKSO, VIII.1964, pp.8-9. In the Rajasuya, messengers take particular presents from the initiate king to 'rival kings' (**pratirājānaḥ**). By accepting the presents, these 'rival' kings demonstrate their allegiance. They are understood to be

an original repository of **brāhman**, and their acceptance of the gifts signals the transfer of that **brāhman** to the initiate king. We may compare the situation here, where the responsibility for the **dhamma** is transferred from the hands of the **pacceka-buddhas** into the hands of the Buddha and the **saṅgha**.

177. M.III.65; Karma Vibh.160; Divy.369.
178. Mvu.II.270. In Epic and Puranic myth Pṛthu (Pṛthu Vainya/Pṛthī) is the first king, the foremost of the **cakravartins** and the archetype and primordial model of any actual ruler. See Gonda (3) pp.128-131; ERE.Vol. 3. p.336; Stutley sv Pṛthu.
179. The derivation of the term **cakravartin** is a complex issue, but in its usage it is indubitably a symbol of universal conquest or sovereignty. See Gonda (3) pp.123-128; ERE. vol.3.pp.336-337; vol.VII.553-557.
180. Vin.I.5.
181. Lamotte pp.8ff.
182. C.Caillat (Isipatana Migadāya, J.A. Vol.256 pp.177-183) makes a thorough analysis of the variant forms of **isipatana/ṛṣipatana** and concludes that the term is a pre-canonical middle indo-aryan reconstruction of **ṛṣya** + **vṛjana** meaning either 'herd of deer', 'deer park or enclosure' or 'company of seers'. As such, it constitutes nothing more than a synonym for **migadāya** (Skt. **mṛgadāya**) - deer park - with which it is always paired in its canonical usage (op. cit. p.179). Clearly, therefore, the original meaning of the term had become lost to the Buddhists and this is why we have diverse interpretations of its meaning in Pali (contrast S.A.III.296 with A.A.II.180) and Buddhist Sanskrit texts. It is interesting to notice that the one passage which Caillot overlooks in her otherwise superb analysis, provides an interpretation

concurring very much with her own, that is, the Sutta-nipāta **pāda** (684c) which may well be the earliest canonical reference and reads: **vattessati cakkaṁ Isivhaye vane** (he will turn the wheel in the forest named after the **isi** - cp. **Kaṅhasiri vhayo isi**: Sn.689a). What is conspicuous about this reference is that, rather than the place name itself, its generic meaning is given.

If Caillot's conclusions are correct, and the significance of the term as denoting a place where **ṛsis** dwelt is pre-canonical, then it provides further support for the theory of the **paccekabuddha**'s identity.

183. Mvu.I.359.
184. cf. La Ville du Cakravartin, RO, 1927, Vol. V. pp.165-185.
185. ERE Vol.11. p.902. The full design of a stūpa may in fact be a representation of a **cakravartin**'s palace - see Przyluski, op. cit., p.182.

Chapter Four
## The Paccekabuddha as Muni

In the preceding chapter we concentrated on the theme of the proto-śramaṇa's **kṣatriya** identity. This we did in order to show how the use of **kṣatriya** concepts in the buddhology of the early Nikāyas was evidence of both a continuity and discontinuity with the antecedents of Buddhism. In this final chapter we shall pursue the same theme of continuity and discontinuity but this time specifically with regard to the **paccekabuddha**'s relationship to Vedic and Brahmanic religion and to the tradition of the **brahma-vihāra** meditations.

Both Brahmanic religion and the practice of the forms of meditation known as the four **brahma-vihāras** are older than Buddhism. They belong to different sides of the 'renunciation' controversy, the former con, the latter pro. By analysing the relationship of Early Buddhism to each of these longer standing traditions we shall develop further the argument that Buddhism operated essentially from the standpoint of a 'cultus'. Firstly, we shall show how Buddhism draws upon many of the Brahmanical cultic concepts in order to communicate its own doctrines. Secondly, we shall show how the **paccekabuddha** is intimately bound up with the **brahma-vihāra** tradition of spirituality. The texts of the main-Nikāya period indicate that the **brahma-vihāras** were the highest expression of spirituality available in the pre-Sākyamuni dispensation. It is a point of view which stands in prima facie contradiction to the doctrine that **paccekabuddhas**, ascetics regarded by Buddhist tradition to be enlightened, existed immediately prior to the time of Sākyamuni. One of the purposes of this chapter is to draw attention to this apparent anomaly and endeavour to explain how the two mutually inconsistent affirmations came into existence.

The chapter has been parcelled into four distinct sections. The first examines Early Buddhism's relationship to the Brahmanic tradition; the second looks at the **brahmavihāras** and their relationship to Brahmanism; the third at Buddhism's own relationship to the **brahma-vihāra** tradition; and the fourth section draws together the various themes of the book - the **paccekabuddha** as an exponent of **iddhi**, as the **proto-śramaṇa** and as an adept of the **brahma-vihāras** - and shows how together, as a totality, they enable us to make sense of the classical Buddhist doctrine that the **paccekabuddha** does not teach **dhamma**.

In the course of our discussion we shall attempt to demonstrate that there is a gradual shift and development in soteriological perspective as we move from one form of religious ideology to another. The pattern of development is indicated by the following Table. Each new phase represents both a critique and an extension of the previous soteriology:

| Tradition | Practice | Salvific goal |
|---|---|---|
| a. Vedic and Early Brahmanic | sacrificial ritual | **loka** and **svarga loka** |
| b. Proto-śramaṇa | **pravrajyā** and **brahma-vihāras** | **brahma loka** |
| c. Later śramaṇa (Buddhist) | the Buddha and his **dhamma** | **nibbāna** |

Historically, phase b. is the rudimentary link between Buddhism and Brahmanism. It comprises both the earliest expression of a critique of Brahmanism and represents the formative phase in the formation of the new tradition of Buddhism itself. It is to this intermediate phase that the figure of the **paccekabuddha** belongs.

## Buddhism's Relationship to the Brahmanic Tradition

### Vedic and Brahmanic conceptions of the world

In this section we draw chiefly upon the extensive work of Gonda and Heesterman for our analysis of the Vedic picture of the world. According to this picture 'being' is defined by 'mobility'. Spatial movement from a fixed point or centre to a surrounding or outlying area is considered an inexorable condition of existence. Such movement is, however, regarded as hazardous because it entails physical and psychological change and disturbance. It is the function of religius ritual to minimise and allay these hazards. The name for the areas of space which have to be traversed when a being sets out from a fixed point or centre is **diśā** (regions; directions of space). The optimum number of **diśās** is ten: the eight points of the compass plus the nadir and zenith. Together these **diśās** represent the totality of space or the entire cosmos and, therefore, all the possible directions in which a being can move. Individual beings aim to navigate a safe passage along these **diśās**. A person's safe passage is assisted by acquiring or obtaining what are called **lokas** (worlds, heavens). **Loka** originally meant 'a glade', 'an opening in a forest', 'a space in which movement is possible'.[1] **Lokas** therefore function as radii or corridors along the **diśās**.[2] Obtaining them assures a person's 'foothold' or 'stability' (**pratiṣṭhā**) during his movement[3], affording him safety (**abhaya**) from the hazards of natural existence.[4]

It seems that the oldest method of obtaining these **lokas** was by political might or force. By 'conquering' (**jayati**)[5] an area of land one acquired a 'sphere of space' (**loka**) in which one could then move freely and safely. The cosmic notion of a **loka** may therefore have developed out of the practical enterprise of obtaining access to land by power and might. Those among the Vedic pioneers who obtained land were referred to as **kṣatriya** (from **kṣatra** meaning 'might', 'dominion').[6]

Since the **kṣatriyas** were the most powerful secular element within Vedic society (hence the prominence of Indra in the early Rg Veda) a comprehensive framework of religious rituals - the Vedic **śrauta** rites - were constructed to assist them in the realisation of their ambitions. This can be illustrated by reference to the two **srauta** rites known as 'mounting the quarters of space' (**digvyāsthāpanam**) and 'offerings of the quarters of space' (**diśām aveṣṭayaḥ**) which figure in one of the most impressive **soma** ceremonies, the Rājasūya.[8] Heesterman writes: 'The two ceremonies represent the two joints in the eternal cyclical process of rising to the zenith and descending to the earth. Having gone ritually through these two terminal stations, the sacrificer secures his safe journey along the road"to heaven and back to the earth".'[9] Of the 'sacrificer' or 'patron of the sacrifice' (**yajamāna**)[10] who performs the first rite, Heesterman says 'through this rite (he) ascends to the zenith....He wins the quarters of space or the seasons, thus mastering the whole of the universe in respect to space as well as to time....The universe is divided into four parts with its centre as the fifth, highest quarter (zenith), which encompasses the whole: "the heaven is the quarters of space"(**diśo vai svargo lokaḥ**)...Thus by performing the fifth step the sacrificer appropriates the whole universe."

The design or construction of the sacrificial apparatus for the performance of these rites is as follows: The three spheres - earth,atmosphere and heaven (**svargaloka**)[12] - are signified by the use of a platform set upon a sacrificial post. A ladder leans against the post and at the top of the post is fixed a wooden wheel which can be turned. In the course of the ceremony the **yajamāna** mounts the platform, ascends the ladder, turns the wheel. The wheel is said to be the **vajra**, (weapon) and, by turning it to the right with his hand, he wins the 'quarters of the universe' and descends again. This ascent and descent by the **yajamāna** signifies a journey taken from one **loka** to another and back again. The successful enactment of this rite ensures that his real life journey will be accomplished successfully.[13]

Another key concept in the Vedic view of reality is that of 'fettering'. To acquire a **loka** means that one can move freely and safely, but to be without a **loka** is to find oneself 'fettered', 'bound','restricted' (**bandhana**).[14] This, again, seems to be a notion that originated within an 'aggrandising' context: 'The gods were afraid of the **rājanya** (king) when he was born. While still within (the womb) they fettered him with a bond. The warrior is thus born fettered. If he were not fettered he would continually slay his enemies'.[15] One of the objects of religious ritual, however, is to liberate the ruler from these 'fetters' so that he may fulfil his function as ruler and extend his conquests and sphere of sovereignty.[16]

In the transition from the Vedic to the post-Vedic era three significant changes took place in the conception of the world:[17]

a. The concept of **loka** was simplified by reducing their number.

b. Safety in one's post-mortem as well as in one's present existence became a central concern (e.g., obtaining a **svarga-loka**).[18]

c. The efficacious power came no longer to reside directly in the sacrifice (**yajña**) but in the knowledge of how the sacrifice worked.

The power inherent in the sacrifice came to be transferred from the rite itself to the agent who performed the rite, the supreme officiant of the rite, the brāhmaṇa (one who possesses the **brāhman** or 'truth power').[19] In time the 'brahmana' acquired a monopolistic hold on the interpretation and performance of **śrauta** rites. This meant they could not be performed without his 'supervision'. To obtain his services the **yajamāna** had to provide him with an 'offering' or 'gift' (**dakṣiṇā**). The **brahmana** distributed the **dakṣiṇā** among the officiants of the ceremony (e.g., the **udgātṛ**, **agnīdhra**, **adhvaryu**) with himself at the head of priority.[20] The **dakṣiṇā** could consist of cattle, gold, land, even whole villages and kingdoms in some cases, depending on the wealth of the **yajamāna** and the precise nature and significance of the sacrifice. Nevertheless it is important to appreciate that the offering was, strictly speaking, not to be understood as obligatory; it was not a 'fee', as the word is sometimes translated, but a voluntary gift. It was understood as a token of gratitude or appreciation directed to the **brāhmaṇa** on behalf of the **yajamāna** and signified the presence of a subjective element (i.e., **śraddhā**) in the proceedings.[21] We may compare this with the function of the **dakṣiṇā** (P.**dakkhiṇā**) in Buddhist merit-earning, which also involves a subjective element - the almsgiver's positive confidence (**pasāda**) in the mendicant. Here the mendicant (**bhikkhu, muni**) is equivalent to the **brāhmaṇa** as deserved recipient of the gift.[22]

## Buddhist use of Brahmanic Conceptions

Buddhism also has its conceptual counterpart to the Brahmanic **digvyāsthāpanam** rite. This rite, we have seen, enables the **yajamāna** to master the whole of the universe in respect to space and time; here the counterpart to the **yajamāna** is the **muni** figure of the early Nikāyas who, we showed in chapter one, succeeds in transcending space and time. In Brahmanic religion the **yajamāna** obtains freedom from 'fetters' through the performance of sacrificial ritual; by contrast, freedom from the 'fetters' in Buddhism comes by renouncing the household life and its attendant duties. We noticed in the Isigili Sutta that **paccekabuddhas** are themselves defined as 'freed from all fetters' (**sabbasaṅgātigate**); we noticed too the prominence given to 'fettering' concepts in the Khaggavisāṇa Sutta.

The symbolically enacted journey from one **loka** to another in Brahmanical ritual is described in terms of the concept of 'bringing across' or 'crossing over' (√tṝ). Hence

Agni, the sacrificial fire which joins heaven to earth, is said in the Rg Veda to be 'our means of crossing over'.[23] In the Puṇṇaka-māṇavapucchā Sutta, however, the Buddha explicitly rejects the Brahmanic belief that **yañña** (Skt.yajña) enables one to 'cross over'(**tarati**) birth and ageing.[24] This same notion of **tarati** is of central importance in Pali Buddhism, where it signifies the process of becoming an **ariya-puggala** or **sāvaka** (a person who has entered the path destined to enlightenment), or the crossing from the **lokiya** (worldly) to the **lokuttara** (supra-worldly) realms.[25] In the Sabhiya Sutta the Buddha qua **muni** carries others across the stream of **saṁsāra**; in response to this act the devotee declares: 'you have carried me across' (**mam atāresi**).

The Pali word patiṭṭhitā is often used in an equivalent sense to the Brahmanic term **pratiṣṭhā** (foothold) where the **yajamāna** is said to gain a 'foothold' in a **loka**. Hence in Buddhist usage one who enters upon the noble path (**ariya-magga**) is described as 'firmly established in the dhamma' (**dhamme... patiṭṭhito**).[27] the Buddha is himself said to be a **patitthāpitar**, 'one who establishes the many-folk in the ariyan method' (**bahuno janassa ariye ñāye patiṭṭhāpitā**),[28] whereas the Buddha's chief disciple, Sāriputta, on a certain occasion 'establishes' (**patiṭṭhapeti**) a person in the inferior (**hīna**) realm (i.e., the **brahma-loka**) by teaching him the way to companionship with Brahmā (**Brāhmaṇam sahavyatāya** maggo) through the cultivation of the **brahmavihāras**.[29] The idea of 'standing firmly' (**thale tiṭṭhati**) seems also to be a distinctive feature of the **muni** concept: 'The world is completely unsubstantial, all regions are unstable (samantaṁ **asaro loko, disā sabbā sameritā**)[30] but 'a muni deviates not from truth, (he is) a **brāhmaṇa** who stands on firm ground; having renounced everything, he is called tranquil indeed' (**saccā avokkamma muni thale titthati brāhmaṇo sabbaṁ so paṭinissajja sa ve santo ti vuccati**).[31] Notice here the implicit adoption of Brahmanic metaphysical imagery:

i. The world is unstable but the **brāhmaṇa** obtains a foothold;

ii. 'Tranquillity' (**santo**) stands in opposition to the 'shaken' (**samerita**) cosmos;

iii. Whereas in the **śrauta** rites, the **yaja-māna** 'renounces' (i.e. makes a **dakṣiṇā** of) some of his wealth or property, the **muni** renounces everything; in other words, he effects the counterpart of the highest form of sacrifice.[32]

In Vedic tradition there are two means of achieving control over the universe: physical 'conquest' and religious power - **kṣatra** (lordly power) and **brahman** (holy power). These two means became combined in the single conception of the religious sacrificial rite. The sacrificial rite is therefore a composition of two basic ideologies, that of the **brāhmaṇa** and the **rājan**. The reason why 'kingly' themes and motifs were a dominant feature of sacrificial imagery is twofold: In the first place the king is the embodiment of the ideal man since it is his sovereign task to conquer and rule;[33] this viewpoint is reflected in ancient mythology where the gods succeed in conquering the **asuras** only after electing themselves a king.[34] Secondly, kings feature as the main **yajamānas** because they are the most 'prosperous' (**gataśrī**) among men and have the most to gain or lose.

It is therefore understandable that the **rājan** should come to serve as the prototype for the conception of the **yajamāna**.[35] The successful functioning of the sacrifice which provides the religious basis to the stability and ordered regularity of the universe depends on both the patron and the **brāhmaṇa**-officiant: 'the priest and king together uphold the laws and activities of the world'.[36] Sacrificial ritual brought together the two antithetical elements of **brāhmaṇa** and **kṣatriya**, sacred and profane, into a symbiotic relationship. Hopkins writes: 'The king only by being united with the holy power, brahma, becomes divine, and is, as it were, brahmanized, made one with the Brahman, to whom, as his domestic priest, he is literally wedded (in the words of the marriage ritual). Priest and king swear mutual fidelity and thus the king becomes 'lord of the whole earth and guardian of the law'.[37]

This unification of the **brāhmaṇa** and the **rājan** effected by the sacrifice (**yajña**) is expressed in the image of an individual corporal man: 'The **yajamāna** is the trunk of the sacrifice, the officiants the limbs' (**ātmā vai yajñasya yajamāno, 'ngany ṛtvijaḥ**).[38] The same Brāhmaṇa further states that the ideal man, Prajāpati, is sacrifice, for he created it in his own image.[39] The integral complementarity of brāhmaṇa and **kṣatriya** is articulated even more plainly in the later Bṛhadāraṇyaka Upaniṣad:

> 'Verily, in the beginning this world was **Brahma**, one only. Being one, he was not developed. He created still further a superior form, the Ksatrahood, even those who are **kṣatra** (rulers) among the gods: Indra, Varuṇa, Soma, Rudra, Parjanya, Yama, Mṛtyu, Īśāna. There-

> fore there is nothing higher than **Kṣatra**. Therefore at the Rājasūya ceremony the **Brahman** sits below the **Kshatriya**. Upon Kshatrahood alone does he confer this honour. The same thing, namely Brahmanhood (**brahma**), is the source (**yoni**) of Ksatrahood. Therefore, even if the king attains supremacy, he rests finally upon Brahmanhood as his own source. So whoever injures him (i.e., a **Brahman**) attacks his own source. He fares worse in proportion as he injures (**hiṁsati**) one who is better'.[40]

In this passage it is the **kṣatriya** who attains supremacy (**paramatā**), that is, who realises transcendence. But he owes that transcendence solely to brāhman which alone is transmitted to him through the person of the **brāhmaṇa**. Because **brāhman** is the **kṣatriya**'s source (**yoni**) and can only be derived from the **brāhmaṇa**, his existence is a derived one. He cannot be said to be 'self-become' (**svayaṁbhū**). In this same passage it is also to be noticed that the relationship of the **kṣatriya** to the brāhmaṇa is characterised by the concept of **ahiṁsā** (non-injury). The **brāhmaṇa**'s livelihood and raison d'etre as mediator of **brāhman** means that his own existence depended as much on retaining the confidence of the **kṣatriya** as the latter's ostensible realisation of his role depended on the **brāhmaṇa**. It is this aspect of the **brāhmaṇa**'s dependence which makes the notion of the **kṣatriya** 'renouncing' his dharmic role such anathema to him, for it signifies loss of confidence in himself as a mediator of religious values and ultimately threatens his own redundancy. If the proper behaviour of the **kṣatriya** to the

**brāhmaṇa** constitutes **ahiṁsā** then '**kṣatriya** renunciation' must be characterised as an abrogation of **ahiṁsā**, and is tantamount to the perpetration of a form of **hiṁsā** (injury) upon the **brāhmaṇa**. 'Renunciation' (**pravrajyā**) therefore can technically be construed a form of 'brahmanicide'. The phenomenon of '**kṣatriya** renunciation' can be symbolically interpreted as a case of withdrawing **ahiṁsā** from the **brāhmaṇa** and applying it in another direction, thereby making possible an altogether wider, 'ethical' notion of **ahiṁsā**. Thus the **brāhmaṇas** had their counterpart to the Sramanic' concept of **ahiṁsā** but it was restricted to the notion of the **kṣatriya**'s duty to the priestly officiant of the sacrifice. It is important to see that in giving **ahiṁsā** a universal application, that is, an 'ethical' significance, the **kṣatriya** achieves an identity of his own (**svayambhū**), a self-deriving quest for realisation that no longer is attributable to a force outside of himself (the **brāhmaṇa**). It is this shift of interpretation that is evidenced in the Jain story of King Nami's renunciation.

In canonical sources the Buddha is presented as a figure who reconciles within himself the antithetical elements of **brāhmaṇa** (for he is 'knower' or 'recipient' of the truth-power viz. **dhamma**) and **rājan** (as the royal Yajamāna mounts the sacrificial ladder to turn the wheel and ritually conquer the quarters, the Buddha conquers the spiritual world by turning the wheel of **dhamma**). Whereas the dualism of **brāhmaṇa** and **rājan** is presupposed within sacrificial ritual and is always there to threaten its efficacy, in the person of the Buddha the two elements are dissolved into one. Within his corporate person he embodies all the components integral to the successful functioning of the **yajña**.[41]

So far in this chapter we have discerned three fundamental ways in which Buddhism adopted concepts functioning within Brahmanic and Vedic sacrificial rites and used them to present its own 'cultus'. Firstly, the **dakṣiṇā** (P.**dakkhiṇā**) is for the upkeep of the **pabbajita**, that is, for the **bhikkhu-saṅgha** instead of the **brāhmaṇa**. Secondly, the **dhamma** not the sacrificial ritual, serves as the 'foothold' (**patiṭṭhitā**); here the Buddha becomes the sacrificial fire (**agni**) that 'carries across' (**tarati**) the supplicant. Thirdly, both the officiating **brāhmaṇa** and the **yajamāna** par excellence are together integrated in the one person of the Buddha. It will be noticed that these three entities, the **saṅgha**, the **dhamma** and the Buddha together comprise the **ti-ratana** (three jewels) of Buddhism, and it is precisely by taking refuge (**saraṇa**) in these that a lay person allies or identifies himself with the Buddhist 'cultus'. In its beginnings, therefore, Buddhism represents its own 'cultus' in such a way as to enter into direct competition with the 'cultus' of Brahmanic religion.

## Buddhism's re-orientation of Brahmanism

We have just indicated that one of the most important differences between Brahmanism and the Śramaṇa Tradition hinges upon the issue of the interpretation given to **ahiṁsā** (non-injury). We shall now see more specifically that the differences between Brahmanism and Buddhism itself also centre around the ethic of **ahiṁsā** (in Pali the term **avihiṁsā** is the preferred form). Whereas the performance of **śrauta** rites require the immolation of a victim, Buddhism stands opposed to the taking of life.[42] However, Buddhism does not reject the principle of 'sacrifice' (Skt. **yajña**; P.**yañña**) per se - as evidenced for instance in the Kūṭadaṇḍa Sutta[43] - but opposes the performance of Brahmanic sacrificial rites and denies their religious efficacy. The Buddhist tradition reinterprets **yanna** to mean obedience to the Buddha's own **dhamma**, either as a lay follower (**upāsaka**) or as a monk (**bhikkhu**).[44]

In so far as Buddhism and Brahmanism together subscribe to the notion of sacrifice but differ radically in their interpretation of it, it is important to grasp the different assumptions upon which these divergent interpretations are based. A principal function of Brahmanic sacrificial ritual is to counteract the inimical forces or hostile beings (**rakṣasas**)[45] which inhabit the **diśās**. In Vedic mythology **rakṣasas** are the archetypal enemies of man, in the same way that **asuras** are viewed as the primordial enemies of the **devas**. The **rakṣasas** threaten the well-being of man by subverting the **yajña**:[46] by interfering in the sacrifice they are said to undermine the overall stability of the **manuṣyaloka** (human world).[47] The very name, **rakṣasa**, means 'that which is to be warded off'.[48]

In the Digvyāsthāpanam ceremony of the Rājasūya, the king, re-enacts an archaic myth in which Indra kicks off the head of Namuci the **asura**, knocks him over and treads upon him with his foot. **Rakṣasas** then emerge from the bulge caused by the pressure of his foot, and 'he (Indra) thereby beats off the fiends, the Rakshas; and in like manner this one (the king) thereby beats off the fiends, the Rakshas'.[49] This mythical motif shows that the cosmological picture is an integrated one: the **rakṣasas** (enemies of man) emanate from the **asuras** (enemies of the **deva**) as an added force in their struggle with the **devas**. But Indra, the distinguished slayer of Vṛtra, is triumphant and all-supreme since he conquers them and 'beats them off'.

Violence is a theme regularly connected with the **rakṣasas**. Since **rakṣasas** are conceived as inveterately injurious, injurious counterparts must be used to repel them. Thus the fire (**agni**) of the sacrifice is said to destroy them,[50] the blood of the victims to appease them,[51] and they are vanquished by the might of the archetypal king, Indra.[52] In Vedic cosmology man is exposed to 'danger' or 'hostility' (**bhaya**) which is personified by the **rakṣasas**. The way of counteracting these inimical forces is to use like against like - to destroy them before they can destroy you. This is in keeping with the Vedic notion of 'conquest' as the paradigm of 'power'.

By contrast, Buddhism does not adopt the principle of violence to repel the dangerous and threatening (**bhaya**) forces in the cosmos, but employs the principle of conciliation instead. This is the nature of the difference in presuppositions which sets apart the Buddhist from the Brahmanic 'cultus'. A major reason why a person undertakes **pabbajjā** is to become extricated from the sorts of conditions and situations which impel one to injure and take life. We earlier mentioned that, according to the teaching of the Buddha, abandoning harming and 'dwelling friendly and compassionate to all creatures that have life' (**sabba-pāṇabhūtahitānukampī viharati**) is the first of the many fruits of becoming a 'renouncer'. In the Aṅguttara Nikāya, **pabbajjā** is seen to be a direct alternative to offering sacrifices (**yañña**), showing that they were mutually exclusive of one another.[53] We may also remind ourselves that in the Daḷhanemi legend the convention of **pabbajjā** is the crucial factor in staving off anarchy and the breakdown of society; the governance of **dhamma** continues only if the counsel of the **rājīsi**, the royal renouncer, is heeded.

To summarise. The institution of renunciation (**pabbajjā**) is the method Buddhism uses to mitigate the play of inimical forces in the world. **Pabbajjā** ensures that the adept does no harm to others. We are about to show how the brahma-vihāras complement **pabbajjā** by ensuring that a person is not harmed by others.

## The Brahma-vihāras

Whereas it has been seen that **yajña** operates on the assumption that force repels force, like is used against like, the **brahma-vihāra** meditations work on the entirely different assumption that 'hostility' should be met and assuaged with 'loving kindness' (**mettā**), etc. We now propose to show that they represent a direct counterpart of the Brahmanic **yajña**, both as a method of transcending dangers and as a salvific scheme. In order to do this, we must examine the practice of the **brahmavihāras** as a type of meditational technique and attainment. In the first place it is to be noticed they comprise a form of meditation which is trans-sectarian. According to C.A.F. Rhys-Davids, sayings on three of the brahma-vihāras - **maitrī**, **karuṇyā** and **upekṣā** - are found in the early Upaniṣads and in the Mahābhārata.[54] They also feature in Patañjali's Yoga Sūtras.[55] The Jains possess a similar procedure with some slight variation in two of the four recognised components: maitrī, **karuṇyā**, pramodā (a cognate of **muditā**) and **mādhyastha** (non-attachment).[56] The **brahma-vihāras** themselves are identified as dispositions of mind or volitional states (**citta-bhāvanā**). The Nikāyas enumerate four: **mettā** (loving-kindness), **karuṇā** (compassion), **muditā** (sympathy) and **upekkhā** (equanimity). These mind-states may be cultivated collectively or individually.[57] One who cultivates them creates an 'abode' (**vihāra**) in which he abides (**vihārati**) in the appropriate mind-state; hence **metta-vihāra**, etc. Cultivating a **brahma-vihāra** involves the process of 'permeating', 'suffusing', 'pervading' (**pharati**) the four quarters (i.e., **sabba loka**) with the appropriate characteristic of mind (**citta**).[58] Here the mind of the adept functions like a force-field. In the case of **mettā**, for example, a force-field of 'protection' is created. The range of this force is said to be far-reaching (**vipula**), wide-spread (**mahaggata**) and unlimited (**appamāṇa**). It permeates (**pharati**) the 'will' of those upon whom it acts, so that they are constrained to respond non-aggressively. The classic example of this in Buddhist legend is the story of the Buddha using **mettā** to quieten and pacify Nālāgiri, the wild elephant. Finally it should be noted that the 'permeating' (**pharati**) and 'abiding' (**vihārati**) technique makes the **brahma-vihāras** a category of **jhāna**. Accordingly, a situation of 'solitude' (**paṭisallāna**) is an important condition for their cultivation.[59]

The **brahma-vihāras** may be said to operate on the principle of **avihiṁsā** (refraining from injury) as distinct from **vihiṁsā**, the principle by which the 'sacrifice' repels the **rakṣasas**.[60] Among the four **vihāras** **mettā** receives most prominence. It occurs more often by itself than any of the other three and appears to be the only one among them having an active 'protective' function.[61] **Mettā** expresses itself as compassion (**anukampā**):

'With a mind of unlimited **mettā** he shows compassion everywhere, To all the inhabitants of the triple world'[62]

According to canonical teaching, **mettā** alone of the four **brahma-vihāras** leads to rebirth in the **brahma-loka**; **karuṇā-vihāra** leads to rebirth among the Abhāssara deities; **muditā-vihāra** among the Subhakiṅha deities; and **upekhā-vihāra** among the Vehappala deities.[63] It may therefore be the case that the practice of **mettā** itself is older than the collective notion of the four **brahma-vihāras**.[64] If this is so, we have a rather interesting form of parallelism existing between (our theory of) the relationship of Nimi to the other three kings who become **paccekabuddhas** and the relationship of **mettā** to the other three **brahma-vihāras**.

Both **mettā** by itself and the **brahma-vihāras** collectively can be seen to function as the counterpart of **yajña** on three distinct fronts: protectively, salvifically and ethically. We have chosen to cite a passage from the Mettā Vagga of the Aṅguttara Nikāya to illustrate all three functions.[65] The Mettā-Vagga passage consists of three parts: The first part lists the 'good consequences' (ānisaṁsa) of developing **mettā**; the second part, states the salvific function of **mettā**; and the third, contrasts **mettā** with the Brahmanic religious ideal. **Mettā** protects in the following ways:

(a) One sleeps happy
One wakes up happy
One has no nightmares
One is beloved **(piya)** among humans **(manussā)**
One is beloved **(piya)** among non-humans **(amanussā)**
One is protected **(rakkhanti)** by **deva**

Fire, poison and sword do not affect one
If one does not penetrate further (**uttarim̊** ie. become an **arahant**) then one attains the **brahmaloka**.
One composes one's mind quickly
One's countenance becomes serene (**mukkhavaṇṇo vippasīdati**)
One dies unbewildered.[66]

**Mettā** saves in the following ways:

(b) For the one who sets his mind to developing unlimited (**appamāṇa**) **metta**
The fetters (**saññojanā**) are loosened, the end to rebirth (**upadhi**) is seen.
If one, pure-minded, develops **mettā** toward just one creature, then one is good (**kusalī**).
So if one's mind is compassionate (**anukampī**) toward all creatures, one makes abounding merit (**puñña**).

**Mettā** is intended to replace Brahmanic sacrifice:

(c) The **rājīsis** (Skt.**rājarṣi**), having conquered the earth go around sacrificing (**yajamānānupariyayā**):
The **aśvamedha**, **puruṣamedha**, **śamyāprāsa**, **vājapeya nirargala**'[67]
These are not worth one sixteenth the practice of developing **mettā**,
Like the moon outshines all the stars.
One who neither kills or causes (others) to kill, who neither conquers or causes (others) to conquer
Regards all living things with **mettā**, he has hate (**veraṁ**) for no one.

It may be noticed that seven out of the eleven 'good consequences' of practising **metta** belong to the theme of freedom from **bhaya** or **hiṁsā**. They are the sorts of results which in Brahmanism **yajña** is expected to achieve. The sixth good consequence, protection by **devas**, echoes the Vedic myth in which Indra drives-away the **rakṣasas**. Since **pacceka-buddhas** practise **mettā**, and one of their most distinctive characteristics is **pāsādika** (serenity), it is not without interest to observe that one of the consequences of **mettā** here is a 'serene' countenance.

We must note too that the king is here represented as the chief patron of sacrifice and that **mettā** is asserted to be a direct alternative to the performance of Brahmanic ritual. The expression 'having conquered the earth' (**sattasaṇḍaṁ paṭhaviṁ vijetvā**; lit. transl. 'having conquered the world of creatures') and the choice of the term **anupariyayā**, which denotes the 'continual' use of sacrifices, together imply that kings are the principal perpetrators of **hiṁsā**: firstly, by the secular act of 'conquest'; secondly, by 'animal sacrifice' which sanctions and sustains their power.

Part (c) of this passage is of particular importance to our general argument, for two reasons. In the first instance it provides evidence of a thematic link between **mettā** and 'kingship'. The objective is the same as the Brahmanicised notion of the 'king' or 'prototype **yajamāna**': universal dominion. But the method is different: conquest without violence. Secondly, as we shall shortly show, the doctrine of **mettā** is older than Buddhism itself and therefore may be seen to represent a bridge between the Brahmanic conception of the ideal king (i.e., **rājarṣi**), the patron of **śrauta** ritual, and the Buddhist notion of the ideal king (**rājīsi**) as the mainstay and upholder of **dhamma**.

Beside the **brahma-vihāra** meditations another important source of 'protection' for Buddhists is the use of the paritta.[68] A

**paritta** consists of nothing other than a formalising or ritualising of the principle of **mettā**. Words spoken by the Buddha (or by **paccekabuddhas** - viz. Isigili Sutta), or words to which he gives his sanction, are formally recited by Buddhists, principally **bhikkhus**. The association of these words with the Buddha (or **paccekabuddha**) affords protection against an impending misfortune or danger. These words, sometimes the length of an entire **sutta**, are called **paritta**. They operate in a similar fashion to the 'act of truth' (**saccakiriya**) discussed in chapter two.

Another term for paritta is **rakkhamanta** (a mantra of protection), a concept which has an equivalent in Brahmanic religion. Certain mantras of the Atharva Veda, for instance, are known as **rakṣamantras**.[69] A comparison of the way one of these works with the way the **khandha paritta** works reveals the contrasting assumptions on which they operate: In the Atharva Veda mantra the snakes in the six regions (diśā) are implored to 'be kind and gracious unto us and bless us'.[70] The Buddhist **khandha paritta** is also directed at the problem of dangerous snakes. The formula that is recited consists of a profession of **mettā** towards the four types of snake (corresponding to the four regions), as well as towards other animals and insects, with an entreaty that they should not harm the reciter.[71] The purpose of this particular **paritta** is to protect **bhikkhus** against snake-bites, etc. when forest-dwelling. It is to be noticed that the Atharva Veda and Buddhist mantras differ in one important respect: the former simply invokes the snakes to be kind to the reciter, whereas the **paritta** makes an affirmation of **mettā** towards the snakes, etc. prior to invoking their kindness. In the case of the **paritta** the initiative or power to create a situation of 'safety' (abhaya) and 'well-being' lies with the reciter. By his identification with 'the word of the Buddha' the reciter has power over these creatures, but the reciter of the Atharva Veda mantra is ultimately reliant on the goodwill of the creature invoked.

## The Upaniṣadic Concept of the Salvific Goal

We have seen that in Brahmanical **śrauta** ritual the **yajamāna** acquires a **loka** or **lokas** that afford him the security and stability to which he aspires. In the ensuing Upaniṣadic period the ideal of security and stability becomes synonymous with the attainment of one **loka** in particular, the **brahmaloka**. We shall now consider how this concept first emerged within the post-Vedic tradition.

We have already indicated that in the post-Vedic era religious cosmology developed an increasing concern with the well-being of the post-mortem person. One of the prime concerns of the yajamāna came to be the desire to obtain a **puṇya-loka** or entry to a **svarga loka** after his death.[72] The **puṇya-loka**, as the term indicates, is acquired through the accumulation of merit which comes predominantly from the observance of sacrificial ritual.[73] A **svarga loka** was a place inhabited by the gods and, since the gods were regarded as the source of protection against, for instance, the **rakṣasas** they epitomised safety and permanence. To share the world of the gods, therefore, was a way of assuring direct access to such permanent safety (**a-bhayam**).[74] Consequently the supreme religious objective was the obtaining of access to the **loka** of the gods in one's post-mortem existence, a goal made possible by following the correct ritual procedures.[75]

Upaniṣadic ideology marked the emergence of a different means than sacrificial ritual to obtain a similar object or goal. It is not within our province here to investigate how far Upaniṣadic thought was a development out of sacrificial ritual or how far its development is attributable to non-Aryan influences, but we do observe that its frame of reference or cosmology was essentially the same as that of the Brāhmaṇas. Obtaining the **brahma loka** was the summum bonum of the Upaniṣadic seer as the **svarga loka** was the summum bonum of the ritualist. Both were places inhabited by gods or God (Brahmā) and both signified a condition of permanence (viz.**amṛta**) according to their own terms of reference.

The use of **brahma loka** instead of **svarga loka** to represent the **parama-loka** (supreme goal) would seem to have to do with **brahman** being a power concept (nb. 'truth power') and with the idea that **brahman** must be present for a project or enterprise to be rendered effective. So, for example, in **śrauta** ritual the rite achieves its efficacy when the **yajamāna** is (ritually) reborn a pure **brāhmaṇa**; here the official **brāhmaṇa** serves as the repository of **brahman** out of which the **yajamāna** is reborn.[76] In so far as **brahman** was required for the complete efficacy of the yajña, the Upaniṣadic seers realised that it was the key which gave access to all reality. Hence the knowledge (**jñāna**) of **brahman** is the 'performing' of the **yajña**: 'whosoever, knowing this, performs this sacrifice'.[77] Consequently, **brahma** comes to represent both the 'goal' (viz. **brahma loka**) and the 'means' (viz. **brahma-carya**).

It is important to understand that in Brahmanical sacrificial theory the **yajamāna**'s fate is wholly determined by the success or otherwise of the ritual; the ritual, as it were, carries or bears (**bibharti**) him and this is why it is vital it should be performed correctly. Just as the **yajamāna** achieves his salvific objective through an exact identification of the ritual with the real cosmos by symbolically enacting in the ritual what he hopes to achieve in reality, so the Upaniṣadic seer achieves his aim by discerning and effecting a similar correspondence between his self and the actual cosmos. We, therefore, have the following set of parallels:

| | | |
|---|---|---|
| Agent: | **yajamāna (ātman)** | Upaniṣadic seer (**ātman**) |
| Means: | **yajña** creates **puṇya** | **dhyāna** creates **jñāna** |
| End: | **svarga loka** (**deva loka**) | **brahma loka** (**Ātman;Brahman**) |

The idea of a situation of permanent safety, whether it be obtained through meditation (**dhyāna**) or through ritual performance, (**yajña**), is synonymous with the idea of being able to move (**carati**) safely and freely in all **lokas**:

> 'he who sees this, who thinks this, who understands this... he is sovereign (**svar-āt**), he moves at pleasure (**kāma-cāra**) in all **lokas**. But they who think differently from this have others for their rulers (**anya-rājānas**), they have perishable **lokas**. They are unable to move at pleasure in all **lokas**'.[78]

In the Upaniṣads, freedom of movement (e.g., through the **diśās**) and the acquisition of secure **lokas** remains the same objective as for Brahmanic ritual, but the secure base or foothold (**pratiṣṭhā**) has been assimilated to the holistic notion of Brahman or Ātman. Thus the attainment of complete freedom from danger is signified by access to the **brahma loka**:

> 'only they (i.e., the **brahmacarins**) possess that **brahma loka**, they move at pleasure in all **loka**'.[79]

## The Upaniṣads and the Brahma-vihāras

The doctrine of the **brahma-vihāras** within the Buddhist Nikāyas suggests definite parallels with Upaniṣadic teaching. The cultivation of either **mettā** itself or the **brahma-vihāras** collectively leads to rebirth in the **brahma loka**. They are a form of **dhyāna** (P.**jhāna**), as we have already noted, and they enable the adept to move safely in each of the four quarters (**cātuddisā**). In fact the sense given here to **vihāra** closely parallels the Vedic meaning of **loka**, as that which acts as a 'pocket' or 'sphere' of protection. Where they do happen to differ quite significantly from the Upaniṣads is in their critique of traditional Brahmanic religion. The Muṇḍaka Upaniṣad, for instance, demotes the accomplishments of sacrificial ritual (**karma**) to a secondary status, namely, the attainment of 'perishable worlds' (**kṣīṇa-lokāḥ**) as distinct from the 'imperishable' (**akṣara**) **brahman** or **puruṣa**.[80] Consequently, it is said that the ritualists 'having enjoyed the high place of heaven won by good deeds, enter again this world or a still lower one'.[81] Ritual is not fully rejected but merely relegated by establishing a hierarchical or priority system in which men are deluded and ignorant if they regard sacrifices and works of merit as the 'most important' (**variṣṭha**) goal. By contrast, **mettā** in Buddhism functions as a direct counterpart that altogether excludes sacrificial rites.

## Buddhism's Relationship to the Brahma-vihāra Tradition

Having ascertained that the **brahma-vihāras** parallel the Brahmanic religious scheme but operate on the contrasting assumption of **avihiṁsa**, we now suggest that they represent an important aspect of the Buddhistic tradition prior to the advent of Sākyamuni. A combination of factors can be adduced in support of this contention. First and foremost, on the basis of evidence provided by the Nikāyas the **brahma-vihāras** antedate the time of Sākyamuni. In addition, the brahma-vihāras' close association with the figures of the **paccekabuddha**, the **ekacarin** and the **muni** is suggestive of their antiquity. Having a pre-Sākyamuni identity means that they are superseded by the Buddha's teaching which comprises a superior soteriology. Albeit the Buddha recognises them as an authentic form of spiritual practice and accommodates them within his own scheme of teaching.

In view of these historical facts the **brahma-vihāras** came to occupy an equivocal status within Buddhism. When practised outside the knowledge of the Buddha's own teaching their salvific value is regarded by Buddhists as singularly limited; but when practised in conjunction with his own teaching they serve as an agency (either directly or indirectly) of transcendence. We shall therefore aim to clarify the relationship of the **brahma-vihāra** meditations historically and doctrinally to Early Buddhism by examining the subject in greater detail. Our chief purpose in so doing is to provide further evidence in support of the thesis that Early Buddhism operated essentially from the standpoint of a 'cultus' centring on the uniqueness of the person and teaching of Sākyamuni. The final part of this discussion will prove to be the longest. It is concerned with highlighting those criteria in Buddhism which determine whether a form of religious practice is conducive to transcendence (ending rebirth) or not, and with showing what can and cannot be regarded as authentic **sāsana** (instruction).

As already indicated the Nikāyas consistently represent the **brahma-vihāra** meditations as a form of ascetico-religious practice that existed before the advent of the Buddha. For example, they report the ancient figure of King Makhādeva of Videha - according to Buddhist tradition the founding-father of 'renunciation'- as one who practised the **brahma-vihāras**. Passages in the Dīgha Nikāya mention two additional mythical figures of the past - King Sudassana and Govinda - as having practised them too.[82] It is noteworthy that these three personalities feature in early **jātaka** tales, where each is identified as the Buddha in one of his former existences. This can be taken as evidence that Buddhist tradition wanted to associate itself integrally with the older tradition of the **brahma-vihāras**. The Nikāyas also list the individual names of a group of ascetics (**titthakaras**) from the past whose sole distinguishing feature is the practice and teaching of **mettācitta** or **karuṇā** leading to rebirth in the **brahma loka**.[83] Their description reads

> 'six famous teachers from the past who observed non-harm, were sweet-smelling, liberated through pity, having traversed

> the fetter of desire; quenching the passion of desire, they achieved the **brahma loka**'.[84]

We note yet again how this passage confirms the link between 'non-harm' (**ahiṁsā**) and the practice of the '**brahma-vihāra**' meditations.

In addition to being older than Buddhism and yet practised by the Buddhists themselves the **brahma-vihāras** were also cultivated and taught by non-Buddhist contemporaries of Sākyamuni, those known canonically as 'wanderers of other views' (**aññatitthiyaparibbājaka**).[85] We shall explore the implication of this fact in a moment.

That the teaching of Sākyamuni was considered by his followers to represent a new and unique form of gnosis is shown by the conclusions to the Majjhima and Dīgha Nikāya versions of the Makhādeva and Govinda legends. These clearly stipulate that the **brahmacariya** of the Buddha, namely, the doctrine of the noble eightfold path (**ariyo aṭṭhangiko maggo**), is an unprecedented teaching and the only means to the realisation of'**nibbāna**'.[86] This affirmation is the culmination of discourses specifically about the **brahma-vihāras**, and its purpose is to make it absolutely clear that no one should mistakenly construe these meditations in themselves to be a sufficient vehicle of salvation. Nevertheless, the Buddha saw fit to incorporate them into his own scheme of spiritual practice, and thereupon recommended them both to his own **bhikkhus** and to other ascetics such as the **tevijjā brāhmaṇas** (learned in the three-fold veda).[87] From the Tevijja Sutta it appears that this branch of the Brahmanic tradition had no knowledge of these meditations, a not unexpected discovery if our earlier analysis is correct that the **brahma-vihāras** arose outside of Brahmanism.

We shall now proceed to summarise the Buddha's teaching on how to be reborn in the company of the **brahma** gods (viz. **brahma loka sahavyatā**), as it is given in the Tevijja Sutta. We do this for two specific reasons: to show that the practice of developing the **brahma-vihāra** meditations is the culmination of a series of graduated steps of training; and to draw attention to the fact that this training involves characteristics which traditionally come within the categories of Buddhist **sīla** (morality) or **samādhi** (meditation) rather than **paññā** (insight). The Sutta teaches that the first step for the Buddhist novitiate is hearing the **dhamma** and having 'faith' (saddhā) in the Tathāgata; the second step is to become a renouncer (**pabbajita**); this is followed by the practice of the lesser morality (**cūḷa-sīlam**); then comes a sense of joy (**sukha**). The remaining stages are characteristics of **samādhi**: 'guarding the doors of the senses' (**indriyesu guttadvāro hoti**), 'mindfulness and attentiveness' (**sati-sampajāna**), 'contentment' (**santuṭṭha**), 'retirement to seclusion' (**vivittaṁ senāsanaṁ**); then the five hindrances (**pañca nīvaraṇa**) are abandoned; in the penultimate stage, the entire body is filled with peace and joy (**pīti-sukha**); finally, the brahmaviharas themselves are cultivated. This is the full extent of the Buddha's teaching on this particular occasion. It is taught that rebirth in the brahma **loka** comes by reason of cultivating those attributes possessed by the god Brahma, namely **avera-citta** (a mind free from hate), **avyāpajjha-citta** (a disposition not to injure), **asamkiliṭṭha-citta** (an undefiled mind) and **vasavatti** (self-mastery). Clearly these are the particular attributes which give rise to the expression **brahma loka sahavyatā** (companionship of the **brahma** world). The basic principle behind the teaching is 'unification' (**saṁsanda**) by means of 'correspondence' or 'likeness' (**sameti**): one achieves entry to the **brahma loka** by adopting the characterists of the god Brahmā. We would remind ourselves that a similar operative principle governs the thinking behind **śrauta** rites: the **yajamāna** becomes 'divine' by unification with the brāhmaṇa (who embodies **brahman**). The **brahma-vihāras** functionally resemble Brahmanic **yajña** but operate instead upon the assumption of the spiritual potency of the **ahiṁsā** ethic.

If it is the case that the **brahma-vihāras** antedate Buddhism yet became incorporated within Buddhism then we would expect some evidence of this situation to be apparent in the representation of the figure of the **paccekabuddha**, a predecessor of Buddhism too. In order to establish whether or not this is so we shall need to refer again to certain passages and personalities discussed earlier.

The Majjhima Nikāya version of the story of King Makhādeva of Videha, The monarch who founded 'renunciation', has a thematic association with the **paccekabuddha** because it belongs within the Nimi complex of legends. This version points to the existence of a connection between the custom of renunciation, the practice of the **brahmavihāra** meditations and a belief in the attainment of rebirth in the **brahma loka**. It also implies that this nexus of beliefs and practices originated in the region of Videha. The legendary figure of Makhādeva serves as the important link between the three variables of the **brahma-vihāras**, renunciation and the region of Videha.

We now turn to the place of the **brahma-vihāras** within the Khaggavisāṇa Sutta which allegedly contains utterances of **paccekabuddhas**. This Sutta is observed to open with the subject of 'renunciation' (v.35) and to finish on the theme of the '**brahma-vihāras**' (v.75). In other words, it is structured in such a way as to conform with the notion of pre-Buddhistic spirituality typified in the Makhādeva era as outlined above. The Sutta is replete with expressions which imply the practice of the **brahma-vihāras** and their conceptual basis:

> 'He goes where he wishes'[88]
> 'He is a man of the four regions and not hostile, being contented with whatever happens; A fearless overcomer of dangers'[89]
> 'Like the wind he is not caught in a net'[90]

In the Commentarial tales illustrating these verses, **paccekabuddhas** are identified as the principal practitioners of these meditations. To take one salient example:[91] The King of Bārāṇasī offers hospitality to four **paccekabuddhas**. Unaware of their true identity he asks whom they are. They reply

> 'We are called those of the four regions' (**cātuddisā nāmāti**)
> King: 'What does it mean, those of the four regions?'
> Paccekabuddhas: 'There is no danger (**bhaya**) or anxiety (**cittutrāsa**) for us anywhere in the four regions.'
> King: 'Why is there no danger for you?'
> Paccekabuddhas: 'We develop loving-kindness, compassion, sympathy and equanimity; that is why there is no danger.'[92]

The king then draws a comparison between **yañña** (sacrifice) and the **brahma-vihāras**, in view of the fact that they are both intended to dispel danger (**bhaya**). He declares that **brāhmaṇas** praise the slaughter of several thousands of beings and therefore attempt to purify the impure by the impure.

However, samanas he observes, are different: they purify the impure by the pure.

Another passage from the Commentaries refers to someone going on to become a **pacceka-buddha** after having first developed **metta-vihāra**: King Brahmadatta of Bārāṇasī became disgusted with military activity owing to the killing (hiṁsā) and the carnage that it involves. Instead he decided to develop the meditation on **mettā**. Using this as a jhanic support (padaka), he came to thoroughly understand (sammasita) the sankhāras and to attain the 'knowledge of enlightenment (paccekabodhiñāṇa).[93]

Clearly **paccekabuddhas** are conceived by Buddhist tradition as closely connected with the practice of **mettā** and the other **brahma-vihāras**.

## The Equivocal Status of the 'Brahma-Vihāras' in Nikāya Doctrine

We have tried to provide some indication that the Nikāyas teach a soteriological distinction between practising the brahma-vihāras from within the Buddhist 'cultus', and practising them outside it. Given the existence of this particular doctrine, we propose to ask why such a distinction should have held currency. In seeking a solution to this question we shall need to further address ourselves to the subject of the historical relationship between Buddhism and the brahma-vihāras. Since the doctrine maintains that this set of meditations can function as a vehicle or agency of transcendence when cultivated in the proper context or under the requisite conditions, then we are intent on explaining the mechanism by which this becomes possible. Here, it will be seen, the Buddha's own teaching turns out to be the crucial catalyst that transmutes these meditations into agencies of transcendence.

Two passages in particular, one from the Aṅguttara and the other from the Saṁyutta Nikāya, set out the distinction between the **brahma-vihāras** as practised by non-Buddhists (e.g., the wanderers of other views: **añña-titthiyaparibbājakas**) and as developed by disciples of the Buddha (i.e.,**sāvakas**).[94] In the latter passage, a group of Buddhist monks become alarmed when they discover that the **brahma-vihāra** meditations are also cultivated by non-Buddhist ascetics. Their concern leads them to seek out the Buddha and question him about whether there is any difference between his own teaching and the teaching of other ascetics on the **brahma-vihāras**. In reply to their question the Buddha explains that all who succeed in cultivating (bhāvanā) the brahma-vihāras, irrespective of their sectarian allegiance, qualify for rebirth as 'spontaneously born ones' (**opapātika**) in one of the heavens.[95] So, for example, success in the cultivation of **metta-vihāra** leads to rebirth as a **brahma-kāyika deva**. However, the Buddha is careful to point out that only disciples (**sāvaka**) of the Buddha proceed on to **parinibbāna** directly from their existence as **opapātikas**. Here the Buddha is providing a description of the classical Buddhist category of the 'non-returner'(**anāgamin**).[96] Canonical Buddhism therefore instances the doctrine that it is not exclusively humans that attain **nibbāna** but that gods can too, when they have achieved a certain status as a disciple (**sāvaka**) in their preceding existence. The non-**sāvaka** (i.e., **puthujjana**) who cultivates the **brahma-vihāras**, however, is not just deprived of entry into **parinibbāna** but also is subject to further rebirth in lower existences as an animal or a **peta**.[97]

There are other Nikāya passages which refer to the **brahma-vihāras** as a positive spiritual accomplishment but without remarking on this explicit distinction. These nevertheless presuppose the **sāvaka** status of the adept.[98] Meanwhile those passages which do allude to the distinction between **sāvaka** and **puthujjana** in respect of the practice of these meditations are careful to define that difference. So, for instance, the **puthujjana** is criticised for not appreciating the significance or seeing the implication of their practice: it is claimed that the object **(gatikā)**, highest attainment **(paramā)**, outcome **(phalā)** and true fulfilment **(pariyosānā)** of the brahma-vihāras are beyond the **putthujana**'s scope **(visaya)**. The only ones in whose scope they do lie are the Tathāgata or Tathāgatasāvakas or 'those who have heard it of them'.[99] Elsewhere it says that among those who develop the **brahmavihāras** there are ones who have not heard' **(assutavanto = puthujjana)** and ones who have heard (sutavanto=sāvaka), leaving it quite apparent that the crucial difference resides in the 'cultic' factor: whether a person has or has not heard and accepted the Buddha's teaching.[100] In terms of further doctrinal elaboration the difference consists in whether one develops the **brahma-vihāras** in association with **(sahagata)** the seven limbs of enlightenment **(bojjhanga)** or develops them complemented by insight into the three marks of existence **(ti-lakkhaṇa)**.[101] In the former instance each **brahma-vihāra** has its own individual category of spiritual realization which it accomplishes: one who develops **mettā ceto-vimutti** (freedom of mind through loving kindness) has as his highest attainment **parama-subha**; one who cultivates

**karuṇā** has the sphere of infinite space (**ākāsānañcāyatana**) as his highest attainment; **muditā**, the sphere of infinite consciousness (**viññāṇañcāyatana**); and **upekhā** has the sphere of nothingness (**ākiñcaññāyatana**). Each of these attainments is understood to be consonant with the insight (**paññā**) or freedom of mind (**ceto-vimutti**) qualifying a person to be an **anāgamin.** Elsewhere it is said that the meditation (**bhāvanā**) on each of the **brahma-vihāras** should be practised (**bahulīkata**), mastered (**yāni-kata**), made a support (**vatthu-kata**), matured (**anuṭṭhitaṁ**), accumulated (**paricita**) and pursued (**susamāraddha**) for the purpose of producing **ceto-vimutti**; on those grounds, the meditations are seen as factors (**dhātu**) conducing to freedom (**nissaraṇīya**).[102] When, however, the Nikāyas represent what the brahma-vihāras mean to the aññatitthiyāparibbājaka's, the notion of **vimutti** or **ceto-vimutti** is noticeably absent.[103] This would seem to be another way of characterising the difference between the two kinds of adept. The disciple of the Buddha is the one who in fact makes the meditations into an instrument of freedom (**vimutti**).

Since the **brahma-vihāras** are acknowledged by the Nikāyas to be pre-Buddhist as well as extra-Buddhist, it seems appropriate to describe their incorporation into Buddhist practice as a form of assimilation. Alternatively it could be maintained that the they were a part of Buddhism's natural heritage but not uniquely so; in this respect they share the same ambiguous position as the phenomenon of **iddhi** (magic power) in that both are practised by non-Buddhists as well as Buddhists. In view of these observations, the 'legitimated' version of the **brahma-vihāras**, the doctrine of them in the Nikāyas, must have constituted an amended or modified version of the original. This leads us to consider the question of why it should have been thought necessary to introduce this modification. A clue to the answer can be found by looking back at the Samyutta passage just cited. It will be recalled that some of the Buddha's **bhikkhus** encounter **aññatitthiyāparibbājakas** who claim that there is no difference between their own doctrine (**anusāsana**) and that of the Buddha, since they both promulgate the teaching of the **brahma-vihāras**. Evidently, these particular **bhikkhus** were unaware of the difference themselves and, had it not been pointed out to them by the Buddha, we may suppose, there would have been no reason for giving their allegiance exclusively to the Buddha in this regard.

An examination of the **brahma-vihāras** in the Nikāyas therefore leads us to conclude that the Buddhists superimposed their own doctrinal interpretation upon these meditations. This conclusion is reinforced by reference to the Makhādeva Sutta which seeks to show that they were an authentic part of Buddhism's own pre-history. In its own conclusion the Sutta implies the existence of two dispensations: the period inaugurated by King Makhādeva (qua the **Bodhisatta**) in which the practice of the brahma-vihāras was the highest attainment, having rebirth in the **brahma loka** as its consequence; and the period which superseded it, which was instigated by the Buddha with his teaching of the Eightfold Path culminating in **nibbāna**.

One issue yet to be resolved is how data which suggests the **brahma-vihāras** were the primary spiritual accomplishment prior to the advent of the Buddha can be reconciled with the doctrine of **paccekabuddhas** which affirms that 'enlightened' ascetics existed before the time of the Buddha. A possible resolution may be found by deciphering the identity and significance of another mysterious group of figures occurring in the Nikāyas, beings referred to as **paccekabrahmās**. We suggest that coincidence of the prefix **pacceka** in the terms **paccekabuddha** and **paccekabrahmā** may here be much more than accidental. We shall argue that the existence of the two terms is an indication that an alteration took place in the definition of a summum bonum in the Buddhistic tradition. The summum bonum was first characterised by the locution **brahma** but, in an attempt to extricate itself once and for all from Brahmanical associations, eventually came to be dropped and substituted by **nibbāna**.

**Paccekabrahmas** are mentioned in the Saṁyutta and the Aṅguttara Nikāyas as deities who inhabit the **brahma loka**.[104] Three are mentioned by name: Tudu, Subrahmā and Suddhavāsa. The latter two are represented as disturbing (**saṁvejeti**) the illusions of a certain **Brahma-deva** who is infatuated with his own magic power (**iddhānubhāva**), and who regards himself as too superior to pay homage to the Buddha. They eventually succeed in persuading him to pay homage to the Buddha. The other named **paccekabrahmā**, Tudu, presents himself before a certain member of the **bhikkhu-saṅgha** and rebukes him for slandering the Buddha's chief disciples, Sāriputta and Mahāmogallāna. In this particular story, the **bhikkhu** seems totally perplexed by the visitation because Tudu the **paccekabrahmā** is supposed to be an an **anāgamin**(non-returner), that is, a class of person who is incapable of returning to the **kāma loka**. The story is significant by virtue of the fact that it identifies the figure of the **paccekabrahmā** with the category **anāgamin**. Although the episode involving the other **paccekabrahmās**, Subrahmā and Suddhavāsa, does not explicitly refer to them as **anāgamin**, some kind of **sāvaka** status must be applicable to them since they are capable of 'instructing' their fellow brahmadevas in **dhamma**. Therefore it does seem to be the case that **anāgamin** is a category which applies (prospectively) not only to one who cultivates the **brahma-vihāras** within the framework of Buddhist doctrine but also to a type of deity called **paccekabrahmā**.

We shall now need to trace the process which led to **nibbāna** supplanting **brahma** as the received concept of transcendence. The teaching of the Upaniṣads and the Buddhist interpretation of the **brahma-vihāras** both express their summum bonum in terms of 'identification' or 'unification' with Brahmā (that is, as entry into the **brahma loka**). Furthermore, the use of **brahma-bhūta** (and other **brahma** epithets) for the Buddha and **arahants** shows that the Buddhistic tradition had affiliations with this conception of a summum bonum at some point in the course of its evolution.[105] The fact that **brahma-bhūta** is also used to denote the **sāvaka** who cultivates the **brahma-vihāras** would lead us to suppose it has a special association with the ascetic tradition which practised these meditations.[106] However, Early Buddhism affirmed its critique of prevailing soteriologies (including the brahma-vihāra meditations), by situating its supreme attainment beyond the notion of a **loka**; in other words it achieved the conceptual distinction of citing transcendence in the principle of **loka** <u>absentia</u> (**nibbāna**) and **kāya** <u>absentia</u> (**anattā**) rather than in **loka** <u>maximus</u> (**brahma loka**). The conception of **loka** <u>maximus</u> is perfectly exemplified by the meditational technique of the **brahma-vihāras** since it is said that the adept's mind (**citta**) expands outwards, pervading (**pharati**) all directions (**sabba loka**; **sabba disā**). Prior to the development of the **brahma-vihāras** the **citta** is said to be **paritta** (small, confined), but through their development it grows or expands (**bhāvitā**) until it becomes **subhāvitā** (well developed) and **appamāṇa** (unbounded). Given such a cosmological framework of **loka** maximus, it seems to us that the conception of **cittaṁ appamāṇaṁ** (unbounded mind) implies transcendence, that is, implies **vimutti** (release). If instead the conceptual framework is **loka** and **kāya** absentia as Buddhism traditionally affirms, then the **brahma-vihāras** would not alone be sufficient for the attainment of transcendence. The **anāgamin** category may therefore have come into existence as a bridging concept intended to reconcile the two contrasting concepts of transcendence. It is just possible that **paccekabrahmā** was the original term for those who achieved the summum bonum before this doctrinal innovation happened and, when the **anāgamin** category was introduced to allow for the possibility of transcendence through entrance to the **brahma loka**, it was incidentally retained.

If we are to posit the idea of an alteration in the conception of a summum bonum, then there is considerable evidence to suggest that the **dhamma** of the Buddha is the new conception which replaces **Brahmā/brahman** as the primary object of knowledge or gnosis for the new 'cultus'. We have already seen that, according to the Nikāyas, developing the **brahma-vihāras** is not of itself a sufficient medium for achieving transcendence unless it is leavened by the **dhamma** of the Buddha. Whether or not Buddhism happened to be familiar with the traditional Upaniṣadic soteriology of **ātman-brahman** it remains to be said that a critique of its standpoint is implicit in the way Buddhism depicts the idea of the

**brahma loka**. Accordingly in the Nikāyas the **brahman** hypostasis becomes anthropomorphised into the single figure of a self-professed supreme deity (Mahā-Brahmā), and the **ātman** is represented by his sons or companions (**brahmakāyika devas**) who rule individual **lokas**. The identification of the 'individual **ātman**' and 'supreme **ātman**' could therefore be picturesquely depicted as individual persons becoming reborn in a **brahma-loka**, it being deliberately left ambiguous whether they become **mahā-brahmā** or one of his sons. These **devas** still have a body (**kāya**) and inhabit a **loka**, therefore remain within **saṁsāra**. By the same token the Nikāyas show the **brahma-vihāra** meditations as having a similar soteriological objective to the Upaniṣads: thoughts or mind states (**cetaso**) such as **mettā**, **karuṇā**, etc. are developed which, correspond in anthropomorphic terms to the mind-state of Brahmā (supra) or, in abstract terms, to the hypostatic principle of brahman.[107] Hence they are described as **brahma-vihāra**: **brahmam etaṁ vihāraṁ idha-m-āhu** (this abode here they say is brahman).[108] And the **citta** is 'made become' (**bhāvaya**) **brahman**.[109]

It can now be shown more precisely in what way the Buddha's religion of **dhamma** supersedes the religion of brahman. The new dispensation is signified by 'turning the wheel of **dhamma**' which is sometimes anachronistically referred to as the **brahma-cakka**.[110] Similarly, the criterion of spiritual power (i.e., **ariyapuggala** status) is no longer the possession of **brahma**-vision (**brahma-cakkhu**) but the acquisition of **dhamma**-vision (**dhamma-cakkhu**); the eye of the Buddha (**buddha-cakkhu; samantacakkhu**) also supersedes the **brahma-cakkhu**.[111] On a number of fronts the Buddha is seen to depose Mahā-Brahmā, the anthropomorphic representation of the hypostatic principle of **brahman**: Mahā-Brahmā is made to entreat the Buddha to teach **dhamma** as though he were either directly or inadvertently dependent or reliant on that teaching;[112] furthermore, the Buddha's **dhamma** enables him to disappear from Brahmā's range (of vision), whereas Brahma does not have the power to vanish from the Buddha's sight. These themes and concepts signify that the Buddhist conception of transcendence is higher than the conception of **brahman**; one of **loka** and **kāya** absentia rather than of **loka** maximus.

It is this new conceptual understanding of what 'transcendence' means in cosmological terms which becomes the principle or criterion for that which in the post-Nikāya period distinguishes authentic **buddha-sāsana** from non-**buddha-sāsana**. Thus the shibboleth of the new 'cultus' becomes **dhamma** rather than **brahman**. As in the Brahmanic religion the **kṣatriya** is born as a 'universal sovereign' out of the **brahman** that comes from the **brāhmaṇa**, in Buddhism the Buddha is born as a **cakkavatti** by reason of the spiritual principle of **dhamma**.[113]

Our basic findings concerning the ambiguous status of the **brahma-vihāra** meditations in Nikaya doctrine can be summarised as follows. In the first place they were recognized to be a genuine form of spiritual practice. In the second place they were admitted to be more archaic than Buddhism itself though they were not practised exclusively by Buddhists. The Buddhists made attempts to reconcile all these propositions with their commitment to the uniqueness and superiority of the Buddha's teaching. In order to alleviate the particular threat posed by the status of the **brahma-vihāras** as a more long-standing tradition than Buddhism, they utilised the device of the doctrine of the Buddha's former lives. It was declared that the Buddha himself had been responsible for discovering this system of meditations in one of his former existences. And the Buddhists succeeded in differentiating between Buddhist and non-Buddhist practitioners of the **brahma-vihāras** by introducing the device of the **anāgamin** category into their doctrines.

## The Brahma-vihāras as a Vehicle of Transcendence

We shall now try to understand how in Buddhism the **brahma-vihāras** came to be recognised as a genuine form of spiritual practice and as a type of salvific agency. In order to do this, it is necessary to link our argument with remarks we made in chapter two concerning the causal relationship between **avihiṁsa** and 'religious transcendence'. We there saw how conduct based upon the principle of **avihiṁsā** proceeds to extinguish the **sankhāras** (purposive activities) and thereby starve **kamma** of its fuel. According to Nikāya doctrine the **sankhāras** consist of three elements-intentions, views, and actions - which correspond, it will be noticed, to the triple faculties of mind (**manas**), speech (**vācā**) and body (**kāya**) respectively. Since **avihiṁsā** is likewise defined in terms of the restraint of the threefold mind, speech and body, we can see how it helps to eradicate the **sankhāras**. In Buddhist doctrine the total extinction of the **sankhāras** is synonymous with transcendence or the ending of rebirth, for they are the producers of **kamma** and so perpetuate conditioned existence - 'all beings are constituted through purposive activity' (sabbe sattā sankhāraṭṭhitikā).[114] Both

**avihiṁsā** and the **brahma-vihāras** promote 'transcendence' by causing the attrition of **kamma**. The Nikāyas provide an example with regard to the practice of **mettā**:

> 'Furthermore, this freedom through the thought of loving-kindness should be developed by man or woman. The man or woman whose mind crosses over death cannot take their body with them. Thus they know: "Whatever evil deed formerly done by me is done through the physical body, if brought to fruition here it will not follow (me across death)... Formerly, this mind of mine was small, underdeveloped, but now this mind of mine is well-developed, so that whatever form of **kamma** there is will not last, will not remain".'[115]

We see here that **mettā** eliminates in the present body **kamma** which would otherwise come to fruition in a future existence. The individual no longer requires to be reborn (as a human) again since the **kamma** which leads to further rebirth will have been eradicated. That person goes on to become a 'non-returning' deity in a non-kamma-inducing existence where all that remains is for him to cultivate the spiritual roots needed to realise **nibbāna**. In another passage from the Nikāyas the transcendent potency of **mettā** is expressed specifically in terms of its stilling (**upasama**) impact upon the **sankhāras**:

> The **bhikkhu** who abides in loving-kindness, has faith in the teaching of the Buddha, wins the sphere of calm and happiness, the stilling of purposive activity.
>
> (**mettāvihāri yo bhikkhu**
> **pasanno Buddhasāsane**
> **adhigacche padaṁ santam**
> **sankhārūpasamaṁ sukhaṁ**).[116]

The phrase 'wins the sphere of calm and happiness' implies that **metta-vihāra** leads not to **anāgamin** status but to **nibbāna** itself, since elsewhere in the Nikāyas **santipada** is a synonym for **nibbāna.**[117] It is not to be forgotten however, that the practice of **metta-vihāra** is here complemented by faith in the Buddha's instruction. The Mahāvastu version of this passage states unequivocally that the combination of faith in the Buddha's teaching with the attainment of the **brahma-vihāras** leads to **nirvāṇa.**[118] In addition, a passage in the Majjhima Nikāya testifies to the transcendent impact of the **brahma-vihāras** when practised within the context of the **dhamma** and **vināya** taught by the Buddha (Tathāgatappaveditam **dhamma-vināyaṁ**).[119]. They are said to result in inward assuaging, **(ajjhattaṁ vupasam)** and liberation of self **(vimuttam attānam)**.

The three passages just cited make it clear that Early Buddhism did not fully resolve the question whether or not the **brahma-vihāras** led to **nibbāna** directly or via the **opapātika** excursion. But they concur on the matter that the meditations must be complemented by 'faith in the teaching of the Buddha' in order to serve as a vehicle of transcendence. Since the conditional clause of 'faith in the teaching of the Buddha' determines whether they function as such a vehicle we must now try to understand how precisely the 'faith' element works.

So far we have seen that the 'spiritual' potential of the **brahma-vihāras** lies in their propensity to tranquillise the **sankhāras**. Earlier we saw that the initial prerequisite for developing these meditations is the practice of **samādhi**, and **samādhi** is valued because it too conduces towards the gradual assuaging and cessation **(nirodha)** of the **sankhāras.**[120] Though always extolled and often represented as indispensable samādhi is not of itself a sufficient condition for the realisation of the ultimate spiritual goal of **nibbāna**. By itself **samādhi** is **lokiya** (mundane) and only becomes transcendent-effective (**lokuttara**) when complemented by insight (**paññā**), that is, by the faculty of 'gnosis'. The attainment of **lokuttara** goals in Buddhism is always defined in terms of 'gnosis' and therefore the **brahmavihāras** (qua **samādhi**) in isolation cannot ensure transcendence. This can be shown through a brief examination of the concept of the **sankhāras** according to the Nikāyas. Firstly entry onto the **lokuttara** that is, acquisition of **sāvaka** path status - comes by insight (**paññā**) into the impermanence and suffering of all **sankhāras**:

> "All **sankhāras** are impermanent;
> When through insight he sees this,
> he is disgusted by suffering:
> This is the way to purity.
>
> All **sankhāras** are suffering,
> When through insight he sees this,
> he is disgusted by suffering:
> This is the way to purity."[121]

The form of **paññā** here enunciated is synonymous with understanding (**pajānāti**) the four noble truths, another way of talking about entering the path, which is also described in terms of dissolving the **sankhāras**:

> 'Those **samaṇabrāhmaṇa** who know, (**pajānanti**) as it really is, the meaning of 'This is **dukkha**, etc....such delight not (**anabhirati**) in the **sankhāras** that lead to rebirth lamentation and despair. Not taking delight therein no accumulation of **sankhāras** takes place, that leads to rebirth, etc.'[122]

**Paññā** is here seen to be the factor which causes release from attachment. Rescue from the **sankhāras** presupposes 'knowledge' of their bankrupt nature. The final stage, **arahant** status, is acquired by insight (**paññā**) too, in this case by insight into the additional third 'mark', **anattā** (no self):

> whatever belongs to the five **khandha**s 'should by means of right insight be seen as it really is (**yathābhūtaṁ sammapaññāya datthabbaṁ**), thus: This is not mine, this am I not, this is not my self. Seeing (**passaṁ**) in this way, monks, the instructed disciple (**sutavā ariya-sāvako**) is disgusted (**nibbindati**) by form, feeling, perception etc. Through disgust he is detached; through detachment he is liberated (**vimuccati**); in liberation there comes to be the knowledge (**ñāṇa**) that I am freed; he knows (**pajānāti**) rebirth is ended, the **brahmacariya** is fulfilled, done is what was to be done, there is no more of being such and such'.[123]

It is therefore to be observed that the first stage of the path involves insight into the universality of **dukkha** and **anicca** (i.e. seeing the macrocosm as **anattā**) and the last stage involves insight into the nature of the self (i.e. seeing the microcosm as **anattā**). Only with this last stage are the **sankhāra**s extinguished once and for all. And this extinction is, once again, conceived as a form of 'gnosis' (**ñāṇa**): 'knowing the extinction of the **sankhāras**, you know the uncreate' (**sankhāranam khayam natvā akatannū**'si).[124]

Therefore, according to Buddhist doctrine, the complete cessation of the **sankhāras** is equivalent to **nibbāna** but it is only finally brought about by a form of insight (**paññā**). This is where the **brahma-vihāras** themselves appear to be insufficient. They can be practised with or without the right soteriological objective, and the right soteriological objective is supplied or tramsmitted solely through the instruction of the **tathāgata** or **tathāgata-sāvakas** or through 'those who have heard it of them'. That the teaching of the Buddha was considered by his followers to represent a new and unique form of 'gnosis' is also shown in the conclusions to the Makhādeva and Mahā-Govinda Suttas which emphasise that the Buddha's way is unprecedented and constitutes the only means to the realisation of **nibbāna**. These conclusions are arrived at in Suttas which have the **brahma-vihāra** meditations as their major theme. And the point is stressed in the text lest anyone should mistakenly construe the **brahma-vihāras** by themselves to be a sufficient means of salvation.

Our discussion has therefore shown us that the Buddhist conception of salvation not only consists of a form of 'gnosis' but of a unique form whose source is the person and teaching of the Buddha. By contrast, the **brahma-vihāras** do not comprise (qua **samādhi**) a 'gnosis', nor are they unique to the Buddha's teaching. Thus in order to become transcendent effective they must be interpreted from within the total framework of Buddhist doctrine. This is the reason why faith in the **dhamma**; of the Buddha is made a prerequisite for their successful practice salvifically.

## The 'Paccekabuddha' and the 'Savaka' Tradition

By way of concluding this chapter we shall endeavour to show the relevance of these observations on the status of the **brahma-**

**vihāra** meditations to our delineation of the **paccekabuddha** concept. In chapter three we argued that the concept of the **paccekabuddha** referred to the tradition of **śramaṇas** which existed prior to the formation of distinct sectarian groups. The beginnings of the Śramaṇa Movement were primarily marked by ways or methods of raising consciousness, namely, the emergence and application of yogic and meditational techniques (**samādhi**). Once these techniques had been developed and systematised, then factors of transmission and choice of emphasis came to play an important part in the tradition; this gave rise to different authorities, each claiming to possess the true and definitive form of 'gnosis'. Accordingly, the **paccekabuddha** conception denotes the form of spirituality which characterised the nascent period of the acquisition of **samādhi** techniques, prior to the articulation of systematic schemes of teaching and transmission. We shall now draw together the different strands of evidence throughout this study into a final, concerted interpretation.

In chapter one we saw how the concept of the **muni** was explicated doctrinally in terms of the three higher super-knowledges (**abhiññā**). The last of these, the 'exhausting' of the **āsavas** (**khīṇāsavā**), represents the supreme attainment of **arahant** status. Although tradition recognizes the existence of four **asavas** - sense-desire (**kāmāsava**), desire for existence (**bhavāsava**), views (**diṭṭhāsava**), and ignorance (**avijjāsava**) - in actual fact the majority of citations with- in the four Nikāyas mention only the first three, omitting 'ignorance'.[125] This leads us to suppose that there were originally just three **āsavas** and this number was later amended to four. Since 'ignorance is specifically defined as ignorance in respect of the four noble truths' it can be seen that its inclusion alongside the other **āsavas** introduced the 'cultic' element into the system of practice; for the four noble truths represent the essential teaching of the Buddha. If, therefore, we see the fourth **āsava** as a 'cultic' accretion, the remaining three form a natural counterpart to the three 'restraints' (**moneyyāni**) which distinguish the **muni**: with 'control of body' (**kāya-moneyya**) we may equate the cessation of bodily or sense desires (**kāmāsava**); with 'restraint of mind' (**mano moneyya**) cessation of the desire to persist as an individual (**bhāvāsava**); and with 'restraint of speech' (**vāci-moneyya**), cessation of the imbalanced dominance of the intellect (**diṭṭhāsava**).

It therefore becomes clear that the emphasis on 'right view' (**sammā-diṭṭhi**) and 'right insight' (**sammā-paññā**) in Buddhism expresses its existence essentially as a 'cultus', that is, as as a tradition having a single authority, Sakyamuni, who makes known (**pakāsati**) the 'gnosis' (**ñāṇa**) to his followers (**sāvaka**). This is formally acknowledged by the occurrence of **sammā-diṭṭhi** (right view) at the beginning of the noble eightfold path and, correspondingly, 'faith in the **tathāgata**' (**tathāgate saddham**) as a precursor to following the path. We therefore suggest that **avijjā** was appended to the **āsavas** in their three-fold formulation in order to accommodate the notion of the **sāvaka**, one who attains access to spiritual attainment by 'hearing from another'.

Our investigations have shown that the dominant ascetico-religious strains of practice in the Buddhist depiction of the figure of the **paccekabuddha** are iddhi, the **brahma-vihāras** and **santi**. In Canonical Buddhism these are all aspects of **samādhi**. Indeed, within the Gandhamādana mythical motif discussed in chapter two the **paccekabuddha** is depicted as an adept of the attainment of the cessation of consciousness and perception (**nirodha-samāpatti**), the highest form of **samādhi** according to Pali tradition, and only possible to those who have already realised either **nibbāna** or **anāgamin** status.[126]

In addition, the **brahma-vihāras** and **iddhi** have in common the fact that they are older than Buddhism, both figure within Buddhist practice, and both possess an ambiguous status: the use of iddhi (**iddhi pāṭihāriyam dasseti**) is regarded as both good and bad, depending on the circumstances; and cultivating the **brahma-vihāras** can lead either to **nibbāna** or to a **duggati** destination. In order to achieve full legitimacy both **iddhi** and the **brahma-vihāras** had to be complemented by **sāsana** (the **brahma-vihāras** by **buddha-sāsana**; **iddhi** by **anusāsana**). **Iddhi** (specifically, **adhiṭṭhāna-iddhi**) and the **brahma-vihāras** (specifically, **mettāvihāra**) also have the following in common: They provide access to the **brahma loka**; their manifestations are non-verbal (viz. visual display and thought power); and they both feature transformations. The fact that they share these same features and are both closely associated with the figure of the **paccekabuddha**, are an indication that a period of revision took place marking the transition from the era of the **paccekabuddha** to that of the hearer (**sāvaka**) or recipient of 'gnosis' from another.

In our analysis of the visual characteristics of the **paccekabuddha** we saw that his essential charm stemmed from his tranquillity (**santi**). Tranquillity and equanimity are also primary distinguishing characteristics of the figure of the **muni** depicted in the earliest Nikāya stratum. In the Māgandiya Sutta, for instance, we find the rather striking description of the **muni** as 'one who professes or holds the doctrine of tranquillity' (**muni santivādo**)[127] rather than the doctrines of 'views' (**diṭṭhī**), 'tradition' (**suta**), 'gnosis' (**ñāṇa**) or 'works' (**sīlabbata**), or their denial.[128] Here, the truly transcendent aspect of the summum bonum prohibits it from being represented in any other terms than 'inward peace' (**ajjhattaṁ santiṁ**).[129] In other words, since it is a 'mode of being' it cannot be conceptualised. It is for this very reason that the notion of transmission is inherently problematic. There was a real danger of misleading or misdirecting the aspirant by providing him with further and perhaps more sophisticated and elaborate objects of 'grasping' (**gahaṇa**), instead of assisting him to achieve self-transformation.[130]

This observation can be used to support the idea that the emergence of recognised forms of transmission was a slowly evolving feature of the Buddhistic tradition, and to account for the existence of a triple buddhology: **paccekabuddha**, **sammāsambuddha**, and **arahant** (i.e., **sāvaka**). Consequently, we can formulate the following pattern of correspondence:

| | | |
|---|---|---|
| **paccekabuddha** | = | 'transmission' in its formative stages |
| **sammāsambuddha** | = | 'transmission' comes of age |
| **sāvaka** | = | beneficiary of 'transmission' |

Thus the **sāvaka** regards the **sammāsambuddha** as exceptional (**sabbaññū** : omniscient) because the latter has resolved the antinomy of transmitting that which is 'untransmittable' in terms of the traditional sources of transmission - emphasis on either doctrines, views, tradition, 'gnosis', and works. But in elevating the Buddha to this special status the **sāvaka**, inadvertently and ironically, creates a 'cultus' and falls into the same trap: he creates yet another form of doctrine, view, etc. [131] The subsequent history of Buddhism (viz. Mahāyanist forms) is a tale of its attempts to extricate itself from this dilemma (that is, the one of doctrine inhibit-practice).

The later and post-Nikāya doctrine of the limited salvific powers of the **paccekabuddha** does not categorically affirm that he did not teach or that he did not intend to teach. To construe the **paccekabuddha** to be a 'silent' ascetic is a misconception, even though 'silence' is a strong element in his make-up. There are three relatively simple explanations for his reticence of speech. Firstly, the 'transcendental' experience is inherently difficult to communicate as is testified by the story of the Buddha's hesitation to teach and his silent gesture of the upheld lotus flower. Secondly, restraint in speech is regarded as a necessary condition of self-discipline and a natural corollary of meditation.[132] Thirdly the **paccekabuddha** is incapable of articulating the **dhamma** in a systematic and all-encompassing way; the capacity to articulate universal truths is the prerogative exclusively of Sākyamuni (and other **sammāsambuddhas**), the founder of the **bhikkhu-saṅgha**. The Commentarial tradition, nevertheless, recognises the existence of a tradition of 'words' (**bhāsitāni**) spoken by **paccekabuddhas**. But one very conspicuous thing about these words, the verses of the Khaggavisāṇa Sutta and the Samanabhadra verses (See Appendix III), is that nowhere among them is there a reference to a doctrine that could be classed as specifically Buddhist or markedly sectarian. The one exception is reference to the **brahma-vihāras** in the Khaggavisāṇa Sutta, and we have seen that these were an archaic and trans-sectarian ascetical practice. There is no mention, for instance, of the four noble truths.

In the Pali Commentaries there are a number of references to persons themselves becoming **paccekabuddhas** through encountering **paccekabuddhas** and listening to their words. There is the story, for instance, of the young **brāhmaṇa**, Susīma: Wanting to find the 'end of learning' (**sippassa pariyosānaṁ**) he is advised to visit the **isis** (i.e., **paccekabuddhas**) at Isipatana. They persuade him to become a **pabbajita** and teach him the basic duties of the ascetic life. In due course he attains **paccekabodhi**.[133] Again, there is mention of an elder called Nāḷaka, who penetrates the knowledge of **paccekabodhi**, after receiving moral instruction (**ovāda**) from **paccekabuddhas**. It is to be noticed, however, that these examples place emphasis on the role of the aspirant's own effort and initiative in bringing about **paccekabodhi** rather than the efficacy of the **paccekabuddhas** instruction. The story of Nāḷaka is in fact an ad hoc one, used by the Commentators to demonstrate the potency of a particular faculty known as 'quick-understanding' (**ugghaṭitaññū**).[135] Such examples do not in principle contravene the dictum that **paccekabuddhas**' attain enlightenment on their own. For the association with **paccekabuddhas** and their 'words' acts as the same sort of triggering mechanism as the 'incident' or 'event' that plays the formative role in the definitive explanations of how **paccekabodhi** comes about.

In terms of our analysis of the derivation of the **paccekabuddha** concept the need was obviously felt, at the stage coincidental with the production of later canonical material, to clarify the soteriological significance of these paragons of the past relative to the figure and persons of the Buddha. We indicated earlier the reason behind this particular imperative. If **paccekabuddhas** could bring others to enlightenment then there is nothing special or unique about Sākyamuni and a fortiori the **sāvaka** tradition which he founded. Here, again, there are analogies with the Buddhist treatment of the **brahmavihāra** tradition: if it is possible to achieve transcendence through these meditations independently of the Buddha's teaching, his teaching cannot be uniquely significant.

Therefore, we are led to conclude that the assertion that the **paccekabuddha** did not teach is to be understood as a technical and doctrinal judgement, the explanation for which belongs to the realm of Buddhist dogma. For the prime motivating force in the growth of the **sāvaka** tradition was the belief in the uniqueness of their 'master' (**satthar**). This is evident from the choice of the figure of **cakkavatti** (universal sovereign) to interpret the salvific role and significance of the Buddha. But having made this point clear, it remains apparent that the dogmatic strictures placed upon the **paccekabuddha** are to some extent backed by the character of the 'utterances' which comprise the alleged sayings of **paccekabuddhas** as well as by the accentuation given to their visual rather than verbal impact. There is little to make us suppose that they had arrived upon a method of transmission which could pilot the aspirant to a prescribed attainment.[136] This instruction is noticeably more exhortatory than systematic or conceptual: emphasising the perils of the senses, the indispensability of renunciation and the formalities of mendicancy. The form of this instruction suggests that they belonged to an earlier, more rudimentary phase in the renunciation tradition.

We have tried to indicate that Buddhism places an emphasis on 'gnosis' and that this was a corollary of the growth of the **sāvaka** tradition, notably, the growth and extension of the Śramaṇa Movement itself. In a similar way, Buddhism's claim to represent a unique form of 'gnosis' is a sign of the appearance of rival sectarian groups within the Śramaṇa Movement. What we are seeing in the representation of the figure of the **paccekabuddha** is by-and-large a picture of a state of affairs prior to the appearance of a form of 'gnosis' that shows signs of advanced adaptation - systematically and doctrinally. It seems that these features are the inevitable result of a change from an esoteric to a more exoterically-grounded tradition, as the impact of the **śramaṇas** upon society gradually increased. However, this effectively meant the growing effeteness of the powers of **samādhi** and abhiññā within the **sāvaka** tradition. There is a sense in which their slow exhaustion - at least within the Theravāda tradition - was already assured by that tradition's de-accentuation on the techniques and powers (knowledge of former lives and of other people's **kamma**) traditionally bolstering their notion of world transcendence.

Both the 'meditational techniques' and 'gnosis' phases of the tradition, however, interpret 'transcendence' to mean 'detachment' (**virāga**). In the initial period, detachment from the sense-faculties, both as a moral (**sīla**) and a meditational (**samādhi**) criterion, resulted in experiences which gave the impression of the faculty through which they took place, the mind or consciousness (**citta**), as superpowerful and transcendent. So, for example, the **brahmavihāras** (specifically mettā-vihāra), a meditational technique typifying this incipient period, were characterised in terms of the **citta** growing and expanding from a small and restricted to an unbounded, immeasurable, transcendent faculty. Irrespective of finer conceptual formulations characterising the doctrine of **anattā**, the realisation of the **brahma-vihāras** presupposes a notion of 'selfless-ness' tantamount to that described by **an-attā**. In this case the 'selflessness' is expressed as a growing, expansive process, rather than as the negation of all wrong 'gnoses'. The Buddhist emphasis on the nega-tion of 'gnoses' (i.e. views) is to be seen as its own particular form of response to a multi-sectarian environment.

Bearing in mind this distinction between a state of affairs in which persons were pioneering states of 'non-attachment' realis-ation and a situation where relative novices were being initiated into doctrines by way of 'verbal' transmission, we can see that the stipulations imposed upon, for example, the **brahma-vihāras** as a means of transcendence were the consequence of the eventual predomin-ance of the **sāvaka** adherent. And the **sāvaka** is, of course, the source and stim-ulus of the 'cultus' organisation itself. Consequently, the so-called problem of whether to characterise Early Buddhism as a religion of 'empiricism' or a religion of 'faith' or 'revelation' is dissolved when we explain the rise of historical Buddhism as the occasion of a transition from a **paccekabuddha** or **muni** (independent striving) to a **sāvaka** (hearing from another) tradition.[137] Early Buddhism retained many of the characteristics of its ascetico-relious experimental background, but these were gradually and increasingly the casualties of the growth of an emphasis on the transmission of 'received' doctrine. This emphasis signifies the transition from a **muni** to a **sāvaka** tradition, and the emergence of the form of 'cultus' which subsequently became the Buddhist religion.

**Notes:**

1. On the Vedic conception of **loka** see Gonda (1) pp.14-21,41-2,55,108-109.
2. 'The quarters (**disāḥ**) are said to be both inside and outside these 'worlds' (lokāḥ), but elsewhere they are in these 'worlds' or between them'- op. cit. p.110 fn.17.
3. On **pratiṣṭhā**, see op. cit. p.97,98, 104. Note that **pratiṣṭhā** is conceptually related to **santi** ('immunity from dangerous influences, appeasement, peace' - op. cit. p.31).
4. For example, the poet appeals to Indra to 'lead us to a broad place, to light consisting of the brightness of heaven, to safety and well-being' (**uruṁ no lokam anunesi vidvān svarvaj jyoti abhayaṁ svasti** - Ṛg.V. VI.47.8). cf. also Ṛg.V. II.30.6; Tait.Brh.2.7.13.3; Śat.Brh. V.4.1. For further discussion, see Gonda (1) p.17,22,23.
5. Gonda (1), pp.36-40.
6. Gonda (2), pp.140-143; (3), p.8.
7. In the Brahmanic religious system there are basically two forms of sacrificial rite: 'great solemn rites' (**śrauta**) performed by the well-to-do; and the 'domestic rites' (**gṛhya**) common to all householders. See Gonda (4), pp.468ff.
8. For a description and analysis of these two rites, see Heesterman, pp.103-105, 196-199.
9. op. cit. p.197.

10. 'The complicated **śrauta** rites are carried out on the invitation, at the expense of and for the benefit, of the patron or sacrificer **(yajamāna)**, a well-to-do member of the higher classes' - Gonda (4), p.468.
11. op. cit. p.104.
12. Gonda (1), pp.91-93.
13. Tait.Brh.I.3.6.1.
14. Gonda (1), p.24.
15. Tait.Sam.II.4.13.1 (cite Gonda (2), p.143.)
16. Heesterman, p.160
17. See Heesterman: 'Brahmin, Ritual and Renouncer', WZKSO, Vol.VIII. 1964, pp.2ff.
18. According to Gonda (1), p.73, **svarga loka** occurs only once in the Rig.V. (at X.95.18).
19. The **brāhmaṇa** is engaged in supervision of the ritual and has to repair every flaw that the other priests might cause. And 'while both the **Brahman** and the **kṣatriya** can offer the sacrifice, only the **Brahman** can operate it' - L.Dumont: 'The Conception of Kingship in Ancient India' p.50.
20. 'His share of the **dakṣiṇās** is as great as those of the other officiants together' (Ait Brh.5.24; Kauś.Brh.6.11) - Heesterman, op. cit. p.3.
21. See, for example, Bṛhad Up.III.9.21:
"On what is the sacrifice supported **(yajñaḥ pratiṣṭhita)**?"
"On the offering **(dakṣiṇā)**".
"And on what are the offerings supported?"
"On faith **(śraddhā)**, for when one has faith, he gives offerings".
22. See, for example, Sn.490 et seq.
23. op. cit. IV 1.5.
24. Sn.1043-8.
25. See D.III.55 (and Dial. pt.III. p.50, fn.1); D.II.41; Sn.318-321.

26. Sn.539-40.
27. S.I.185.
28. A.V.66
29. M.II.194-6.
30. Sn.937
31. Sn.946 cp. also, the statement in the Bhagavadgītā (II.56): '**sthitadhīr munir ucyate**' (he is called a stableminded **muni**).
32. See Sn.484-485: 'the muni endowed with **moneyya** has become the sacrifice' (munim **moneyya-sampannaṁ** tādisam **yaññam** āgatam); 'with clasped hands pay homage, and with food and drink worship (the **muni**) - thus the offerings will prosper (**pañjalikā namas-satha, pūjetha annapānena - evaṁ ijjhanti dakkhiṇā**).
33. 'But when he thinks that he is a god, as it were, that he is a king, as it were, that I am all this, that is his highest world' (**atha yatra deva iva rājeva; aham evedam, sarvo 'smīti manyate; so'sya par-amo lokaḥ** - Bṛhad.Up.IV.3.20).
34. See Ait.Brh.I.14.
35. See Heesterman, op. cit. p.3,227.
36. Śat.Brh.V.4.4.4.5.
37. 'The Divinity of Kings, JAOS, Vol.51, pp.309-310.
38. Śat.Brh.IX.5.2.16.
39. Śat.Brh.XI.1.8.2.
40. op. cit. I.4.11.(trans. Hume).
41. D.III.84; M.III.195,224; S.IV.94; A.V. 226.
42. See D.I.127,148; A IV.41-6; Sn.307; It.27.
43. D.I.127ff.
44. D.I.145ff.
45. On the **rakṣasas**, see Macdonell, pp.162-164. They are the subject of two Ṛg.V. hymns (VII.104; X.87) and Ath.V. VIII.4.
46. cf. Ṛg.V. VIII.104.18,21; I.76.3.
47. Heesterman p.197.

48. Macdonell p.164.
49. Śat.Brh.V.4.1. (trans. Eggeling).
50. Ṛg.V. X.87.3,6,7.
51. See Walker sv 'animal sacrifice'.
52. At Ṛg.V. X.87 note the aggressive tone of the vocabulary describing Agni's power: 'attack with teeth of iron', 'rend', 'pierce to the heart', track his 'mangled body','tear','strike','demolish','crush', 'cast down','burn up','exterminate','consume', etc.
53. A.I.166.
54. The Unknown Co-Founders of Buddhism: A Sequel, JRAS 1928, pt.II. p.278.
55. op. cit. Section I.33.
56. See Tähtinen p.64.
57. cf. D.I.235-53; S.V.115-21; A.II.129; III. 225.
58. A.V.299.
59. D.II.186; 237f.
60. See, for example, S.IV.320-1 which shows how these meditations are a development of the principle of **avihiṁsā**.
61. According to C.A.F. Rhys-Davids (op. cit. p.24) **mettā** on its own is mentioned twenty-three times in the Sutta Piṭaka.
62. J.II.61.v.37.
63. A.II.129.
64. Since the pre-eminent Buddhist ethical value is the principal of conciliation or **avihiṁsā**, made religiously potent by means of the meditational technique of **mettā**, etc and since the practice of **mettā** itself is archaic, we shall examine some of the significances of the Vedic figure Mitra, a name etymologically linked with the word **mettā** (Skt. **maitrī**).

**Mitra**

The god Mitra may be said to possess two distinctive associations according to his representation in the Ṛg.Veda. These are associations with conciliation or concord and with contract or concordat, two conceptions which are quite clearly interconnected.

(a) Conciliation

The word **ahiṁsā** occurs only twice in the Ṛg.V. (I.141.5; V.64.3) and on one of these occasions it is as an attribute of Mitra : His devotees proclaim of him 'men go protected in the charge of this dear friend who harms us not' (**ahiṁsāna** - V.64.3). Śat.Brh. later confirms this description by remarking that 'Mitra injures (**hiṁsati**) and is injured by no one, for Mitra is every one's friend' (V.3.2.7). Mitra is therefore conceived of particularly as a 'protective' deity eg against fire, disease, enemies (Gonda, op.cit., Indologica Taurinensia Pt.1. p.84; cf., also Śat.Brh.VI.I.23.6; 41.1; 156.1; III.111.59) and as difficult to provoke (Ṛg.V. X.12.5).

(b) Contract

Mitra embodies the principle of 'reliance' and 'trust' because he epitomises true friendship. This is a particularly crucial concept in Vedic and post-Vedic times since the struggle for hegemony between different groups and tribes and the gradual migration into N.W. India presupposed 'alliances' and concordats as much as strife. Mitra, symbolising the necessity of trust between the members of a community and between communities, is therefore called 'Lord of the **kṣatra**' (XI.4.3.11).

In Vedic mythology, Varuṇa and Mitra often form a pair or twin-head, complementing one another. Gonda ('Mitra in India' in Mithraic Studies, vol.I.p.48) writes: 'in the rites relating to the consecration of a king, Varuṇa is invoked as particularly interested in the established order of things (**dharman**), Mitra is closely associated with **satya**: 'that which is really existent and in agreement with fundamental being, what is true, real and essential, truthfulness in mind, speech and action'. Thus Varuna and Mitra epitomise the twin requirements of true **kṣatriya** status: 'sovereignty' and 'conformity with reality or natural law'. It may be noticed that these are exactly the two principles which the Buddha as **dharma-rājā** embodies: he is sovereign, and yet he also rules without the **daṇḍa**, that is, by the principle of non-violence (**ahiṁsa**) which is according to Buddhism the principle by which the stability and order of things is maintained.

65. A.IV.150-1.
66. The last three items listed are additions from a parrallel passage in the same Nikāya. See A.V.352.
67. aśvamedha = horse sacrifice
    puruṣamedha = man sacrifice
    samyāprāsa = the throwing of the peg. cf. Śat.Brh.III.5.1.24- 30.
    vājapeya = the drink of victory
    nirargala = the bolts (obstruction) removed.

    On these particular rites of the Brahmanic 'cultus', see 'The Questions of King Milinda', transl. T.W. Rhys Davids, SBE XXXVI. p.16, n.3; KS.I. p.102 n.1.
68. See Dial. pt.III. p.185 for a list of Buddhist **parittas**.
69. See for example, Ath.V. III.26 and 27.
70. trans. Griffiths
71. Vin.II.109-10; A.II.72.
72. See Śat.Brh.II.2.3.3.9; X.1.4.14; Kauś. Brh.VI.15; Pañc.Brh.VI.8.15; Tait.Brh.I. 3.7.5; and cf. also Gonda (1) p.89 fn.2.

73. Gonda op. cit. p.81 fn.41; p.108; p.150 fn.3.
74. See Śat.Brh.XII.8.1.22.
75. See Jaim.Brh.I.218: 'By means of a special ritual technique which "leads to heaven" (**svargya**) the gods reached "these **lokas**"; the man who knows and imitates them will reach the **svarga loka**'. (cite Gonda, op. cit. p.94).
76. See Heesterman, op. cit. WZKSO, Vol. VIII. 1964. p.7: 'The ksatriya's transformation into a brahmin is made even more explicit in the **rājasūya**; when the king has been annointed and enthroned, he addresses each of the four leading brahmins with **brahman**, whereupon each answers with: 'thou, O king, art **brahman**'.
77. Śat.Brh.XI.4.3.20.
78. Ch.Up.VII.25.2; cp., also Ch.Up.VII.3.2; Bṛhad.Up.IV.3.12.
79. Ch.Up. VIII.4.3.
80. compare Muṇḍ.Up.I.2.9. with II.2.2.2-3.
81. Muṇḍ Up.I.2.10.
82. See D.II.186ff and II.250 et prev. Govinda is also referred to in Mvu.III.198ff.
83. The names are Sunetta, Mugapakkha, Aranemi, Kuddālaka, Hatthipāla and Jotipāla. Jotipāla is probably the same as the aforementioned Govinda, whose original name was Jotipāla (D.II.230). He is also said to have taught the **brahmavihāras** and had followers who were reborn in the **brahma loka**. See A.III.373; IV.10.4. The passage at A.IV.104 lists an additional figure by the name of Araka.
84. A.III.373.
85. See S.V.115-21.
86. See M.II.82.3 and D.II.251-2 respectively.
87. D.I.235-53.
88. Sn.39.
89. Sn.42.
90. Sn.71.

91. Sn.A.87.
92. Sn.A.87.
93. Sn.A.63.
94. See A.II.128-30; S.V.115-21.
95. An **opapātika** is one who is reborn without nativity; the term is usually translated 'spontaneous uprising;. It is a category which only applies to those types of **deva** who are so ultra-mundane that the anguished and messy process of womb-birth is inappropriate for this class of being. It is a concept shared by Jainism.
96. An **anāgamin** (non-returner), as the name implies, spends his final existence in a **deva loka** and enters **parinibbāna** directly from there. According to canonical doctrine one must have fully destroyed the 'five lower fetters' (**pañcoram bhāgiyāni** saṁyojanāni), which tie a person to the **kāma loka**, in order to become an **anāgamin** (S.V.177,178). These 'fetters' comprise **sakkāya-diṭṭhi** (soul-theories), **vicikicchā** (doubt) of the teacher (**satthar**) and the teaching (**dhamma**), **sīlabbata-parāmāsa** (attachment to rules and rituals), **kāmacchanda** (sense-desire) and **vyāpāda** (ill-will).
97. cf. A.II.127-8. The use of the term **puthujjana** (lit. one of the many-folk) in the Canon is extremely complex. For the purposes of this discussion, a **puthujjana** is a non-**sāvaka**.
98. See D.I.250: '**so tam dhammam sutvā Tathāgate saddhaṁ paṭilabhati**'; A.V.299: **ariyasāvaka**; Dh 368: **pasanno buddha-sāsane**.
99. S.V.118.
100. A.II.128-9,130.
101. S.V.119ff.
102. D.III.247-8.
103. ibid.

104. S.I.146-9 and A.V.170-1.
105. See D.III.84; M.I.III; III.195,224; S.III.83; IV.94; A.II.206; V.226.
106. A.I.193-6. At D.III.233 and A.II.206 one who neither torments himself nor others is called **brahma-bhūta**. Here is another example of how **brahma-bhūta** is associated with the conception of 'non-harm'.
107. See D.I.247.
108. Sn.151; Kh.8.IX.9
109. Sn.149,150.
110. M.I.69; A.II 24; III.9,417; V.33.
111. compare, for instance, D.II.239-40 with Vin.I.11.13.
112. Vin.I.5; Mvu.III.319.
113. See A.I.110.
114. D.III.211.
115. A.V.300-301.
116. Dh.368.
117. A.II.18.
118. Mvu.III.421-2.
119. op. cit. I.283-4.
120. S.IV.217-8.
121. Dh.277-8.
122. S.V.451-2. cf. also S.III.60.
123. Vin.I.14.
124. Dh.383.
125. See Nyanatiloka, sv **āsava**.
126. Vism.702.
127. Sn.845.
128. Sn.837-9.
129. ibid.
130. Sn.847.
131. See, for example, the reason behind the Buddha's rebuke of Ānanda at D.II.99-101.
132. See Sn.850.
133. Separate versions of the story occur at Kh.A.198-9; Dh.A.III.446-7.
134. A.A.II.192.
135. At Pb.Ap.3 it says that persons who have very acute insight **(sutikkha-paññā)**

become **paccekabuddhas**.

136. By comparison, see the formula that defines the Buddha as a teacher (satthar): 'But consider...where a teacher has appeared in the world who is worthy, supremely enlightened; where a doctrine has been well proclaimed, well made known, leading to salvation, conducive to tranquillity, well made known by one who is supremely enlightened; and where the religious life is made clear to them entire and complete, manifested, with all its stages co-ordinated and made a thing, of saving grace, well-revealed to men.'- Dial. Pt.III.p.163

137. See Jayatilleke pp.383.ff. (esp. pp.391-2).

## Conclusion

The purpose of this study has been to show that the **paccekabuddha** is an ascetic figure of crucial importance to our understanding of the origins of the Buddhist religion. If **paccekabuddha**s actually existed, as we have argued, then questions have to be raised about their relationship historically and doctrinally to Sākyamuni, the founder of Buddhism. The process of determining their identity has important implications for determining the identity and uniqueness of the figure of the Buddha also. Another reason for contending the importance of the **paccekabuddha** revolves around the subject of what existed before Buddhism - its historical antecedents. Our explorations into the topic of the **paccekabuddha** have of necessity drawn us into examining the ascetico-religious background to the emergence of the Buddhist tradition.

The key factor in our search after the identity of **paccekabuddha**s has proved to be the custom and institution of 'renunciation'. The kinds of spirituality and modes of conduct which are the hallmarks of Buddhism could not have come into being had they not been long-nurtured by means of the ascetic phenomenon of renunciation. The evidence produced in this study points towards the **paccekabuddha**s as the first renouncers or earliest **śramaṇa**s. This evidence has principally centred around a core of legend common to a number of sectarian traditions which relates the story of a mythical king of Videha. Analysis of the different versions of this story have revealed this king to be the mythical progenitor of the custom of renunciation - the primordial **śramaṇa**, the prototype **paccekabuddha** and a paradigm of spirituality.

Our conclusion with respect to the identity of the **paccekabuddhas**, therefore, is that they are the common ascetic tradition out of which the Śramaṇic Movements of Buddhism and Jainism emerged as sectarian manifestations. This theory of their identity explains the presence of the concept in both Buddhism and Jainism and accounts for the resemblance of these traditions - doctrinally, ethically and soteriologically.

We have tried to explain the **paccekabuddha**'s ambiguous status within Buddhism by arguing the case that there existed two distinct phases in the evolution of the Śramaṇa Tradition: the **paccekabuddha** and the **sāvaka** phases. The figure of the **paccekabuddha** can be assigned to the period in the evolution of the Śramaṇa Tradition from its inception as a movement of renunciation among the **kṣatriyas** of the region of Videha to a time when, owing to the increased impetus toward proselytisation, it splintered into different sectarian groups with variant interpretations of doctrine and practice. This growth in proselytisation gradually gave rise to the concept of the **sāvaka** (disciple) or adherent. The notion of the **sāvaka** was eventually to supersede the prior concept of the **muni** or **ekacarin**, the pre-sectarian individual ascetic. An interesting historical counterpart to this kind of transition occurs also at a later period in the development of the Buddhist tradition, namely in the rise of the Mahāyāna. Here the notion of the **śrāvaka** or **arahant** was overtaken by the concept of the **bodhisattva** as a religious ideal.

The religious and philosophical characteristics of the pre-sectarian phase in the Śramaṇa Movement may be summarised as centring upon the perception or awareness of the universality of suffering (**dukkha**) and impermanence (**anicca**). This contemplative or meditational orientation gave rise to the notion that there is a causal stimulus (e.g. **pratyaya, nimitta**) underlying these forms of awareness. This causal stimulus was the **śramaṇa**'s counterpart of the **veda** or **śruti**. For the **śramaṇas** the principle of 'revelation' resided (immanently - and therefore dynamically) within the world rather than in a fixed object of reference (oral tradition) and with a select body of intermediaries (the Brahmanical priesthood). The notion of truth being 'immanent' made it all that much harder for the 'transmission' of truth to take place; hence the earliest conception of a **buddha** (one who has 'awoken' to the truth) is synonymous with 'self-realisation' only. The concept of 'teacher' or 'instructor' therefore emerged only gradually within this tradition and would have applied to those who possessed the capacity to identify the appropriate 'causal stimulus' for a given individual. Both the Buddha and Mahāvīra were reputed to have possessed such powers (qua doctrines of 'omniscience').

The theory of the **paccekabuddha**'s presectarian identity is supported by his representation in terms of **samādhi** characteristics, that is, in terms of his meditational technique and accomplishments rather than as a purveyor of doctrinal assertions. We have also noted the importance of the use of 'light' imagery as a graphic way of showing these meditational accomplishments . We therefore submit that the concept of 'light' plays a central role in the 'phenomenology' of religious meditational attainment characterising the pre-Buddhist tradition. The reader may note with some interest that this phenomenology re-emerges as a conspicuous feature within the Mahāyāna tradition.

An ancillary theme within this study has been the argument that the moral and philosophical postulate of **avihiṁsā** (refraining from harming) provides the clue to understanding the development of ascetico-religious powers in the proto-**śramaṇa** tradition. In its proper articulation, **avihiṁsā** entailed discipline of the triple faculties of 'body', 'mind' and 'speech' which, in turn, necessitated withdrawal from the outside world. A practice which centred itself upon the heart of man's volition led to the expansion of volitional powers. These gave rise to the two types of religious experience which characterise this tradition: 'world-transforming' and 'world-transcending' power. Both forms of power characterised the Buddha and the **paccekabuddhas**. Our argument with regard to **avihiṁsā** has implied that these forms of power were originally part of a single integrated conception. When, in the post-Sākyamuni era, it was perceived that there were inherent dangers in manifestations of magic for a tradition intent upon winning adherents or converts then a doctrinal distinction was created between the two forms of power. That the figure of the **paccekabuddha** seems to be something of a janus in the Buddhist sources - a solitary wandering mendicant (**muni**) and an adept of magic (**isi**) - is not therefore because the concept was based on more than one type of ascetic, rather, it is attributable to Early Buddhism's insistence that a distinction be maintained between them.

We have seen that to pose the question of whether **paccekabuddhas** still existed at the time of the Buddha is in some respects to misunderstand the significance of the **paccekabuddha** within Buddhism. Buddhist legend presents **paccekabuddhas** as existing until the time of the Buddha's birth, when suddenly they cease to exist. To be excluded from existing by this kind of doctrinal fiat only goes to show how far doctrinal categories have been superimposed upon their interpretation. We are therefore led to conclude that the concept of **paccekabuddha** functions as the canonical and post-canonical designation for the category of persons who, in the period prior to the advent of the Buddha, were regarded as sufficiently worthy in status to be canonised as 'enlightened' ones. Nevertheless we have maintained that they passed into the Buddhist tradition already conferred with this or a kindred status and that therefore the title '**paccekabuddha**' was merely a de jure recognition of a de facto situation. In short, the transition from a pre-Buddhist to a post-Buddhist situation was not marked by a break or dislocation in the tradition but itself formed a historical continuum. The Buddhist tradition could no more disassociate itself from these forerunner paradigmatic figures than a new-born child can sever its own umbilical cord.

In the light of the gradual spread, growth and impact of renunciation, however, there are strong grounds for supposing that the term '**paccekabuddha**' may not itself have been the oldest appellation for these ascetics. In this regard we have seen that the term '**muni**' has a heritage reaching back to the Ṛg Veda and is used exclusively to refer to 'enlightened' persons in the oldest stratum of Buddhist sources. We have also argued that even the Buddhistic description for this figure may have undergone revision, such as from '**paccekabrahma**' to '**paccekabuddha**'.

Apart from denoting an 'enlightened' being the concept **paccekabuddha** we have seen also denotes in Buddhist doctrine someone who is incapable of teaching '**dhamma**' or initiating another into '**sāvaka**' status. We have suggested that this is a dogmatic stricture superimposed by the **sāvaka** tradition itself, in order to differentiate its own master from a long-standing tradition of **buddhas** or spiritual paragons. Nevertheless it is vital that this type of formal pronouncement should be seen in its proper context. The issue of 'transmission' has a special problematic significance of its own in Buddhism. The nature of 'truth' in Buddhism is such that it is not essentially credal but concentrated in individualised religious experience. In view of this basic premise it would have taken some time historically for an adequate and public conceptual apparatus to appear, and there would always be room for a category of person who was specifically deficient in this dimension of spirituality. Owing to this flaw in his make-up the **paccekabuddha** has, in Mahāyāna teaching, become synonymous with the idea of the selfish and short-sighted ascetic. But we have shown, contrary to this interpretation, that he is not lacking in goodwill or intention. His soteriological limitations should not be construed as an indication of flawed intentions on his part.

We have submitted that originally there was just a single buddhology represented by the figure and conception of the **muni**. The dual buddhology signified by the terms **paccekabuddha** and **sammāsambuddha** was developed by followers of Sākyamuni as a way to sanction and justify their claims for him to be regarded as unique. The inspiration for the distinction between the **sammāsambuddha** and the **paccekabuddha** they derived from the prestigious secular concept of the 'universal sovereign' **(cakravartin)**. Meanwhile it has never been the purpose of this study to answer the question why it happened to be the person of Siddhattha who was selected out in this way. The 'Napoleonic' question of how and why a great man arises is one of the imponderables of history and sociology: personal charisma, individual originality, a coming together of historical forces, etc. This study has simply striven to show that the figure of the Buddha formed part of a historical continuum of spirituality – the paradigm **śramaṇa**. We have tried to argue that the mythical concept of a plurality of **buddhas**, acknowledged by Buddhist tradition and accredited textually, must have had some basis or expression in historical fact.

# Appendices

## APPENDIX I

<u>**Paccekabuddha** Linguistic Forms and Translations</u>

We here list

A. terms directly associated with the **paccekabuddha** in the Pali texts.

B. various English translations of the word **paccekabuddha.**

C. forms of the term in Sanskrit, Prakrit, Tibetan, Chinese.

A.

| | |
|---|---|
| **paccekabuddha** | |
| **paccekabodhisatta** | (cp.meaning and usage of **bodhisatta** in Pali) |
| **paccekasambuddha** | (cf.M.III.69; S.I.92vl.) |
| **paccekajina** | (cf.Ap.248 No.301; PbAp.51) |
| **paccekamuni** | (cf.Ap.289 No.366; Nd.I.58) |
| **paccekabodhi** | (the enlightenment of a **paccekabuddha)** |
| **paccekabodhiñāṇa** | (the knowledge or realisation of the enlightenment of a **paccekabuddha**) |

B.

| | |
|---|---|
| **buddha** by and for himself | I.B. Horner: Milinda's Questions, Luzac, 1964. |
| independent **buddha** | Humphreys: Buddhism, Pelican, 1951. |
| private **buddha** | H.W. Schumann: Buddhism, Rider, 1973. |
| solitary **buddha** | Sangharakshita: The Three Jewels, Rider, 1967. |
| isolated **buddha** | A.K. Warder: Indian Buddhism, Motilal Banarsidas, 1970. |
| hermit **buddha** | Nanamoli: Minor Readings. |
| self-styled **buddha** | H. Guenther: Buddhist Philosophy in Theory and Practice, Pelican, 1972. |

| | |
|---|---|
| silent **buddha** | C.A.F. Rhys Davids: 'Kindred Sayings' Vol. I. PTS, 1950. |
| enlightened only for one | T.W. Rhys Davids: 'Hibbert Lectures 1881', Williams & Norgate. |
| personal **buddhas** | T.W. Rhys Davids:'Buddhism',SPCK, London, 1912. |
| separate **buddhas** | E.J. Thomas: 'The History of Buddhist Thought', RKP, 2nd Ed. 1951. |
| small **buddhas** | Winston L. King:'A Thousand Lives Away', Bruno Cassirer, 1964. |
| englightened singly | R.Gombrich:'Precept and Practice', Oxford, 1971. |

C.
Sanskrit

| | |
|---|---|
| **pratyekabuddha** | |
| **pratyekajina** | (cf.Mvu.I.197,357;PbBhūmi 375) |
| **pratyayairbuddha** | (cf. Lal. 319) |
| **pratyayabuddha** | (cit. BHSD. sv **pratyaya**) |
| **pratyaya-jina** | |

Prakrit

| | |
|---|---|
| **patteyabuddha** | (Ardha Māgadhī.cf. Pischel p.198) |
| **pracaga-buddha** | (Gāndhāri Prākrit.cf. Sten Konow, Corpus Inscriptionum Indicarum vol.II. Pt.1: Kharosthi Inscriptions, Calcutta, 1929, 77.) |
| **pracīya-sambuddha** | (NW Prākrit. cf. Khot, Śūrangama Sūtra, p.125) |

Tibetan

| | |
|---|---|
| **raṅ-saṅs-rgyas** | (cf.C.Das.Tibetan-English Dictionary) |
| **rten ḥbrel bsgom** | (='who meditates on **prātītya**') - ERE Vol.X. 153 |
| **rkyen gcig rtogs** | (='who understands only the causes') - ERE Vol.X. 15 |

Chinese

| | |
|---|---|
| **tu chüeh** | (= **pratyekabuddha**) |
| **yüan i chüeh** | (= **pratyayikabuddha?**) |
| **yüan chüeh** | (= **pratyayabuddha**) For a discussion of the relationship of **'yüan chüeh'** to **'yüan i chüeh'** and of what Indian form the latter seemed to be a translation, see de Jong, Es B.Vol.X. No.2. Oct.1977,pp.173-4,Fujita, JIP Vol.3. Nos.1/2 March/April, 1975,p.100,126fn.81ab,128fn.89,90. |

## APPENDIX II

<u>Sanskrit Formulae Associated with the Pratyekabuddha</u>

| | | Divy | Av Sat | Other texts |
|---|---|---|---|---|
| A | **asati Buddhānām utpāde Pratyekabuddhā loka utpadyante hīnadīnānukampakāḥ prāntaśayanabhaktā ekadakṣiṇīyā lokasya** (Divy 88)<br><br>'when there are no **Buddhas, pratyekabuddhas** arise in the world who are compassionate to the unfortunate and imperilled, inhabit remote places and whose worthiness of offerings is unique in the world.' | 132<br>191<br>538<br>541 | 108<br>113<br>199<br>226<br>230<br>244 | PbBhūmi.<br>375 |
| B | **kāyaprāsādikaś cittaprāsādikaś ca śānteryāpathaḥ.(ibid)**<br><br>'graceful in body, serene in mind, tranquil in movement.' | 132<br>312 | 108 | |
| C | **kāyikī tesham mahātmanām dharmadeśanā na vācikī** (Divy 313)<br><br>'these majestic ones teach **dhamma** by means of the body not by means of words.' | 133<br>296 | | PbBhūmi.<br>375 |
| D | **sa tasyānukampārthaṁ vitatapakṣa iva haṁsarāja uparivihāyasam abhyudgamya jvalanatapanavarṣana-** | 134<br>313<br>539 | 199<br>226 | |

| | | | | |
|---|---|---|---|---|
| | **prātihāryāṇi kartum ārabdhaḥ.**<br>**(ibid)**<br>'out of compassion for him, rising into the air like a regal swan with its wings outspread, he commenced to perform magical feats, creating fire, heat, rain and lightning.' | 583 | | |
| E | **āśu pṛithagjanāsy ṛiddhir āvarjanakarī** (Divy 83)<br>'magic converts the unspiritual person quickly.' | 133<br>192<br>313<br>539 | | PbBhūmi.<br>375 |
| F | **prāsādikābhiprasannadevamanuśyāḥ** (Mvu I. 302)<br>'men and gods have faith in these serene ones.' | 226 | | Mvu III. 27<br>171, 414 |
| G | **praṇidhānam kṛtam, evaṁvidhānāṁ ca dharmāṇāṁ (guṇānāṁ** - Divy 584) **lābhī syāṁ, prativiśiṣṭataraṁ cātaḥ śāstāram ārāgayeyaṁ ma virāgayeyam iti.** (Av Śat. 226)<br><br>'he made a vow: "May I also obtain these modes and qualities (i.e. of the **arhat**); may obtain access to and win the favour of a more distinguished teacher than this one (the **pratyekabuddha**).' | 133<br>192<br>313<br>539<br>584 | 199<br>229<br>230<br>255<br>259 | |

## APPENDIX III

<u>**samanabhadragāthā** (stanzas on the blessings of the **samaṇa**)</u>

There are 8 **gāthās** in the Pali version and just 6 in the Mvu. Four of these overlap Each stanza is accompanied by the refrain: 'This is the first (etc) blessing of the poor, homeless monk' (P.**sadāpi** bhadram **adhanassa anāgārassa bhikkhuno;** Skt.**prathamaṁ khu bhadramadhanasya anāgārasya bhikṣuṇo**)

| Jātaka V. 252-3 | Mahāvastu III. 452-3<br>(transl. Jones) |
| --- | --- |
| 1. They (the **samaṇas**) do not hoard for themselves in basket pot or jar; Seeking what others provide, they live virtuously. | |
| **na tesaṁ kotthe upenti na= kumbhe na kalopiyā paraniṭṭhitam esānā tena yāpenti subbatā.** | **nate koṣṭhamiṁ osaranti na kumbhena kulopakam paritiṣṭhati eṣāṇo tena yāyanti suvratā** (g.5) |
| 2. His food is eaten blamelessly and without opposition. | |
| **anavajjo piṇḍo bhottabbo na ca koc' ūparodhati.** = | **na kocidūparudhyati** (from g.2) |
| 3. His food is eaten in peace and without opposition. | (no equivalent) |
| **nibbuto...** | |

| | | |
|---|---|---|
| 4. He wanders in freedom throughout the kingdom, knowing no fetter | cp. | I go from village to village, traverse kingdoms and towns, heedless of all (from g.2) |
| **muttassa raṭṭhe carato saṅgo yassa na vijjati.** | | **yo haṁ grāmāto prakramāmi rāṣṭrāṇi nigamā tathā anupekṣo va prakramāmi** |
| 5. When the town burns, nothing of his is burnt. | = | When Mithila is ablaze, nothing of his is burned (g.4) |
| 6. When the kingdom is ransacked nothing of his is plundered. | | (no equivalent) |
| **raṭṭhe vilumpamānamhi nāssa kiñci ahīratha.** | | |
| 7. Protected on the way against robbers and other dangers,<br>Taking bowl and robe these virtuous ones go in safety. | = | Though there be robbers on the way he goes,<br>With his bowl and robe he ever moves secure (g.3) |
| **corehi rakkhitaṁ maggaṁ ye c'aññe pāripanthikā pattacīvaram ādāya sotthiṁ gacchanti subbatā.** | | **panthena gacchamānasya ye bhonti paripathakā pātracīvaramādāya sukhaṁ gacchati survato** |
| 8. In whichever region he travels, he goes with indifference. | | |
| **yaṁ yaṁ disaṁ pakkamati anapekho va gacchati** | cp. | **anapekṣo va prakamāmi** (supra g.2) |

The Mvu includes within its version of the '**samaṇabhadra-gāthās**' two stanzas not found in the Pali:

What is a kingdom to a man who fares all alone? (g.1)

**ekasya carato rāja kiṁ me rāṣṭraṁ kiriṣyati.**

Wanderers are maintained by various families and by various country districts; with one and all they have friendly relations. Behold the role of dharma. (g.6)

**nānākule pravrajitā nānā-janapadāśritā anayamanyaṁ priyāyanti paśya dharmasya dharmatā.**

## ABBREVIATIONS

| | |
|---|---|
| A. | Aṅguttara-nikāya |
| A.A. | Manorathapūraṇī |
| A.Aś. | Arts Aśiatique |
| Ait.Brh. | Aitareya Brāhmaṇam |
| Anav. | Anavataptagāthā |
| Ap. | Apadāna |
| Ap.A. | Visuddhajanavilāsinī |
| Ath.V. | Atharva Veda |
| Ausg.Erz. | Ausgewahlte Erzahlungen in Mahārāṣṭrī |
| Av.Śat. | Avadāna-śataka |
| BD | Buddhist Dictionary |
| BHSD | Buddhist Hybrid Sanskrit Grammar and Dictionary |
| Bṛhad. Up. | Bṛhadāraṇyaka Upaniṣad |
| Bv.A. | Madhuratthavilāsinī |
| Ch. Up. | Chāndogya Upaniṣad |
| CJS | Ceylon Journal of Science |
| Comies. | Commentaries |

| | |
|---|---|
| Comy. | Commentary |
| Cp | Buddhavaṁsa and Cariyāpiṭaka |
| Cp.A. | Paramatthadīpānī Vol. VII. |
| Cpd | Compendium of Philosophy |
| CPD | Critical Pali Dictionary |
| CPS | Catūṣpariṣatsūtra |
| D. | Dīgha-nikāya |
| Dial | Dialogues of the Buddha |
| Dh | Dhammapada |
| Dh A | Dhammapadaṭṭhakathā |
| Divy | Divyāvadāna |
| DPPN | Dictionary of Pali Proper Names |
| Dvmsa | Dīpavaṁsa |
| EB | Encyclopaedia of Buddhism |
| ERE | Encyclopaedia of Religion and Ethics |
| Es B | The Eastern Buddhist |
| g | gāthā |
| IA | The Indian Antiquary |
| IHQ | Indian Historical Quarterly |
| It. | Itivuttaka |
| IT | Indologica Taurinensia |

| | |
|---|---|
| J. | Jātaka |
| JA | Journal Aśiatique |
| Jaim Brh. | Jaiminīya Brāhmaṇa |
| JAOS | Journal of the American Oriental Society |
| JIBS | Journal of Indian and Buddhist Studies |
| JIP | Journal of Indian Philosophy |
| Jmala | Jātakamāla |
| Jones | The Mahāvastu, (trans.) |
| JRAS | Journal of the Royal Asiatic Society |
| Karma Vibh. | Mahākarmavibhañga et karmavibhañgopadeśa |
| Kauṣ.Brh. | Kauṣītaki Brāhmaṇa |
| Kh.A | Khuddaka-pāṭha together with its commentary Paramatthajotika I |
| Khg.S. | Khaggavisāṇa Sutta |
| Khot. | Khotanese Śūrangamasamādhisūtra |
| KS | Kindred Sayings |
| Lal | Lalitavistara |
| M. | Majjhima-nikāya |
| MA | Papañcasūdanī |
| Manu | Mānava Dharma-śāstra |
| Mahavyut | Mahāvyutpatti |
| Mbh | Mahābhārata |

| | |
|---|---|
| Mc | Maṇicūdāvadāna |
| Miln | Milindapañho |
| MLS | The Middle Length Sayings |
| MMK | Mañjuśrīmūlakalpa |
| Mvṁsa | Mahāvaṁsa |
| Mvu | Mahāvastu |
| MWD | Monier-Williams Dictionary |
| NAGW | Nachrichten von der Akademie der Wissenschaften in Gottingen Philologisch Historisch Klasse |
| Nd.I. | Niddesa, Mahā- |
| Nd.II. | Niddesa, Cula- |
| Netti | Nettipakaraṇa |
| Norman | K.R. Norman, 'The Pratyekabuddha in Buddhism and Jainism' in Denwood, P. and Piatigorsky, A. |
| P | Pali |
| Pañc.Brh. | Pañcaviṁśa-Brāhmaṇa |
| PAPA | Proceedings of the American Philosophical Society |
| Pb.Ap. | Paccekabuddhāpadāna = (Apadāna pp.7-14 vv. 1-58. |
| Pb.Bhūmi | Pratyekabuddhabhūmi |
| PED | Pali-English Dictionary |

| | |
|---|---|
| PEW | Philosophy East and West |
| Pkt. | Prakrit. |
| Ps.A. | Saddhammappakāsinī |
| PTS | Pali Text Society |
| Pug. | Puggalapaññatti |
| Pv. | Petthavatthu |
| Pv.A. | Paramatthadīpanī IV |
| Rel.St. | Journal of Religious Studies |
| Ṛg V. | Rigveda |
| RO | Rocznik Oryentalistycby |
| S | Samyutta-nikāya |
| SA | Saratthappakāsinī |
| Śat.Brh. | Śatapatha-Brāhmaṇa |
| SBE | Sacred Books of the East |
| Śiks | Śikshāsamuccaya |
| Skt. | Sanskrit |
| Sn | Sutta-nipāta |
| Sn A | Paramatthajotika II |
| Tait.Brh. | Taittirīya Brāhmaṇa. |
| Thag | Thera-therīgāthā |
| Thig A. | Paramatthadīpanī VI |

| | |
|---|---|
| Ud. | Udāna |
| Up. | Upaniṣads |
| Upās. | Upāsakajanālankarā |
| Utt. | Uttarādhyayanasūtram |
| V. | Vajracchedikā Prajñāpāramitā |
| Vin. | Vināyapiṭaka |
| Vism. | Visuddhimagga |
| Vv | Vimānavatthu |
| Vv A. | Paramatthadīpanī III |
| WZKM | Wiener Zeitschrift fur die Kunde des Morgenlandes |
| WZKSO | Wiener Zeitschrift fur die Kunde Sud-und Ostasiens |

# BIBLIOGRAPHY


Aṅguttara-nikāya, 1885-1900, 5.vols. ed. Morris, R. and Hardy, E. PTS. London.

Aitareya Brāhmaṇam, 1863, vol.1. text, vol.2. trans., ed. Haug, M. Bombay.

Anavataptagāthā und die Sthaviragāthā, Die. 1961, Buddhistischer Verssammlungen vol. 1. ed. Bechert, H. Sanskrittexte aus den Turfanfunden VI: Berlin.

Apadāna, 1925-27, 2 vols. ed. Lilley, M.E. PTS. London.

Atharva Veda, Hymns of the 1897, trans. Griffiths, R. Benares.

Ausgewahlte Erzahlungen in Mahārāṣṭrī, 1886, von Jacobi, H.

Avadāna Śataka, 1958, ed. Vaidya, P.L. Darbhanga.

Barth, A. 1921, (5th Ed), The Religions of India, Kegan Paul, Trench, Trubner.

Barua, D.K., 1971, An Analytical Study of Four Nikāyas, University of Calcutta.

Basham, A.L., 1951, History and Doctrines of the Ājīvikas, Luzac.

Bloomfield, M., 1919, The Life and Stories of the Jaina Saviour Pārśvanātha, John Hopkins, Baltimore.

Buddhavaṁsa and Cariyāpiṭaka, 1882, ed. Morris, R1 PTS: London.

Buddhist Dictionary, (3rd Ed. 1972), Nyanatiloka, Frewin, Colombo.

Buddhist Hybrid Sanskrit Grammar and Dictionary, 1972 (1st Ed. 1953), 2 vols. Edgerton, F. Motilal Banarsidass.

Buhler, J.G. 1963 (1st Ed. 1903), The Indian Sect of the Jainas, Susil Gupta: Calcutta.

Cakraborti, H. 1973, Asceticism in Ancient India, Punthi Pustak, Calcutta, 1973.

Charpentier J. 1908, Paccekabuddhageschichten, Studien zur Indischen Erzahlungsliteratur: Upsala.

Catūsparisatsūtra: The Sūtra on the Foundation of the Buddhist Order, 1973, trans. Kloppenborg, R. Leiden.

Clarifier of the Sweet Meaning, The. (Buddhavaṁsa Commentary), 1978, trans. Horner, I.B. PTS: London.

Compendium of Philosophy (Abhidhammattha- saṅgaha), 1972, Shwe Zan Aung, PTS: London.

Cooray, 'paccekabuddha', specimen article submitted to EB.

A Critical Pali Dictionary, 1924- ed. Trenckner, V. a.o., Copenhagen.

Dayal, Har, 1932, The Bodhisattva Doctrine in Buddhist Sanskrit Literature, Kegan Paul, Trench, Trubner: London.

Denwood, P. and Piatigorsky, A. ed. 1983, Buddist Studies Ancient and Modern, Curzon Prefs: London.

Dhammapada, Text and Translation, 1970, Narada, Mahā Thera Mahā Bodhi Society of India: Calcutta.

Dhammapadaṭṭhakathā, 1909-25, 5 vols. ed. Smith, H. and Norman, H.C. PTS: London.

Dialogues of the Buddha (Dīgha Nikāya), 1899-1921, 3 vols. Rhys Davids, T.W. Luzac.

Dictionary of Pali Proper Names, 1937-38, 2 vols. Malalaskera, G.P. PTS: London.

Dīgha Nikāya, 1890-1911, 3 vols. ed. Rhys Davids, T.W. AND Carpenter, J.E. PTS: London.

Dīpavaṁsa, 1879, ed. and trans. Oldenberg, H., Williams and Norgate: London.

Dowson, J. (6th Ed. 1928), A Classical Dictionary of Hindu Mythology and Religion, Geography, History and Literature. Kegan Paul, Trencher, Trubner.

Elders' Verses I, The. (Theragāthā), 1969, trans. Norman, K.R. PTS: London.

Eliade, M. 1958, Yoga, Immortality and Freedom, Bollingen Series LVI: New York.

Encyclopaedia of Buddhism, 1961-71, 3 vols. ed. Malalasekera, G.P. Ceylon.

Encyclopaedia of Religion and Ethics, 1908-26, 13 vols. ed. Hastings, J., T. & T. Clark: Edinburgh.

Erghardt, J.T.E. 1977, Faith and Knowledge in Early Buddhism, E.J. Brill.

Geiger, W. 1916, Pali Literatur und Sprache, Trubner: Strassburg.

Gonda, J. (1) 1966, Loka - world and heaven in the Veda, North Holland Pub.Co: Amsterdam.

Gonda, J. (2) 1976, Triads in the Veda, North Holland Pub.Co: Amsterdam.

Gonda, J. (3) Ancient Indian Kingship from the Religious Point of View (rep. from Numen III and IV with Addenda and Index), E.J. Brill.

Gonda, J. (4) 1977, The Ritual Sūtras, History of Indian Literature Vol.1 Fasc.2. Wiesbaden.

Gopalan, S. 1973, Outlines of Jainism, Wiley Eastern Private Ltd: New Delhi.

Heesterman, J.C. 1957, The Ancient Indian Royal Consecration. Mouton: The Hague.

Hiriyanna, M. 1932, Outlines of Indian Philosophy, Allen & Unwin: London.

Hodgson, B.H. 1971 (1st Ed. 1874), Essays on the Languages, Literature and Religion of Nepal and Tibet, Bharat-Bharati.

Hopkins, E.W. 1968, Epic Mythology, Indological Book House.

Itivuttaka, 1889, ed. Windishch, E. PTS: London.

Jaina Sutras, 1884, 1895, trans. Jacobi, H. SBE Vols.XXII and XLV. OUP.

Jātaka or stories of the Buddha's former births, The. 6 vols. ed. Fausboll, V. PTS: London.

Jātakamāla, 1959, ed. Vaidya, P.L. Dharbhanga.

Jātakamāla or Garland of Birth Stories, 1895, trans. Speyer, J.S. London.

Johansson, R.E.A. 1979, The Dynamic Psychology of Early Buddhism, Curzon Press: London.

Kathākośa or Treasury of Stories, The. 1895, trans. Tawney, C.H. London.

Khotanese Śūrangamasamādhisūtra, 1970, ed. and trans. Emmerick, R.E. OUP.

Khuddakapātha together with its Commentary Paramatthajotikā I. 1915, ed. Smith, H. PTS: London.

Kindred Sayings, The Book of (Samyutta Nikāya). 1917-30, 5 vols. trans. Rhys-Davids, C.A.F. and Woodward F.L. PTS: London.

Kloppenborg, R. (1) 1974, The Paccekabuddha. A Buddhist Ascetic, E.J. Brill.

Kloppenborg, R. (2) 1983, The Paccekabuddha A Buddhist Ascetic, Kandy, Sri Lanka.

Lalitavistara, 1958, ed. Vaidya, P.L. Dharbhanga.

Lamotte, E. 1958, Histoire du Bouddhisme Indien, Louvain.

Macdonnell, A.A. 1963, The Vedic Mythology, Varanasi.

Mahābhārata, The. 1834-39, 4 vols. Calcutta Ed.

Mahābhārata, The. 1933, 19 vols. ed. Sukthankar, V.S. Poona.

Mahābhārata, The. trans. Roy, P.C. 12 vols. Calcutta.

Madhuratthavilāsinī nāma Buddhavamsatthakathā (commentary on the Buddhavaṁsa) 1978, ed. Horner PTS: London.

Mahāvaṁsa, 1908, ed. Geiger, W. PTS: London.

Mahāvastu, 1882-97, 3 vols, ed. Senart, E. Paris.

Mahāvastu, The. 1949-56, 3 vols, trans. Jones, J.J. Luzac & Co. London.

Mahāvyutpatti, 1915-25, 2 vols. ed. Sakaki, R. Kyoto.

Majjhima Nikāya 1888-1902. 3 vols. ed. Trenckner, V. and Chalmers, R. PTS: London.

Maṇicudāvadāna, 1967, text and trans. Handurukande, R. PTS: London.

Mañjuśrīmūlakalpa, 1920-22, 3 vols. ed. Ganapati Sastri, T. Trivandrum.

Manorathapūranī (Commentary on the Aṅguttara Nikāya), 1924-40, 5v. ed. Walleser, H. Hermann Kop, PTS: London.

Middle Length sayings, The (Majjhima Nikāya), 1954-59, 3vols. ed. Horner, I.B. PTS: London.

Milindapañho, 1880, ed. Trenckner, V. PTS: London.

Miller, J. and Feurerstein, G. 1971, A Reappraisal of Yoga. Essays in Indian Philosophy, Rider.

Minor Anthologies Pt. III. (Buddhavaṁsa and Cariyā piṭaka), 1975, trans. Horner, I.B. PTS: London.

Minor Readings and Illustrator (Khuddakapāṭha and Commentary), 1960, trans. Nanamoli, Bhikkhu PTS: London.

Mithraic Studies, Vol.1. 1975, ed. Hinnells, J. Manchester U.P.

Monier-Williams, M. 1899, A Sanskrit-English Dictionary, Oxford.

Nettipakaraṇa, 1902, ed. Hardy, E. PTS: London.

Niddesa, Cula-. 1918, ed. Stede, W. PTS: London.

Niddesa Mahā-. 1916-17, 2 vols. ed. La Vallee Poussin, Louis de. and Thomas, E.J. PTS: London.

Pali-English Dictionary, 1921-25 (rep. 1972), ed. Rhys-Davids. T.W. PTS: London.

Pañcaviṁśa-Brāhmaṇa, 1931, trans. Caland, W. Calcutta.

Pande, G.C. 1974 (2nd Ed.) Studies in the Origins of Buddhism, Motilal Barnasidass.

Panikkar, R. (ed and trans.), 1977, The Vedic Experience. Mantramañjari, Darton, Longman and Todd: London.

Paramatthadīpani III (Commentary on the Vimānavatthu), 1901

Paramatthadīpani IV (Commentary on the Petavatthu), 1894, ed. Hardy, E. PTS: London.

Paramatthadīpani VI (Commentary on the Therigāthā), 1893, ed. Muller, E. PTS: London.

Paramatthadīpani VII (Commentary on the Cariyāpiṭaka), 1939, ed. Barua, D.L. PTS: London.

Paramatthajotikā II (Commentary on the Sutta-nipāta), 1916-17, 2 vols. ed. Smith, H. PTS: London.

Petavatthu, 1888, ed. Minayeff, PTS: London.

Pischel, R. 1965 (1st Ed. 1879), Comparative Grammar of the Prakrit Languages, Motilal Barnasidass.

Pratyekabuddhabhūmi, 1960, ed. Wayman, A. JIBS. Vol.III. No.1.

Puggalapaññatti, 1883, ed. Morris, R. PTS: London.

Renou, L. 1953, Religions of Ancient India, University of London.

Rigveda, Die Hymnen des. 1963 (1st Ed. 1889), 2 vols. ed. Aufrecht, T. Varanasi.

Rigveda, The Hymns of the. 1963 (1st Ed. 1889) 2 vols. Varanasi.

Saddhammappakāsinī (Commentary on the Patisambhida-magga), 1933-47, 3 vols. ed. Joshi, C.V. PTS: London.

Samyutta Nikāya, 1884-98, 5 vols, ed. Feer, L. PTS: London.

Saratthappakāsinī (Commentary on the Samyutta Nikāya), 1929-37, 3 vols. ed. Woodward, F.L. PTS: London.

Śatapatha-Brāhmaṇa, The. 1882-1900, 5 vols. trans. Eggeling, J. SBE: OUP.

Schubring, W. 9162, The Doctrine of the Jainas, Motilal Banarsidass.

Śikshasamuccaya, 1957, ed. Bendall, C. Indo-Iranian Reprint, Mouton & Co.

Soothill, W.E. and Hodous, L. 1937, A Dictionary of Chinese Buddhist Terms, Kegan Paul, Trench, Trubner: London.

Sternbach, L. 1974, Subhasita, Gnomic and Didactic Literature, Vol.4. Fasc.1. Wiesbaden.

Stevenson, Mrs. S. 1915, The Heart of Jaimism, OUP.

Stutley, M. and J. 1977, A Dictionary of Hinduism, Routledge and Kegan Paul: London.

Sutta-nipāta, 1913, ed. Andersen, D. and Smith, H. PTS: London.

Tähtinen, U. 1976, Ahimsā. Non-Violence in Indian Tradition, Rider.

Thakur, U., History of Mithila (circa 3000BC - 1556AD) Darbhanga.

Therī-theragāthā, 1883, ed. Oldenburg, H. and Pischel, R. PTS: London

Thomas, E.J. 1951, The History of Buddhist Thought, Routledge, Kegan and Paul: London.

Udāna, 1885, ed. Steinthal, P. PTS: London.

Upaniṣads, The Principal. 1953, text and trans. Radhakrishnan, S. Allen & Unwin: London.

Upaniṣads, The Thirteen Principal. 1931 (2nd Ed.), trans. Hume, R.E. OUP.

Upāsakajanālankarā, 1965, ed. Saddhatissa H. PTS: London.

Uttarādhyayanasūtram, 1959, ed. Vadekar, R.D. & Vaidya, N. Poona.

Uttarādhyayana Sūtra, The. 1921, ed. Charpentier, J. Upsala.

Vajracchedika Prajñapāramitā, 1957, ed. and trans. Conze, E., Roma.

Vimalakīrti, The teaching of.(Vimalakīrtinirdeśa) 1976, annot. trans. Lamote, E. PTS: London.

Vimānavatthu, 1969-83, 5 vols. ed. Oldenburg, H. PTS: London.

Visuddhajanavilāsini nāma Apadānātthakathā (Commentary on the Apad.) 1954. ed Godo, PTS: London.

Vināyapiṭaka, 1869-83, 5 vols. ed. Oldenburg, H. PTS: London.

Visuddhimagga, 1920-21, 2 vols. Rhys-Davids, C.A.F. PTS: London.

Walker, B. 1968, 2 vols. Hindu World. An Encyclopaedic Survey of Hinduism, Allen and Unwin: London.

Warder, A.K. 1963, Introduction to Pali, PTS: London.

Winternitz, M. 1933, History of Indian Literature. Vol. II. Buddhist Literature and Jaina Literature, Oriental Reprint, Calcutta, 1933.

# INDEX OF PALI, PRAKRIT AND SANSKRIT TERMS